THE
ELAN VALLEY
RAILWAY

The Railway of the
Birmingham Corporation Waterworks

by
Colin Judge

THE OAKWOOD PRESS

© The Oakwood Press 1987

ISBN 0 85361 353 2

Typeset by Gem Publishing Company, Brightwood, Wallingford, Oxon.
Printed and bound by S & S Press, Abingdon, Oxfordshire

Note to reader
The spellings of the various names in this book are based on the reports of the time. Many variations of hyphenation, capital letters and even spelling are to be seen on the maps, photographs and reports. Where possible the current Ordnance Survey map annotation has been used.

Author

Dedicated to my wife Jane, whose love of
the Elan Valley is as great as my own.

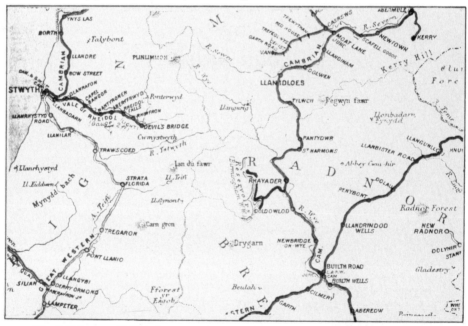

The RCH map of 1917, showing the area and railways around the Elan Valley.

Published by
THE OAKWOOD PRESS
P.O.Box 122,
Headington, Oxford.

Contents

		Page
	Introduction	5
Chapter 1	The Problem and the Solution	11
Chapter 2	Early Developments and Construction of the Railway	21
Chapter 3	The Model "Navvy" Village of Elan	51
Chapter 4	The Route Described	79
Chapter 5	Locomotives of the Birmingham Waterworks Company	113
Chapter 6	Coaching and Goods Stock	145
Chapter 7	Operation of the Railway	165
Chapter 8	The Dams, Aqueduct and Pipeline	193
Chapter 9	The Royal Visit — 21st July, 1904	205
Appendix 1	Walking the "Line" today	219
Appendix 2	Walks from the Elan Visitors Centre	223
Appendix 3	Richard Eustace Tickell	226
Appendix 4	Alterations to the 1892 City of Birmingham Water Act	227
Appendix 5	Cambrian Traffic Statement (1893–1895)	228
Appendix 6	The Cambrian Railways siding at Cerrig Gwynion	229
	Acknowledgements	230
	Index	231

Maps

	Page
RCH map of the area, c.1917	2
Ordnance Survey (area), c.1904	4
Birmingham Corporation Water, Elan Supply, c.1900	15
Railways No. 1 and No. 2, c.1894	45 and 46
Elan Village, c.1893	50
Railway No. 1 and Village buildings, c.1895	52
GWR Rhayader Station, c.1923	80
Elan Valley Junction, c.1900	81
Noyadd Sidings, c.1900	84
Elan Valley Junction, c.1910	177
The Dams and Reservoirs today	192
Walking today map (4 walks)	222

1904 Ordnance Survey map of the area showing the BCWW Railway main line only.

Introduction

The area around the Elan Valley is rugged with wooded promontories, frowning crags and scree surrounded by hills rising to over 2,000 feet. From the vast plateaux of moorland and numerous peat bogs, two rivers rise, namely the Elan and Claerwen. As with other streams, these rivers derive their strength, tumbling through bracken and woodland on their way down to join forces in the Vale of Nantgwilt, on the borders of Radnor and Brecon. The new river, now called the Elan, continues eastward to join up with the River Wye just south of the little market town of Rhayader (this being the largest populous in the area).

In the earliest times many of these valleys were the central Wales crossing points and several ancient roadways were established.

The etching (*plate 1 overleaf*) portrays one such crossing bridge of the River Elan, which carried the Wye to Ystwyth road. Many of the local names contain the words PONT or ELAN which were the ancient words for "bridge" and the "meetings of the ways".

There is evidence of early settlements in the valleys, undertaking farming (goats, sheep and horses) and with mining also being carried out, mainly at Nant-y-Car* and Cwm Elan mines by the Builth Lead Mining Company. At the town of Rhayader a special tannery was established using oak bark in the tanning process, reportedly the last of its kind in Mid-Wales.

A Wiltshire gentleman once described this area as a "paradise of 10,000 almost worthless acres"; so this wilderness was chosen, rightly or wrongly, by the Birmingham Waterworks Committee as the site of their "cyclopean construction" of reservoirs, dams etc. to store and feed water for the needs of the growing city of Birmingham, some seventy miles away.

The formation of these reservoirs not only submerged for ever some of the most charming valleys in Great Britain but caused the destruction of two large houses of some pretensions and literary interest, namely, "Cwm-Elan (*plate 2*) on the right bank of the River Elan, and "Nantgwillt" (*plate 3*) on the left bank of the River Claerwen (*see fold-out map at rear*). Both of these houses, the sites of which are now situated some forty and sixty feet below the top water level of the Caban Coch Reservoir, were associated with the poet Shelley. Shelley visited his uncle, Mr Thomas Grove, at "Cwm-Elan" in July 1811, returning with his bride, Harriet Westbrook, to take up a short residency in Nantgwilt house during 1812.

---

* This mine had been reopened by Downes and Hadley, and as late as the 1860s was still operating but closed soon after because of its non-profitability.

Plate 1: The Pont-ar-Elan as depicted in an etching by R.E. Tickell in 1893.
Courtesy: Severn-Trent Water

Plate 2: Cwm-Elan house on the right bank of the River Elan, seen here as the
waters were rising in the reservoir.   *Collection C. Edwards, Rhayader*

Plate 3: The house of Nantgwillt on the left bank of the River Claerwen as etched by R.E. Tickell in 1893. *Courtesy: Severn-Trent Water*

Plate 4: "Capel Nantgwillt" etched by R.E. Tickell in 1893.
Courtesy: Severn-Trent Water

Plate 5: The new Baptist church (*left*) built by the BCWW to replace the chapel now under the Caban Coch Reservoir. The Foel tower in the middle is where the water is piped from the reservoir to the filter beds, and then on to the City of Birmingham. The arched bridge carrying the road is supported on piers on a dam below the surface. This submerged dam maintains the level of water, even in drought conditions, and is known as the Careg-Ddu viaduct. The inset portrays a close

Plate 6: The new Baptist chapel at Llanfadog built by the BCWW, seen here from the railway embankment, in December 1900; the building still stands today. *Reproduced by permission of the Reference Library, Birmingham*

Plate 7: The village of Nant Gwyllt with the impending reservoir water level indicated by an ink line drawn by the Water Committee surveyor in the 1890s. *Courtesy: Severn-Trent Water*

At the meeting of the two rivers, Claerwen and the Elan, there existed the Chapel of Nantgwillt (a small picturesque ivy-covered church) (*plate 4*) with an old Baptist Chapel and burial ground nearby. Further down the stream was situated the small Nantgwilt school-house. Under the Birmingham Water Acts all these structures were to be submerged to a depth of 90 feet by the new reservoir and so the Corporation of Birmingham was empowered to construct replacement dwellings. The new Baptist Church now stands at the end of the Careg-Ddu viaduct (*plate 5*) with the replacement Baptist Chapel constructed at Llanfadog, near to the Elan village (*plate 6*). With the village of Nantgwilt being submerged the problem of the school was automatically resolved with a new school being incorporated in the Elan village and any children from the surrounding district would be taught there. In addition to the buildings named above, a further twenty dwelling houses (farms and cottages) were lost to the rising waters. The accompanying official photograph (*plate 7*) shows the water level of the reservoir above the submerged village.

So these man-made dams and reservoirs were constructed in some of the most picturesque and rugged mountain scenery in Britain and today provide 76 million gallons of water daily (by gravity) to the Midlands (mainly Birmingham District) from the four large reservoirs capable of storing over 22,000 million gallons.

This water is the result of an average rainfall of 70 inches per year in an area of Wales which now supports farming, 45,000 sheep and over 100 people living and working in the area.

The turn of this century therefore saw the Elan and Claerwen valleys transformed and changed in character by the massive stone structures. This book sets out to record how this was achieved, mainly by the construction and running of a railway; the Elan Valley Railway, a village and above all, hard work. In fact one wonders if this enormous constructional task could have ever been completed without the railway; we will never know.

The text includes many extracts from the Birmingham Corporation Waterworks minute books reproduced in full, as these give precise details of the problems and decisions made at the time and, if re-written, history could have been altered. Newspaper articles and contemporary reports are also included to try and capture fully and accurately the more important decisions made at the time.

Much more could have been included but I hope the material reproduced enlightens the reader into the events that took place in the few short years of the Railway's existence.

Colin W. Judge
June 1987

Chapter One

The Problem and the Solution

"Gentlemen there has been yet another outbreak of smallpox and diarrhoea in our City; we need pure water. Our existing supplies are woefully inadequate. We depend on local wells, rivers and streams which cannot meet our current needs, let alone our projected demands. Therefore as Chairman of the City's Water Committee I propose that we undertake a survey of possible sources of supply and initiate the necessary legalisation in Parliament and seek the necessary finance to improve the situation for our citizens and industry, for remember, fellow Councillors, "Cleanliness is next to Godliness".

Chairman Birmingham Water Committee

Quoted from the Museum at the
Elan Valley Visitors Centre

Over the last one hundred years in Great Britain many social problems have arisen but none more pressing than the question of the adequate provision of the basic supplies to our ever-growing towns and cities. One such problem had always been the supply of ample fresh water to sustain the ever increasing population. In the late nineteenth century many of our larger cities were already drawing water from afar: Manchester from Cumberland; Glasgow from Loch Katome and Liverpool from Lake Vyrnwy in Montgomeryshire. The City of Birmingham, whose population had grown rapidly during the Industrial Revolution, faced cramped and squalid housing conditions and poor sanitation which lead to many deadly epidemics. To combat these problems the city needed more and more water and, as Birmingham's population by 1890 was 725,000 persons, it was estimated that 688,500 inhabitants were using water. From 8,300,000 gallons of water per day consumed in 1876, the daily demand had doubled to 16,500,000 gallons per day by March 1891. So the Water Committee of Birmingham began to look further afield away from their current sources of supply. This was being drawn from the local springs and brooks and stored in local service reservoirs. This supply was only just sufficient to meet the demand and left no margin for the growth or expansion taking place at this time. The wells at:

Aston	yielded	3	million gallons per day			
Witton	"	$2\frac{1}{2}$	"	"	"	"
King's Vale	"	$\frac{1}{4}$	"	"	"	"
Perry	"	2	"	"	"	"
Selly Oak	"	$1\frac{1}{4}$	"	"	"	"
Longbridge	"	$1\frac{1}{2}$	"	"	"	"
	Total	$10\frac{1}{2}$	million gallons per day			

whilst certain other streams contributed a further 7,500,000 gallons per day more as follows:

Plants Brook	„	2	million gallons per day				
Perry & Witton streams	„	1	„	„	„	„	
River Blythe	„	2½	„	„	„	„	
River Bourne	„	2	„	„	„	„	

7½ million gallons per day

The total daily yield therefore was approximately 18 million gallons and as the average demand was approximately 17 million gallons (with "peaks" of 22 million gallons) it was obvious that problems were imminent.

It was therefore no surprise that more than thirty years before, the solitary hillsides of Wales were marked down as a very suitable place for the collection and storage of water (in particular the Elan Valley). The project was critically examined at this time on behalf of Sir Robert Rawlinson and on the 6th April, 1871 brought it to the notice of the Corporation of Birmingham, in particular the Water Committee.

Nothing came of these proposals at this time but by 1890 the matter had reached "such urgency" that a report on the "Valleys" was prepared with a resolution in Council as early as the 7th October, 1890 (No. 15406). This stated,

> . . . that the water committee be authorised to consult with certain Engineers as to the further powers to be obtained by the Corporation with reference to the additional works and sources of Water Supply necessary to meet the future requirements of the district supplied by the department.

The report suggested that if the City of Birmingham did not act soon, the possibility of London using the area chosen, could not be ruled out.

As Birmingham was situated on elevated ground it meant that the cost of pumping water at present from the wells etc., relieved the ratepayers of £20,000 per year and, although Wales was "far distant" from the City, the report suggested the "Welsh" water could be supplied by "gravitational means", thus a vast saving could be achieved in the long term. Sir Thomas Martineau was Chairman of the Water Committee at this time and was firm in his belief that this new scheme could meet the city's demands for water over the next 50 years.

He then requested that a certain civil engineer named James Mansergh (Fellow of the Royal Society) be contacted to work secretly with the City of Birmingham's resident water engineer Mr Gray, to survey the proposed area and to submit a detailed report.

It was not by sheer chance that the gentleman chosen, namely Mr James Mansergh, had ventured across the beautiful Elan and Claerwen Valleys as early as 1862, when he was constructing the Mid-Wales Railway. On studying these valleys, he also had recognised their enormous potential and suitability for storage of water for use in our growing towns and cities. In late 1890 he finalised his detailed survey (commissioned by the City of Birmingham Water Committee) and concluded his report with the statement, "that no better source could have been found or desired".

The report was dated 8th January, 1891 and presented to the full committee accompanied by a fine scale model of the scheme (made by James Mansergh and his son).

As early as February 1891, the Birmingham Water Committee secretly visited Wales, and in particular the village of Rhayader, to see for themselves the suggested area. Proof of this early visit is supported by the copy of the visitors' register (*see below*) from the Lion Hotel at Rhayader where signatures of the members of the committee are clearly seen.

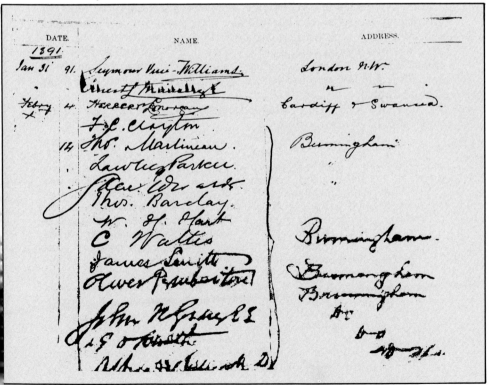

Signatures from the Visitors Book in the Lion Hotel, Rhayader. They are all members of The Committee who went in 1891 to view the proposed site.
Courtesy: Birmingham Reference Library

The City council in their wisdom deliberated during 1891 on the scheme and, after long and hard discussions, finally approved the document on 13th October, 1891.

The next step was to promote the Bill in Parliament and this was to be helped by Joseph Chamberlain (the M.P. for the City of Birmingham) aided by Sir Thomas Martineau and Alderman Rawley Parker, plus many leading members of City council. The initial report by James Mansergh was actually used as a basis to form the first draft of the Water Act, and with expert witnesses and appropriate legal advisers, the Birmingham Corporation Water Act finally received the Royal Assent on 27th June, 1891 but not without a struggle. The debate apparently lasted twenty-two days with "fights" in both houses of Parliament and opposition from all quarters.

The Act allowed the Corporation of the City of Birmingham to obtain a supply of water from the rivers Elan and Claerwen in the counties of Radnor, Brecknock and Montgomery (see Appendix 4 for the relevant revisions and amendments to the Act over the subsequent years).

The scheme involved initially purchasing 71 square miles of "gathering grounds" at Elan and the construction of six reservoirs, with stone dams (see accompanying map). In addition to the construction of a model village, a new chapel and church, there would also need to be a 73 mile aqueduct to allow the water to gravitate to a new reservoir just within the City of Birmingham at Frankley (near Kings Norton).

For a more detailed appraisal of the scheme the relevant parts of the Water Act have been included.

Works

Power to construct works. **19** Subject to the provisions of this Act the Corporation may make construct lay down and maintain in the situation and lines and according to the levels shown on the deposited plans and sections relating thereto the several works shown on the said plans together with all proper embankments dams sluices weirs outlets overflows washouts bridges roads approaches wells tanks basins gauges filter-beds discharge-pipes adits shafts tunnels aqueducts culverts cuts channels conduits drains mains pipes junctions valves telegraphs telephones and other means of electric communication engines apparatus houses buildings and conveniences connected with or auxiliary to the said works or any of them or necessary for inspecting maintaining repairing cleansing managing and using the same.

The works shown on the deposited plans and sections comprise the following principal works (that is to say):

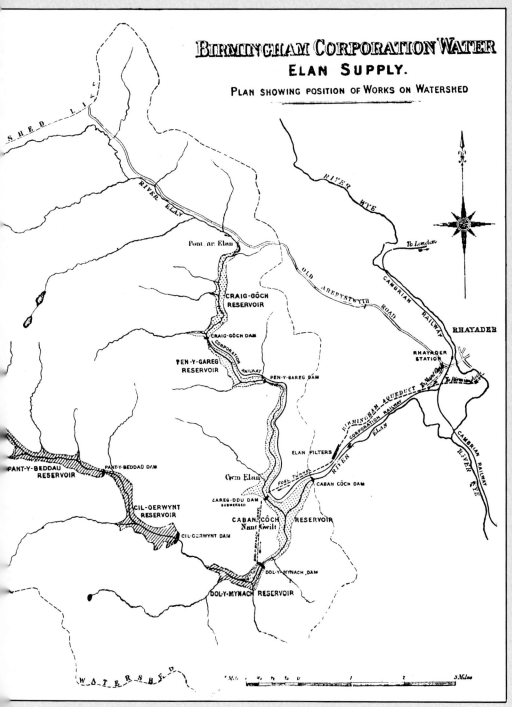

A map showing the initial six reservoirs envisaged but the two on the upper Claerwen were replaced by just one in 1952.

(1) CRAIG-YR-ALLT GOCH RESERVOIR.—A storage reservoir (to be called the Craig-yr-Allt Goch Reservoir) in the parish of Llansantffraid-cwmdeuddwr to be formed by means of a dam across the River Elan.

(2) PEN-Y-GAREG RESERVOIR.—A storage reservoir (to be called the Pen-y-Gareg Reservoir) in the parish of Llansantffraid-cwmdeuddwr to be formed by means of a dam across the River Elan.

(3) CABAN COCH RESERVOIR.—A storage reservoir (to be called the Caban Coch Reservoir) in the parishes of Llansantffraid-cwmdeuddwr and Llanwrthwl to be formed by means of a dam across the River Elan.

(4) PANT-Y-BEDDAU RESERVOIR.—A storage reservoir (to be called the Pant-y-Beddau Reservoir) in the parishes of Llantsantffraid-cwmdeuddwr Llanwrthwl and Caron-Uwch-Clawdd to be formed by means of a dam across the River Claerwen.

(5) CIL-OERWYNT RESERVOIR.—A storage reservoir (to be called the Cil-oerwynt Reservoir) in the parishes of Llansantffraid-cwmdeuddwr and Llanwrthwl to be formed by means of a dam across the River Claerwen.

(6) DOL-Y-MYNACH RESERVOIR.—A storage reservoir (to be called the Dol-y-Mynach Reservoir) in the parishes of Llansantffraid-cwmdeuddwr and Llanwrthwl to be formed by means of a dam across the River Claerwen.

(7) SUBMERGED DAM.—A dam (to be called the Submerged Dam) in the parish of Llansantffraid-cwmdeuddwr in the Caban Coch Reservoir across the River Elan.

(8) DOL-Y-MYNACH TUNNEL.—A tunnel or conduit in the parish of Llansantffraid-cwmdeuddwr commencing in the River Claerwen and terminating in the Caban Coch Reservoir.

Then followed items 9 to 46 which consisted of the construction of tunnels, aqueducts, reservoirs at Warley and pipe lines, followed by the two relevant entries concerning the railway:

BIRMINGHAM CORPORATION WATER

(47)   RAILWAY No. 1 – A railway 3 miles 0 furlongs 3.5 chains commencing in the Parish of Llansantffraid-cwmdeuddwr, in the county of Radnor, at a junction with the Mid-Wales Railway at a point 100 yards or thereabouts, measured in a southerly direction along the said railway from the southern entrance to the first tunnel on the said railway south of Rhayader Station, and terminating in the Parish of Llanwrthwl, in the County of Brecknock, on the right bank of the River Elan, at a point 430 yards from the north end of the footbridge crossing that river at Cwnch Wood, and which railway will be wholly situate in the said Parishes of Llansantffraid-cwmdeuddwr and Llanwrthwl.

48. RAILWAY No. 2 – A railway 5 furlongs, 9.5 chains wholly situate in the Parish of Llansantffraid-Cwmdeuddwr, in the County of Radnor, commencing by a junction with Railway No. 1, at a point on the existing road from Rhayader to Nant Gwylt, 160 yards or thereabouts from the south-west fence of Coed Troed-y-rhiw-fach, measured along the said road in a north-easterly direction, and terminating on the left side of the River Elan, at a point 250 yards or thereabouts from Abernant, and 440 yards or thereabouts from the north end of the footbridge crossing that river at Cwnch Wood.

One other item of interest is the Act's commitment to the Baptist Chapel and its graveyard which was to be buried under the water, by the scheme. Item 24 read as follows:

Removal of bodies from Carig Ddu Baptist Chapel graveyard.

24 The Corporation shall cause the remains of any person interred or deposited in any portion of the graveyard attached to Carig Ddu Baptist Chapel in the parish of Llansantffraid-cwmdeuddwr in the county of Radnor which they may acquire under the powers of this Act to be removed under the superintendence of the medical officer of health for the said county and interred in some other unconsecrated ground where burials may legally take place and shall cause any monuments and tombstones in any such portion of the graveyard to be removed to and fixed or re-erected. Provided that the heirs executors administrators or relations or friends of any person whose remains shall be interred or deposited in such graveyard may if they so prefer (at the cost of the Corporation such cost not to exceed ten pounds in each case) and under such superintendence as aforesaid remove the remains of such person to any burial ground wherein burials may legally take place and remove the monument or tombstone erected to the memory of such person to any place they may think fit.

Mr James Mansergh also supplied to the Water Committee in his report of 1891, a full estimate of the project. This showed a comparison between two 44 inch pipes running to Birmingham and five pipelines. The totals were £3,340,700 and £5,654,953 respectively. Of these amounts, he had allowed £45,000 for the railway construction and operation, with a further £20,000 if the pipeline was laid with five pipes instead of two.

The area chosen was said to have been relatively inaccessible as the nearest station on the main Cambrian Railways, was some miles away at Rhayader (*plate 8*) from the proposed work site. The Water Committee's reports commented that the Cambrian Railways system "was not renowned for its speed and efficiency". Obviously, as with every new enterprise, the Birmingham Water Committee came up against local opposition and several booklets appeared opposing the

Plate 8: A view of Rhayader station in 1900, the nearest station to the construction site of the reservoirs.   *Real Photographs, Courtesy Ian Allan Ltd*

Rhayader.

Plate 9: A view of Rhayader in 1898 from the south, showing the new pipeline of the BCWW aqueduct running across the picture. The Cambrian Railways station is just left of the centre of the photograph (arrowed) with an engine in steam.

Collection Mr C. Edwards, Rhayader

scheme. In March 1892 a booklet by Councillor Samuel Lloyd (price 1s.) briefly listed why Birmingham should not use Welsh Water.

1. The Quality of the Water. It was Storm Water, surface water being soft and insipid. Water to be hardened artificially.
2. There had been NO public consultation and it was rushed secretly through council.
3. Public Health would suffer and the Public Health offices not consulted.
4. Excessive costs with rise in water rates.
5. Fear of "locals" sinking private wells and thus the risk of pollution.
6. No *local* experts consulted.
7. There *was* extra local water available according to engineers.
8. Cost of soap, using hard water, would rise considerably.

Another attempt to stop the project from going ahead was made in February 1892 when Messrs Barlow and James deposited a Private Member's Bill in Parliament against the proposed Water Bill with a desperate plea, "praying to be heard".

A letter written on 22nd February, 1892 by Mr F. Newton stated that "the debt per head of persons would increase and that Birmingham at present had £10 1s. 8d. per person but this new water scheme would double this to £20 per head or nearly as much as Paris". (London was £9 3s. 8d. and Manchester £8 2s. 5d.). He concluded that the Rates would soar!

Obviously the people of Wales themselves also objected to the loss of 32,000 acres of their common land but, as one sensible local reporter stated in June 1893:

> It is understood that Birmingham had been lucky in securing so eligible a source for its water supply: for it is an open secret that had there been any hesitation on their part in securing Parliamentary powers for its acquisition, London would have stepped in and snapped it up.

So it seems the Welsh opposition was futile as the land was apparently destined to be used in any case for water storage for some distant city, somewhere.

Chapter Two

Early Developments and Construction of the Railway

Once the newly appointed consultant Engineer Mr James Mansergh was given a free hand to commence this enormous undertaking, he submitted on the 9th December, 1892 a set of "notes" to the Water Committee.

These clearly set out his needs, ideas, solutions for a swift commencement of the railway and main works and stated that he had only three men at the works near Rhayader at the present time. This report is included below; slightly condensed and with additional punctuation for ease of reading, and sets the scene to the early stages of the construction of the Railways of the Elan Valley. The pullout map at the back of the book should help the reader identify the area and the railway network.

Notes for Meeting with Water Committee at Birmingham at 4 pm Friday December 9th, 1892 by J. Mansergh

Since I received instructions to prepare for proceeding with the works under the Act of 1892, I have been taking steps to provide for the necessary increase to my staff of Assistants and supplement the work of Richard Tickell.

I want as far as is practicable to put on the surveying and setting out work required in making the plans for notices to treat such men as will subsequently be fitted to supervise the construction.

Early in 1893 I hope to have some half dozen men at work.

At present I have three at Rhayader, one on the railway and two on the aqueduct.

I have issued all the Notices required on the Railway under Section 84 of the Lands Clauses Act 1845 and similar notices, 50 in number, for the aqueduct from 4 m 6 chs to 7 m 57 chs.

I propose to get as much of the line of Aqueduct definitely located as possible at the Welsh end as far as Knighton before we are interfered with byleaves, say the beginning of May.

This would include 27 miles of the Aqueduct where the works are heaviest. The setting out of the remainder may in my opinion be deferred for another year.

The works I wish to get in hand as soon as possible are:

1st. The railway from the Mid-Wales Railway near Rhayader, past the Caban Coch Dam and up to the Craig-yr-Allt Goch dam
2nd. The three dams on the Elan
3rd. The two big tunnels between Dolau and Knighton.

Before we can do much even on the setting out of the railway above the Caban, the woods ought to be cleared away, and I have already been in

21

correspondence with the town Clerk as to making arrangements for obtaining speedy possession of the necessary lands.

I have had an interview with the Secretary and Engineer of the Cambrian Railway [sic] and am assured (as is natural) of their cordial cooperation.

I had prepared a general plan of the junction arrangements showing cabin (see page 30), signals etc. which the Engineer approved, but all this work and the putting in of the rails of our branch clear of their road they will require to do with their own men and materials, charging the cost to the Corporation.

The Secretary also informed me that the Company makes a charge for an easement (I think £100) and desires to be put into communication with the Town Clerk with a view to entering into formal agreements on these matters.

In connection with the work in the Elan Valley I am anxious as early as possible to be investigating the question of obtaining stone for the dams, and with this object I am on the look out for a thoroughly competent practical quarry man accustomed to working in the Lower Silurian.

At Vyrnwy there was of course a very large quarry and I may pick up a man who was employed there.

On the hillside just below the Caban on the left bank there are many thousands of tons of stone fallen from the cliffs above which I believe would be available for building.

I presume if we had acquired the Manorial rights over this part of the Common we might have taken this stone. It may now be desirable to purchase the whole area within the limits of deviation for both Aqueduct and the two railways.

I have had under serious consideration the question of how to do the works of the dams of the Caban, Pen-y-Careg and Craig-yr-Allt Goch reservoirs, that is, whether with or without contractors and I have very nearly come to the conclusion to advise that the latter of these courses should be adopted.

If I can secure the services of the gentleman who has acted as my Resident Engineer for over eight years in Teesdale I shall certainly do so.

My reasons are:

1st. That this work must be done in an absolutely sound and faultless manner, and I believe the chances of getting it so done are greater without, than with, a contractor no one about the job having any inducement to hurry or scamp.

2nd. That it will be practically impossible to draw a specification for these almost unique works in which there would be no weak places upon which a contractor could found claims for extras. Nowadays, with the big contractors likely to tender for such jobs, extra claiming has become a fine art. I believe they employ experts who from the moment a contract is commenced are engaged exclusively in devising and formulating such claims but this I am not prepared to guarantee.

3rd. I believe the work would probably be somewhat more cheaply done without, than with, a contractor.

4th. I can foresee only one reason why this should not be the case, viz, that a large amount of costly plant will have to be purchased which at the end of the job will probably be worth less money to the corporation than it would be to a contractor.

If this course is adopted you will of necessity require the services of a much larger staff than if a contractor were employed.

I am not now in a position to state exactly what should be the constitution of this addition but for the engineering and general direction there should be:

One principal Resident to supervise the whole of the works in the Elan Valley having an engineering assistant and a shorthand and copying clerk.

On each of the three reservoirs a junior resident having a similar assistant and clerk.

Into each of these four offices I should probably place as assistants, one of my pupils who had already had some office experience, but who of course would receive no pay.

The principal resident should be provided with a house, horse, trap and groom.

The gentleman I have before referred to has had fourteen years continuous experience of reservoir construction and will require, and is worth, a good salary. He has been getting from the Board and me together from £500 to £550 a year. I should not be unwilling rather than not secure him to pay 10% of his salary if you consider what he asks is high. He will probably expect a yearly advance.

The junior residents will probably be got for salaries commencing at about £300 a year.

For the aqueduct a Resident Engineer of about this class or somewhat more experience will be wanted for each length of seven or eight miles. They will of course require a horse and conveyance each and one engineering assistant and clerk at least.

I have secured the services of a very good young fellow who has had charges of some of the difficult works on the Vyrnwy aqueduct (notably the tunnel under the Mersey), and he will begin for me the setting out of the length between Dolau and Knighton embracing the two long tunnels early in January.

I have also engaged one of my old assistants who has for the last three years been superintending the construction of two reservoirs and other works for me in South Wales.

I hope also to get another of my old pupils who has had considerable experience and is a very reliable and promising man.

I have had a great number of applications for appointments and have little doubt that when the time comes I can lay my hands on a sufficient number of Engineers but I am not so sure about Inspectors. In this class it is not so easy to find men who are at once competent and thoroughly trustworthy.

The question of housing the large number of men (and their following) who will be required upon the works in the Elan Valley has been engaging my anxious attention. Whether these works are done with or without contractors, the provision of the necessary accommodation must be made in such a way as to ensure good and safe sanitary conditions, with so much comfort and convenience as will induce men to settle on the works for so long as they last. I believe that when all the works about the Caban are in full swing, 500 men of all classes will be engaged and that housing accommodation will be required for 1000 or 1100 persons [i.e. including families].

The location of a village sufficient for this number has exercised me a good deal. The flat lands below Nantgwilt would have been suitable, were it not that when the building of the Caban dam has attained a certain height, we shall require to hold up the water by temporary works in order to change the culverts which will then have to pass the river so that the village would be flooded. I have in fact come to the conclusion that we ought not to erect any buildings below top water level in either of the three reservoirs, and this conclusion has resulted in the selection of a site for the Caban Colony on the right bank of the Elan some distance below the dam, where it will be clear of the works and outside the range of quarrying and blasting operations.

Of this village I have prepared a plan which I now submit (*see page 50*).

It will have to be properly drained and provided with a good water supply and should have a place of worship, school and hospital.

In addition to this village another will be required higher up the valley for the people to be employed upon the Pen-y-Careg and Craig-yr-allt-goch reservoirs. For this the only site available appears to be near Tynant about half way between the two dams at the place coloured red on the plan produced.

A great many thousands of pounds will have to be spent upon these houses, but it is an absolute necessity that they should be erected if we are to keep upon the spot a sufficient force to complete the works in a reasonable time.

This work and its cost is of course not specifically stated in the priced Bill of Quantities although it is assumed to be covered by the estimates of the various works, that is to say, if let to contractors it would be one of the items of expenditure which would determine the price tendered.

If you decide on erecting the dams etc. without contractors you will of course have to build the villages. This is a class of work which is rather out of my line and it has struck me whether our ubiquitous friend Mr Stephen Williams would not be glad to undertake it with my advice and assistance.

The permanent houses for caretakers at each reservoir and the house for the Fishery Board's watcher are (as regards the former at all events) in my estimate and I would suggest that they be put in hand without delay so as to be available for early occupation by some of your staff.

Plate 10: Early site offices at Nantgwilt which would be submerged when the water of the Reservoir started to rise.   *Courtesy: Severn-Trent Water*

Plate 11: Mr G.N. Yourdi (Resident Engineer) who was of Graeco-Irish origin and is featured in *Plate 94.*

I have received a letter from Mr Stephen Williams with regard to the continuance of interments in the burial ground attached to the chapel near Careg-ddu – Mr Lewis Lloyd has raised the question of stopping this as early as possible by the selection and preparation of another site for both the church and the chapel grave yards, and I think it is a matter which should have your attention.

———

Since the foregoing notes were written for the meeting on the 9th inst, I have been assured that the Stockton and Middlesborough Water Board will release Mr Yourdi from his present engagement whenever you desire to secure his services and I have had some conversation with Mr Yourdi himself.

He began for the Stockton and Middlesborough Board in the spring of 1884 and will therefore have been nine years on the Teesside works by the time he leaves, having been engaged in a similar position previously for the Bradford Corporation.

He very properly says that he considers himself worth twice as much now as he was nine years ago, and his salary on engagement with the Stockton & Middlesborough Board was £365 a year. If you will offer him £600 a year now with a yearly advance of £50 I will undertake to make up the salary to such a figure as I believe he will accept.

Mr Yourdi is very much in favour of working on the dams without a contractor and as he has had 14 or 15 years continuous daily experience principally with a good substantial firm I attach considerable weight to his opinion and judgement. At the same time I wish you to give the matter very careful consideration before coming to any decision.

I know there is a prevailing opinion that men working for public bodies will not do as much for them as for contractors. My own opinion is that the majority of men of this class will earn their money as easily as possible whoever is paying them, and I have been told by contractors that the only chance of getting their money's worth out of men is to let them do piece work, and this you know the Unions are trying to stop.

I should like you to decide this matter as soon as possible because if the works are to be let the quarrying of the stone should be included in the price of the finished dams. If not let, then we should go to work in the quarries without delay, and I may have to ask you to advertise for a master quarryman as I cannot lay my hands on the class of man I want.

As can be imagined the Water Committee were more than impressed by these extremely comprehensive and thorough "notes", and instructed the Secretary to write to Mr Yourdi (*plate 11*), offering him the post of Resident Engineer. Mr Yourdi only took just over a week to deliberate, replying with the following letter on 27th February, 1893:

Cotherstone, Darlington
27th February 1893

Dear Sir,

I have given your letter of the 18th instant my most careful consideration and beg to submit the following proposals:

1st £600 per annum to start, increasing by yearly increments of £75 until the sum of £1050 has been reached, remaining at the last mentioned figure to the completion of the first instalment of your undertaking.

or

£700 per annum to start, increasing by yearly increments of £50 until the sum of £1000 has been reached, remaining at the last named figure to the completion of the first instalment of your undertaking. Engagement in either case to terminate with six months notice on either side.

2nd There being no houses on the site or adjacent to it to select from, I shall expect the Corporation to provide me with quarters as well as coal free.

3rd Pony and trap kept for my use to get about with.

4th Six weeks holiday in the year, viz. four weeks in the summer and two in the winter with the Corporation's and Mr Mansergh's approval.

5th Travelling and out of pocket expenses when on business connected with the works when ordered by Mr Mansergh or the Corporation.

6th Office, furniture for same, stationery etc. to be all found.

I believe I have noted all I can think of and shall be glad to hear from you the result of the Committee's deliberations.

I have sent Mr Mansergh a copy of this letter.

Yours truly,
G.N. Yourdi

It is interesting to note that the committee objected only to one point in Mr Yourdi's reply and this was his proposals for holidays, and informed Mr Mansergh accordingly. The reply from Mansergh to the committee makes interesting reading:

5 Victoria Street
Westminster S.W.
March 10th, 1893

Dear Sir,

In accordance with your instructions I have considered Mr Yourdi's letter to you for the 27th ult. and beg to make the following remarks upon it taking up the several points as they occur in order.

1st With regard to salary, I advise the Committee to offer Mr Yourdi £600 a year to start, with a rise of £50 a year to the completion of the first instalment of the works.

2nd and 3rd.   If you provide Mr Yourdi with quarters and coal say at Nantgwillt or Cwm Elan or in any other house adjacent to the works, a trap would be of little use to him because there is but a short length of road upon which he could drive, and after the first year the railway would be available to some extent. If he has to live in Rhayader he should find his own house but in that case I think you ought to bear the cost of keeping a pony and trap for his use.

4th   I am very much surprised that Mr Yourdi has made this suggestion about holidays, for during the nine years he has been on my works, the difficulty has been to get him away. I am quite sure, if it is put to him that you will not object to his having such reasonable holidays as I may approve at times when the works will not suffer from his absence, he will fall in with that view.

5th and 6th.   Of course he should be paid travelling and out-of-pocket expenses when away on business connected with the works, and an office with proper furniture and all stationery etc. should be provided for him.

The committee then finally resolved that Mr Yourdi should be offered the appointment of Resident Engineer, and the Secretary wrote to that effect on the 24th March, 1893. The reply was by return and dated the 27th March:

27th March 1893

Dear Sir

I have carefully considered the offer of the Water Construction Committee of the Birmingham Corporation as set forth in your letter of the 24th instant and am prepared to accept the appointment and sign the Agreement when ready.

May I ask you to give me a hint how soon I am likely to be wanted to start work, in order that I may make final arrangements with my people here, and thus in a measure avoid any unnecessary delay.

Yours truly,

G.N. Yourdi

He was further asked that his services be available on the 1st June, 1893, he reporting to the office in Rhayader.

During March 1893 a further appointment was made, to the growing staff. This was the Social Estate Agent, Mr Stephen Williams whose main work was to assign and settle all the relevant land leases. In May the Water Committee authorised James Mansergh to finalise all the specifications and Bills of Quantities, for the construction of the initial railways within the 1892 Act, i.e. Railways 1 and 2 (*see plans on pages 45 and 46*). At the same time the Birmingham City Town Clerk was authorised to advertise for Tenders to the construction of Railway No. 1; the contract to include all fencing, the entire construction of the line but with Birmingham Corporation providing the rails, sleepers and small irons. The gauge quoted was standard at 4 ft 8½ in.

The advert was placed in *Industries and Iron Journal* on 30th June, 1893 and read as follows:

> BIRMINGHAM CORPORATION. Tenders invited by Tuesday, 4th July 1893, for the construction of about 5,000 yards of railway on the left bank of the River Elan, commencing by a junction with the Mid-Wales Railway, near Rhayader, in Radnorshire.

Whilst all the office work regarding the Water Undertaking Railway contracts was being carried out, Mansergh was in regular correspondence with the Cambrian Railways trying to conclude a satisfactory agreement to the joining up of his "Elan Valley" railway to the Cambrian. He had received an estimate, based on sketches of the suggested junction at a cost of £4269 18s. 0d.

The Secretary of the Cambrian Railways wrote to his Directors on 26th April, 1893, setting out the problems he was experiencing with Mr Mansergh and the Birmingham Water Committee:

CAMBRIAN RLY CO.   *Secretary's Report 26th April, 1893*

To the Chairman and Directors

My Lord and Gentlemen,

BIRMINGHAM CORPORATION RAILWAY

I beg to place before the Directors a draft Agreement with the Birmingham Corporation. This has been prepared in pursuance of the Birmingham Corporation Water Act 1892, and provides that this Company shall put in the junction with the proposed Water Works railway at about ½ mile from Rhayader station. I may state that this will be an expensive junction, as the Board of Trade, whose opinion has been taken, have intimated that as the junction will join your line on a gradient of 1 in 66, a double junction will be necessary. The Agreement also provides for payment by the Corporation to this Company of £100 for the respective Wayleaves in perpetuity in respect of the aforesaid junction. A very important clause, however, has been struck out by the Birmingham Corporation. This Clause provided that the traffic required by the corporation for the new works, should be forwarded by the route most favourable to the Cambrian Railways Company, so long as the route was a reasonable one. Mr Stephen Williams, the surveyor who has acted for the Corporation in this matter states in his letter dated 17th of April that the "Corporation wish to work in harmony with the Cambrian Railway but they cannot consent to bind themselves by Covenants which may become most prejudicial in the future". The three routes by which the traffic will be sent from the Midlands Counties and the North are Welshpool, Builth Road and Three Cocks. As the Mid-Wales section of your line is outside the London and North Western route arrangement, the traffic can be sent either via Welshpool or Builth Road as consigned. The Welshpool route is the shorter by 9 miles, taking Shrewsbury as a common point and the difference between the latter route and Builth Road to the Company is of the very greatest importance. I have arranged to meet the Town Clerk of Birmingham on my way up to town today and will report to the Directors, the result of my interview on this subject.

The initial plan submitted to the Cambrian was in fact a sketch on a scrap of paper drawn by Mansergh whilst on location and looked as follows, showing a simple head shunt and junction to the single line:

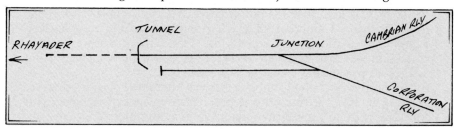

As stated in the letter this was not accepted and the actual junction agreed to, and estimated on, is shown on page 81.

On 4th July, 1893, the Mayor of Birmingham was summoned to the meeting of the Water Committee and requested to open up the en-velopes received containing the Tenders for the railway contracts and to "initial every one". He was then asked to list them and forward to James Mansergh for his decision, and this to be made public at the next available committee meeting in July 1893.

The full list of the 20 tenders received is included to show the great distances these contractors were prepared to travel to obtain work, and the enormous cost differences between the quotes. Note how Mansergh has corrected No. 6 to a higher figure; in an accompanying letter he states "he is not sure whether this error was accidental or not", hinting that the error could have won them the contract. Mr Mansergh had already decided that £13,000 should be the limit of the cost of these works and attached an initial report on these companies and their relevant tenders which makes interesting reading:

> Of the nine, the lowest is by Mr James Dickson of St Albans, the amount being £10,082 4s. 5d. and the highest by Mr Abram Kellett £12,890 1s. 0d., my own estimate being £12,584 2s. 0d.
> Of these tenderers three have done sewerage work for me before viz: Mr Dickson, Mr Ridley and Mr Kellett, the latter having now in hand the main drainage of the City of York.
> At the prices they have tendered you might safely entrust the work to either Mr Ridley or Mr Kellett.
> Mr Dickson so far as I know is a very respectable man and has had large

The following is a list of the tenderers with the totals corrected where required up to N° 9

No	Name & Address	Amount		
1	James Dickson, St Albans and Grays Inn R° London	10082	4	5
2	Arthur Matthews Diglis Worcester	11041	12	.
3	Francis C. Caffin, Broadway	11315	.	.
4	Henry Lovatt, Wolverhampton	11793	9	8
5	J & J Lawton, Twickenham	12000	10	.
6	Lloyd & Powell, Bristol and Pontypridd	12022	17	10
	Engineers Estimate	12584	3	.
7	John Price, G' George Street Westminster	12800	.	.
8	Thomas D. Ridley, Middlesbrough	12828	17	6
9	Abram Kellett York	12890	1	.
10	J & E Bentley, Leicester	13340	1	8
11	William Jones, Neath	13629	19	.
12	Mears & C° Liverpool	13998	13	.
13	Enoch Tempest Mallock Bridge	14155	5	6
14	Cruwys & Holbrough Gloucester	14,380	13	2
15	Watts & Wilson, Glasgow	16,138	13	9
16	John Aird & Sons Lambeth, London	16,403	18	7
17	James Watson & Sons, Glasgow	16,747	3	6
18	Perrin & Long, Sutton Surrey	19476	4	7
19	J. H. Davies Cardiff	19582	11	6
20	Thomas Evans, Cardiff	22104	14	8

A reproduction of the complete list of tenders submitted to the BCWW appertaining to the contracts for the Railway construction.

experience of sewers and drain laying work but I don't know what he has done in Railways.

My impression is that he could not finish this job without incurring considerable loss, and for many years I have made it a practice to advise against the acceptance of any tender under such circumstances, and I am bound to do so in this case.

The second tender is by Mr T.A. Matthews of Diglis Worcester, his corrected total being £11,041 12s. 0d.

There is one item in the tender viz. lighting and watching etc. (£750) which is three times as much as the next highest quoted by the whole twenty.

If this were brought down to £250 his price for the work would be £10,541 12s. 0d. This you will see by comparison with my own estimate I consider £2000 too low.

The third tender is by Mr F.C. Caffin of Broadway. It was correctly worked out and the total therefore stands at £11,515.

It is just possible in my opinion, if everything turns out favourably and with the best possible management, that the work can be done for this money without leaving any profit.

It may be worth while to enquire as to Mr Caffin's experience and his competence generally to carry out a contract under these circumstances.

The fourth tender is by Mr Henry Lovatt of Wolverhampton whose amended total is £11,790 9s. 8d., still nearly £800 below my estimate. It is probable that this gentleman may be known to some of you. I am not acquainted with him nor with

Mr Lawton	£12,000 10s. 0d.
Messrs Lloyd & Powell	£12,022 17s. 10d.
nor Mr John Price	£12,800 0s. 0d.

I believe Mr Price is a man of position and experience.

As I have said before I should be quite content with either Mr Ridley or Mr Kellett.

Messrs J. & E. Bentley have omitted to price an item which would increase their tender (by) £4000 and Mr Thomas Evans of Cardiff has evidently priced the permanent way, as though he had to provide the materials. His tender therefore would be reduced by something like £3750.

As Mr Yourdi's full time appointment was now imminent, the house at Nant Gwyllt was made ready for him. The Estates office, under Mr Stephen Williams, had also been busy with meetings and correspondence concerning three major landowners of the proposed line of the railway, i.e. Messrs Lloyd, Prickard and E.D. Thomas. One small owner, namely Mr Evan Jones wanted far more for his piece of land (£517) than was on offer, but a court order was obtained and the agreement only reached before a magistrates court. All was now signed and sealed and the total fees for the land for the railways amounted to £1360 11s. 6d.

By the end of July 1893, with all the land now secure for the construction of the railway, the Secretary had compiled a more detailed report on the five tenders that James Mansergh had personally not known. This again graphically describes the works that these railway contractors undertook, and scrutinises in depth each company's previous employment:

17th July 1893

To the Chairman & Members
 Water Construction Committee

Gentlemen,

In pursuance of Minute No. 142 I have made enquiries relative to the five contractors No. 3 to 7 in Mr Mansergh's report on the tenders for Railways etc, as to their experience on railway work and as to their financial ability to carry out the contract, and beg to report as under:

No. 3 Francis C. Caffin, Broadway

Mr Caffin has been employed on railway construction works since 1875. For five years he was under the Engineers, Mr N.H. Barlow and Mr C. Barlow. He was then employed as Contractor's Engineer and Agent upon the construction of a railway 75 miles long in Brazil. Afterwards he returned to Messrs Barlow, and was engaged upon the construction of the new Tay Bridge and other undertakings. On the completion of the bridge, he was engaged as Contractor's Agent on the Dore and Chinley Railway. Last year he began to take contracts in his own name. He give particulars of two only. These were both for the Warwickshire County Council, and involved the taking down and rebuilding of an important Masonry Bridge over the river Avon at Warwick. Mr Caffin is highly spoken of by Mr I. Willmot of this City, and gives the names of other good referees, from some of whom I have made enquiry, but have not received reports. As to his financial status, his Bankers say they have a very good opinion of him, but consider that some guarantee should be asked for as the figures quoted (twelve to fifteen thousand pounds) are large. Mr Caffin offers the guarantee of Mr Lewis Firth, Director of Thomas Firth & Sons Limited, Sheffield. I have made enquiry as to Mr Firth's sufficiency as a Guarantor, but up to the present have not received a report. Mr Caffin says he has a credit up to a £1000 with an Insurance Society, and has of his own some Plant that will be suitable for the work in question.

No. 4 Henry Lovatt, Wolverhampton

I have received from Mr Lovatt a long list of railway works in which he has been engaged for the past 20 years. They comprise works for the Great Northern, Midland, Great Western, and Great Eastern Railways. The amount of the Contracts he named are: £113,000, £90,000, £110,000, £140,000, £52,000, £82,000 and £90,000. The list appears to include railway work of every description and in my opinion marks Mr Lovatt as a Railway Contractor of the first rank. Mr Lovatt's financial sufficiency is so well known in this district that I have not considered it necessary to make enquiry relative thereto.

No. 5 I.H.J. Lawton, Twickenham

Mr Lawton on reply to my enquiries names no specific works on which he has been engaged but says that he has carried out over £750,000 of railway work, and that nearly all his Contracts have been for over £100,000 apiece.

He refers to two Divisional Engineers of the Great Western Railway. Mr N.K. Lawrence, writing from Reading, says that Mr Lawton carried out railway works at Bristol in a satisfactory manner, under his superintendence to the extent of £100,000, and Mr Roberts, writing from Newport, Monmouth, says that Mr Lawton has carried out in a satisfactory manner several contracts for this Company (Great Western Railway) under his supervision, and he thinks he may under ordinary circumstances and subject to strict superintendence, be relied upon to carry out a contract of the amount named, £15,000, efficiently and promptly. Mr Lawton mentions a Mr Hothard Thomson as his surety. I have received a very unfavourable report as to Mr Thomson which concludes with the remark "his means are very small and £100/150 could be nearer the mark".

No. 6 Lloyd & Powell, Bristol

Mr Lloyd writes giving an account of his experience extending over 35 years. During the first ten years he was on the late Mr Brassey's Contracts with Mr John Mackay. Afterwards he was with Mr Mackay, who started on his own account, and was one of his chief Agents up to five years ago. Since then he has been taking contracts for himself. He sends me copies of letters, one from Mr John Wilson, the Engineer of the Great Eastern Railway, saying that as Agent for Mr Mackay he carried out two important works with entire satisfaction. Another letter is from Mr Inglis, Engineer to the Great Western Railway, dated from Plymouth. This also refers to Mr Lloyd as Manager for Mr Mackay and speaks well of Mr Lloyd's work. In reply to my enquiry for financial references Messrs Lloyd & Powell simply say that they are prepared to carry out the Contract if entrusted to them.

No. 7 John Price, Great George Street, Westminster

Mr Price says he was Chief Agent for the late Mr T.A. Walker on Severn Tunnel on Gloucestershire side, and the Barry Dock Railways. He also had charge for some years of 22 miles of the Manchester Ship Canal. He refers· to two Engineers at Westminster, from both of whom I have very favourable reports. As to his financial position Mr Price refers to a firm of Solicitors, and to the Executors of the late Mr Walker. I have thought it unnecessary at present to write to either of these, but have made enquiry as to Mr Price's position. I have not yet been able to get any information as the Enquiry agency has been unable to identify him, his name not appearing in the Directory.

After careful deliberation of all the companies, it was agreed unanimously in committee that Mr Henry Lovatt be offered the contract and that the appropriate Bonds, Sureties and agreements be prepared.

Also during July, tender specifications were raised and advertised for the rails, sleepers and associated equipment that the Corporation were to purchase for the contractor to use on Railways No. 1 and No.

2 (*see plans on pages 45 and 46*). The detailed development of the Model Village, which was also well in hand at this time is dealt with in the next Chapter.

Having resolved the question of contractors, Mansergh was now confronted with the choice of which company offered the best materials and delivery for the hardware, i.e. rails, fish-plates, fang bolts and sleepers. He listed details for Railway No. 1 as follows:

Contract No. 1a for Steel Rails & Fish Plates		£	s.	d.
Richard White	Widnes	1868	4	0
Ebbw Vale Steel, Iron & Coal Co. Ltd.	122 Cannon Street, London	2029	5	3
John Hutchinson Darlington Steel & Iron Co.	Darlington	2299	17	0

Contract No. 1b for Fish and Fang Bolts		£	s.	d.
Wilkes Ltd	Grand Junction Works, James Bridge, Darlaston	548	5	0
Phoenix Bolt & Nut Co.	Handsworth, Birmingham	620	16	2
Baylis, Jones & Baylis	Wolverhampton	633	15	0
Patent Nut & Bolt Co. Ltd.	London Works, Nr. Birmingham	636	18	9
Hortons & Sons Ltd.	Alina Works, Darlaston	646	13	9
*Ibbotson Bros & Co. Ltd.	Globe Steel Works, Sheffield	692	12	6
Richard White	Widnes	702	10	6
The Patent Rivet Co.	Smethwick, Nr. Birmingham	972	15	0

* Messrs Ibbotson Bros also quoted for their Patent *Steel* Lock Nuts & *Special Steel* Fish Bolts at an increase of 10s. *per ton.*

Messrs William Barwell sent in a tender for the Fish Bolts etc. at £10 9s. per ton, but do not quote for the Fang Bolts.

Contract No. 1c for Sleepers		£	s.	d.
Richard White	Widnes	1072	16	0
Alexander Bruce	45 West Nile Street, Glasgow	1161	10	0
Burt Boulton & Haywood	64 Cannon Street, London	1200	0	0
Alexander & Co.	Cardiff	1200	0	0
John Bland & Co.	Cardiff	1288	16	0
Robert Lander & Co.	West Hartlepool	1425	0	0

I understand that Mr White is an agent or dealer and not a manufacturer and I would advise that you go in preference to a well known firm of repute for the rails and fish-plates and accept the Ebbw Vale Company's tender for Contract No. 1a.

For Contract No. 1b, I think Wilkes Limited may be taken if, as you may know, the Company is of good standing and repute.

Before finally accepting I should like half a dozen bolts (3 fish and 3 fang) as samples of what they are prepared to supply.

Contract No. 1c, I understand Mr Lees is making enquiries about Mr White and has learned so far that he is a metal dealer. I can't understand how he is in a position to supply sleepers so much lower than timber merchants and personally I would prefer that he be passed over in favour of Bruce of Glasgow or Alexander & Co. of Cardiff.

Mr Mansergh's recommendation for Contract 1a was followed and the Ebbw Vale Steel and Iron Co.'s tender accepted. So far as the sleepers were concerned, a sample sleeper was requested from Mr White, and, in due course, the Secretary reported:

On Contract No. 1c, acting on Mr Mansergh's advice, I requested Mr Richard White of Widnes, who had sent in the lowest tender for sleepers viz. £149 0s. 0d. per thousand, to submit a sleeper for inspection. This sleeper was sent to Rhayader and was reported on by Mr Yourdi as being very unsatisfactory both as regards dryness and creosoting. Mr White is a Metal Dealer and probably has not the proper appliances for thoroughly impregnating the sleepers with creosote, and Mr Mansergh advised that if his tender were accepted it would be necessary for an Agent of the Corporation to attend at the works and watch the process throughout.

Under these circumstances I have accepted the next highest tender viz. that of Messrs. Alexander Bruce & Co. of Glasgow at £161 9s. 2d. per thousand amounting to £1161 10s. 0d.

So, with this problem solved, the contracts for Railway No. 1 were finally placed and the Contractor's Agreement (with H. Lovatt of Wolverhampton) was signed and sealed on 29th September, 1893. All was now set for the first section of the railway to be built.

By 25th October, 1893, Mr Mansergh reported that Mr Lovatt had made a start and that he, Mansergh, had already made one inspection of the works. A first consignment of rails was about to leave Ebbw Vale and Messrs Wilkes, likewise, had 30 tons of fish- and fang-bolts ready. All these products had been tested and found satisfactory. The Cambrian Railways had laid in the new junction but signalling was not complete and Mr Mansergh was in touch with them concerning the delivery of the aforementioned materials by rail.

The local newspaper reported in November 1893 that:

The rough line of railway to the Birmingham waterworks is being sharply laid down. On Monday last an engine belonging to Mr Lovatt, the con- tractor, and called THE SCOTT proceeded with several trucks of rails as far as Aberceithon, a distance of one mile. It could not proceed further owing to a bridge being in the course of erection at Aberceithon. Several new large houses are being erected near Glanyrafon for the staff or head officials of the works. The number of men working at present is said to be about 800.

Having now settled all the initial problems and started the construction of the main railway line to the first dam site of Caban Coch, Mansergh requested more men and equipment to secure his base workshops and railway sidings for the construction of the first of the dams at Caban Coch. The following report was submitted to Birmingham:

(A) For working and opening out the Quarry.

(B) For laying the road to the Mason's yard and placing same in working order.

(C) For opening out the Caban trench.

(D) For putting workshops into working trim, and laying down the roads as well as making connections with Railway No. 1. and Timber for Cement sheds, vertical band-saw shed, gantries and goliaths. Also additional powers for offices, building in connection with clerical staff and assistant Engineers where required.

1. Two 10 ton steam travelling cranes with proper lifting and driving gear with large drum and pulley for wire rope interchangeable with chain.

2. Two 5 ton travelling cranes, ditto, ditto.

3. Winding drum for working incline from Quarry.

4. Four travelling cranes with chains to lift 10 tons for mason's yard.

5. One 5 ton breakdown or bogie crane for taking about the works (iron and wood or iron altogether).

6. One platform crane to lift 2 tons for general stores (iron frame).

7. Ropes, chains, clips, etc necessary for the above.

8. Small locomotive for working mason's yard, 4 ft 8½ in. gauge, 9 in. cylinders.

9. Machinery for sawing slate, circular saw and 10 hp portable engine, double cylinder.

10. Stone dressing machinery as used in granite quarries.

11. Horizontal band saw 4 ft pulley for band to take log 30 in. x 24 in.

12. Temporary half round sleepers
         9 ft x 10 in. x 5 in.

13. 250 tons of 55 lb. steel rails (s.d.) points, switches, fish plates, and signals, bolts and nuts and metal dogs.

14. 20 x 3 cubic yard wagons, 10 side tip, and 10 end tip.

15. 20 stone bogies 7 ft x 6 ft.

16. Six good draught horses, and one of lighter build to run when required in a spring cart.

17. One dozen strong carts, Scotch make.

18. Two timber lorries with break chain and draw out gear; Bradford make.

19. One strong spring cart.

20. Timber for temporary bridges, gantries and goliaths.

21. Loco. shed, 80 ft x 20 ft.

22. Horizontal band saw shed, 30 ft x 16 ft.

23. Cement shed for cooling as shown.

24. Cement Warehouse, as shown.

Plate 12: The workshop site at Caban Coch in 1901 showing the engine shed (*right*) and cement sheds (*central*).   *Courtesy: Severn-Trent Water*

Plate 13: Nestling under the enormous Caban Coch dam is the Elan Visitor Centre, converted from the former site workshops. Here one can spend many hours in the informative museum, film show and restaurant.

Author's Collection

25. Cot-bolters shed in wagon yard.
26. Horsekeepers hut.
27. Horse drivers hut.
28. Harness room, harness spring bars and all fittings.
29. Corn, hay and straw rooms.

This site at Elan, with all the locomotive sheds, sidings etc., can be seen in (*plate 12*) and is now the car park and Elan Visitors Centre site (*plate 13*).

Also included in the document was a request for considerable "crane power" and a note that Mr Yourdi was dealing with this matter. The eventual purchase of the cranes is dealt with fully in Chapter 6.

A progress report printed very early in 1894 and circulated to the Water Committee in Birmingham, included the following details regarding the railway development of works:

A contract has been entered into with the Cambrian Railways Company, for the construction of the railway junction at Rhayader with the Corporation railway, and another contract has been entered into with Mr Henry Lovatt, of Wolverhampton, for the construction of the railway itself as far as the Caban Dam, a distance of 2 miles 1,463 yards. This work is now well in hand, and it is hoped it will be completed some time in May.

Mr Lovatt's contract, the amount of which is £11,793 9s. 8d., comprises the earthwork and the laying of the permanent way, the sleepers, rails, and small ironwork being provided by the Corporation. The following contracts for the supply of these have been entered into: for rails, with the Ebbw Vale Iron, Steel, and Coal Company; for fish and fang bolts, &c., with Messrs Wilkes, Limited, Darlaston; for sleepers, with Messrs Alexander & Co. Cardiff.

The land, which will be occupied by cement and other stores, workshops and railway sidings below the Caban Dam, is being levelled and formed by Corporation workmen.

Possession has been obtained of the land immediately required for opening out the Gigfran quarry (which is the work that must be first undertaken), and operations have been carried on there for the last four months. Preparations for the purchase of cranes and other machinery for working the quarry are being proceeded with.

The Committee have appointed Messrs W.P. Marshall and Son, of Birmingham, Engineering Inspectors of machinery purchased.

The erection of the various temporary buildings required for the works at Caban Coch, such as stables, stores, carpenters' and smiths' shops, etc., and the provision of machinery and fittings for working them, are well in hand. The erection of wooden buildings for the chief offices and houses for the staff is also being proceeded with. Arrangements have been made at Cwm Elan House (one of the two large houses on the estate purchased by the Corporation) to provide quarters for the Assistant Resident Engineers. Nant-Gwyllt, the other considerable house on the estate also has been adapted.

The removal of an old Baptist Chapel which stands below the water line, and the erection of a new church in its place is necessary. Some sixty bodies and graves are to be removed from an ancient burial site to be resited in the new grave yard (*plate 35*).

In April 1894, Mansergh received the invoice from the Ebbw Vale Steel, Iron & Coke Co. Ltd for Railway contract 1, and is interesting that it shows the quantities and equipment needed for the railway.

Rails supplied by the Ebbw Vale Steel, Iron & Coke Co. Ltd for contract 1

Description	Weight				Rate per ton	Amount		
RAILS 68 lb. per yard	tons	cwts	qts	lbs		£	s	d
Railway straight	222	7	1	8				
Railway curved	206	11	0	6				
Shops site straight	68	12	3	23				
Shops site curved	28	17	0	0				
RAILS 56 lb. per yard								
Railway straight	250	4	0	0				
Total	776	12	1	9	4/10/–	3,494	15	6
EXTRA for curving rails	235	8	0	6	3/6	41	4	0
EXTRA for cutting to special length	97	9	3	23	1/–	4	17	6
FISH PLATES								
for 68 lb. rails	15	18	0	24				
for 56 lb. rails	6	8	3	2				
Total	22	6	3	26	6/2/6	136	17	7
TOTAL						£ 3,677	14	7

18th April, 1894.

Points and crossings were also required in connection with the railway sidings at the Caban and after putting their requirements out to tender, the Committee accepted on James Mansergh's recommendation, the bid of the Isca Foundry Co. at £185 2s. 0d. This company, a neighbour of the Ebbw Vale Co., would obtain the rails from the latter firm, supplied at the same price as the other rails already bought by the Birmingham Corporation. Despite this, it is interesting that the Isca Foundry's bid was some £30 lower than the Ebbw Vale Co., who had bid in their own right for the job!

By July 1894, it was obvious all was going well, but several letters and arguments between the Cambrian and the Corporation over wagon loads and weights are in evidence in the minute books. So Mr Yourdi requested that a weighbridge of 20 tons capacity should be sited on the railway to check wagon contents and in the long term save money. A location in the vicinity of the Suspension Bridge level crossing (near the village) was chosen, but clear of the highway; the building still survives today and at the time of writing one can see the sole remaining sections of the running rails. The platform area requested was 14 ft x 6 ft fitted with rails of 68 lb. section and sunk flush with it, set to standard gauge of 4 ft 8½ in. In this way railway trucks, as well as ordinary horse-carts could readily be weighed. Two tenders were asked for from W. & T. Avery of Birmingham (£105) and H. Pooley of Liverpool (£105). The tender from W. & T. Avery was accepted as they were prepared to send a man down to erect the machine "to total satisfaction".

Also in July 1894, the Board of Trade Inspector, Major Yorke came and inspected the whole of the Cambrian Railways junction and passed it for use, naming it officially Tunnel Junction and so the Elan Valley Railway Branch was officially born. Unfortunately in September Mr Mansergh received a copy of the Cambrian Railways invoice for the said work at the junction and, although the total was £293 6s. 5d. less than quoted, he still was not pleased. He wrote immediately to the Committee's secretary saying that he thought the money could have been better spent in extending the sidings at Rhayader station, if the Board of Trade had not been "given into" regarding their insistence on a double junction. The total amount for the work done by the Cambrian came to £3976 11s. 7d. (Estimate £4269 18s. 0d.).

As a considerable amount of Birmingham's public money had been already spent on the scheme, the Water Committee thought it prudent to invite dignitaries, officials and other selected persons, to make the first "official visit" to the area and site. This was arranged for Tuesday 10th July, 1894.

A copy of this invitation is shown on the following pages.

The sub-committee had arranged for this special train to convey visitors by the Great Western Railway and Cambrian Railways to Rhayader. The train was made up of GWR third class saloon carriages and left Snow Hill Station, Birmingham, at 8.00 am arriving at Rhayader at 11.15. The remainder of the journey to the Works Site was made over the new private railway of the Corporation and to a newly constructed halt near the suspension bridge to the village (*see page 46*).

CITY OF BIRMINGHAM, WATER DEPARTMENT

ELAN SUPPLY.

Inspection of Works in the Elan Valley, near Rhayader.

TUESDAY, 10th JULY, 1894.

THE WATER COMMITTEE,

IN ACCORDANCE WITH A RECOMMENDATION CONTAINED IN THEIR REPORT, WHICH WAS APPROVED BY THE CITY COUNCIL AT ITS MEETING ON THE 5th INSTANT,

HAVE THE PLEASURE TO INVITE

TO AN INSPECTION OF THE ABOVE WORKS.

THE PARTY FROM BIRMINGHAM WILL ARRIVE AT THE ELAN VILLAGE ABOUT NOON, WHEN LUNCHEON WILL BE SERVED IN THE PUBLIC HALL

AS MANY ARRANGEMENTS DEPEND UPON THE NUMBER OF THE PARTY, AN EARLY ANSWER, ADDRESSED TO MR. E. ANTONY LEES, SECRETARY, WATER DEPARTMENT, 44, BROAD STREET BIRMINGHAM, IS ESSENTIAL.

BIRMINGHAM,

JUNE, 1894

Memorandum.

A Special Train to convey the Visitors from Birmingham will run as under :—

BIRMINGHAM (G.W.R. Station, Snow Hill)	Depart 8-0 a.m.	
BUTTINGTON	Arrive 9-45 a.m.	Depart 9-50 a.m.
MOAT LANE JUNCTION	,, 10-30 ,,	,, 10-35 ,,
RHAYADER	,, 11-15 ,,	,, 11-20 ,,

If it will be convenient for you to join the Train at one of the above stopping places, kindly name the place when accepting the invitation, and I will arrange accordingly.

E. ANTONY LEES,
SECRETARY.

City of Birmingham Water Department.

❊ ELAN SUPPLY. ❊

INSPECTION OF WORKS IN THE ELAN VALLEY, NEAR RHAYADER.
TUESDAY, 10TH JULY, 1894.

44, BROAD STREET,

BIRMINGHAM,

7TH JULY 1894.

DEAR SIR,

Herewith I beg to hand you Photograph of the model of the Watershed, with notes on the Works to be constructed ; also a Plan showing the Buildings and Works constructed and in course of construction, to be inspected, and the route to be followed. Be kind enough to bring the Photograph and the Plan with you, as it will not be possible to supply duplicates.

The special train leaves Snow Hill Station (Livery Street side) at 8 a.m., and will run as follows :—

BUTTINGTON	-	-	arr. 9-45	-	-	dep. 9-50
MOAT LANE JUNCTION	-	,, 10-30	-	-	,, 10.35

Your railway ticket will be handed to you on joining the train.

The more interesting part of the journey commences after leaving Moat Lane Junction. At eight miles distance, the railway passes the small manufacturing town of Llanidloes, containing about 3,500 inhabitants. At this point the line rapidly rises to the summit at Pantydwr, situated about 800 feet above the level of the sea. Here the Watershed of the Severn is left and that of the Wye entered, and the course of the Afon Marteg is followed to its junction with the River Wye, about four miles distant. The railway then follows closely the Wye to Rhayader Station, which is reached in about three miles. The tickets are issued to this Station, and the train is timed to arrive there at 11-15 a.m.

Rhayader was formerly the county town of Radnorshire, and now contains about 1,000 inhabitants ; it is situated on the left-hand in the direction the train travels.

At Rhayader Station it will be necessary for the visitors to alight and take seats in the special train which will be awaiting their arrival.   No responsibility attaches either to the Cambrian Railways Company, or any other party, beyond Rhayader Station, either going or returning.

A short distance from Rhayader Station, the line passes through a tunnel, and immediately beyond is the junction with the Corporation line.   From this point, the route is shown on the accompanying Plan.

The train will stop at the temporary platform at the Elan Valley Station, immediately opposite the new suspension bridge across the Elan leading to the Village.

Luncheon will be served at 12 o'clock punctually in the Village Public Hall, which will be recognised by the flag on the hillock adjoining.   A cloak room will be provided near the entrance to the Hall.

At the conclusion of the Luncheon, the Chairman will propose the toast, " The Queen," and Mr. Mansergh will give a short description of the Scheme and Works, cartoon plans of which will be exhibited on the wall of the building.

The party will then start on the tour of inspection of the Buildings and Works, which will be explained *en route* by Mr. Mansergh.   The distance to be walked is nearly four miles   The time allowed at the various stages has been carefully worked out and is ample, provided the party keep well together.

Ten minutes before the departure of the train, a signal (an explosion from the quarry) will be given, and five minutes before the departure, another signal (two explosions).   The exact time for the departure from the Elan Valley Station will not, under any circumstances, be earlier than 4-45 p.m.   The party must again change carriages at Rhayader, and the train for Birmingham will leave Rhayader at 5-35.

At Moat Lane, where the train is timed to arrive at 6 o'clock, a stop of half-an-hour will be made for Tea, which will be provided at the Station.

The journey will then be resumed, the train being due at Snow Hill at 9 p.m.

Your obedient Servant,

E. ANTONY LEES,

SECRETARY.

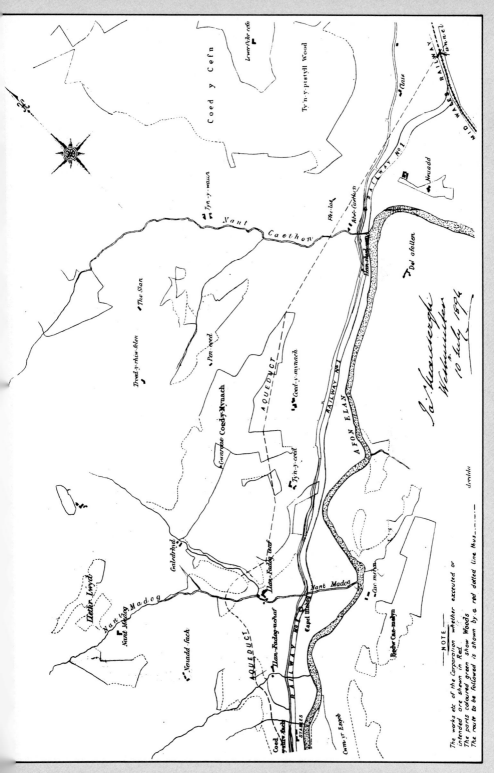

Plan dated 10th July, 1894 for Railways No. 1 and No. 2, signed by James Mansergh.

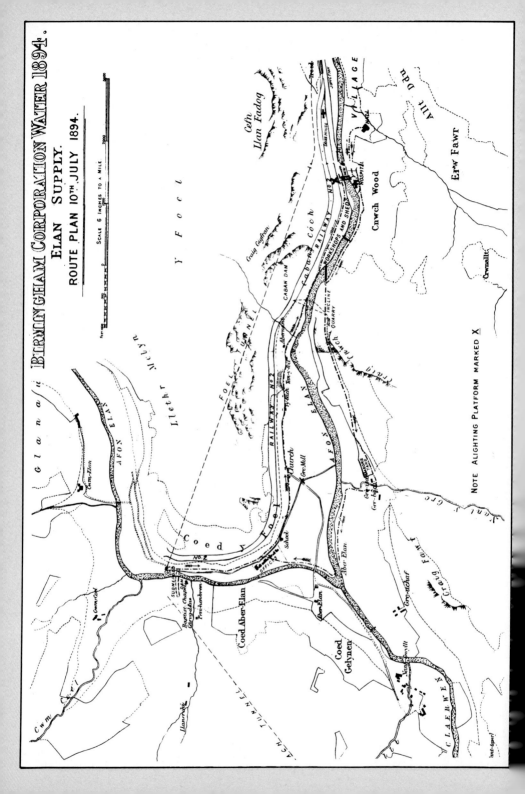

As the Great Western saloon bogie carriages would not travel round the curves on the Corporation line, it was necessary to arrange for another train, made up of Cambrian Railways four-wheel third class coaches to take the party from Rhayader station to the station in the Elan Valley, with the visitors changing carriages at Rhayader station. The fares for this special train were ordinary third class return fare from Birmingham to Rhayader, costing 15s. 11d. per head.

The sub-committee, at a late stage, were informed that the Corporation locomotives were not fitted with automatic brakes, and asked the Cambrian Railways Company to convey the train over the whole Corporation line, using one of their tank engines. They agreed but stated that the Cambrian Railways Co. would bear no responsibility in respect of the journey over the Corporation Railway.

The official list included:

Mr John A. Bright, MP
Mr George Dixon, MP
Mr John S. Dugdale, Recorder
Mr T.M. Colmore, Stipendiary Magistrate
Rt Hon. Joseph Chamberlain, MP
Rt Hon. Henry Matthews, MP
Judge Chalmers, County Court Judge
Sir Walter Foster
Members from other Corporations' Waterworks Committees:
   Sir John Harwood, Chairman of Manchester Water Committee
   Mr R.C.F. Annett, Liverpool Water Works
The Chairman of the Cambrian Railways Company:
   Mr J.F. Buckley
The local dignitaries:
   Rt Hon. Lord Ormathwaite, Chairman of Radnorshire County Council
   Mr Charles Evan Thomas, Chairman of Brecknockshire County Council
   Mr R.D. Cleasby, Chairman of Brecknockshire Standing Joint committee
and, of course, members of the Press:
   Illustrated London News
   Graphic
   Press Association
   Central News

Everything went according to plan and the influential members were treated to a "good day out", thus allowing the project to be advanced without dissension at the next committee meeting; the whole aim of the exercise by Mansergh!

By now with winter approaching, and as the Caban shop site railway sidings had been completed with the 17 sets of points laid and all the extra track fitted, Mansergh was keen to start the laying of the track to Railway No. 2 (*see map on page 46 for Railway 2*) and so

Plate 14: "Devil's Gulch", the nickname for the deep cutting on Railway No. 4 which held up the construction. Seen here looking north in October 1895.
Courtesy: Severn-Trent Water

Plate 15: Another view from the top of "Devil's Gulch" looking north towards the top dam site. October 1895.
Courtesy: Severn-Trent Water

asked the committee for rails for this railway, i.e.:

Rails	666 tons
Fishplates	19¼ tons
Fish bolts	5⅜ tons
Fang bolts	69¼ tons

By the time that Railway No. 2 was completed, the reports on further railway development were not recorded in detail within the minutes as many more important notes and meetings were now held concerning the "real" purpose of the project, namely the dam construction.

Thus Railways No. 3 and No. 4 (*see pullout plan at back*) were constructed relatively swiftly during 1895 and early 1896 and by the middle of July 1896 "traffic" was capable of travelling to the terminus at the Craig Goch Dam site, the furthest dam. The following report stated:

Other Railways and Road Diversions

Considerable progress has been made since the Committee last referred to these. The railway is now workable for traffic right through to the highest point to be reached, that is, the site of the Craig Goch dam, a distance of about six miles above the junction with Railway No. 1, and nine miles from the junction with the Cambrian Railway Company's line. The total cost of the railways above the Caban dam, and of the highway diversions to March 31st, 1896, has been £40,338 9s. 11d.

One problem in the delay of completing the railway main line had been the blasting of the cutting mid-way along the route of Railway 4 (known as Devil's Gulch) which held up construction by about 3 months and the curve had to be slightly more acute than previously envisaged to allow for this obstruction (*see plates 14 and 15*).

This then concludes the construction of the basic "main line" railway system of the Birmingham Corporation Waterworks*, but details of the route and the sidings including spurs and layout changes (due to operational difficulties) are shown on the main map and are dealt with in Chapter 7. The purchase of all the locomotives, rolling stock etc. is set out in Chapters 5 and 6.

---

* The whole track of the railway was initially constructed using both half round and flat sleepers with spikes holding down the rail. There is evidence that in later years some chairs were used on the main line.

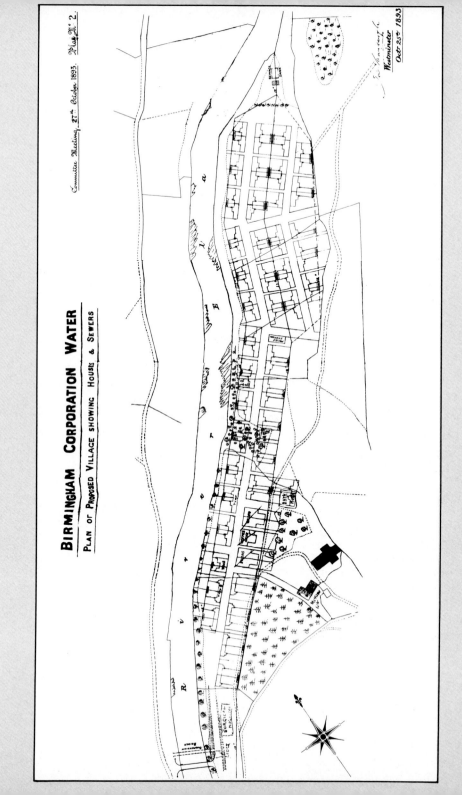

BIRMINGHAM CORPORATION WATER

PLAN OF PROPOSED VILLAGE SHOWING HOUSES & SEWERS

Committee Meeting, 27th October 1893. Plan No. 2.

Westminster
Oct 25th 1893

Chapter Three

The Model "Navvy" Village of Elan

Although this book was written to cover the history of the railway of The Elan Valley, it would not be complete without looking at the new "model" village associated with construction of the works.

Acting on very sound advice, the Corporation of Birmingham decided from the outset that, in the interests of their citizens, they would employ their own engineering staff to carry out the project and, in the words of the committee:

> The contractor, with all his human tendency to scamp work, and by such means to enlarge his own profit, should be dispensed with, and the scheme carried out by "administration".

This brave decision immediately presented the department with enormous problems, for there were no surplus houses in the locality, therefore nowhere to house the hundreds of navvies, labourers, masons and other trades needed to complete the scheme. The area was somewhat "remote" and it was obvious that the nearest village of Rhayader could not cope with the influx of such large numbers and even if it could, was some eight miles from some of the "works" on the Elan Valley project. Also it was obvious that the Corporation employees could not be "stowed away" (as the report phrased it) in the disgracefully crowded fashion in which working men were compelled to be on other large scale works of the time. Such living standards were known on other projects to have consisted of one large sleeping room containing perhaps a dozen or more beds in each, and each of these beds probably occupied both day and night, week in and week out. It was even reported, that "two per bed" had been found in certain works projects. This was not condusive to a good physical or moral atmosphere, especially when families were involved.

The corporation decided in their wisdom therefore that they would set a good example, to quote: "in this respect, as in other matters of modern social science, and inaugurate a plan worthy of their civic status".

In light of this statement and the corporation having already acquired the land from Mr Lewis Lloyd (in 1893), it was decided to build without delay a "model village" on a site situated below the proposed bottom dam of Caban Coch, and on the banks of the river Elan (some 4 miles from Rhayader).

The term "model village" was, architecturally speaking, not very true as will be seen later, but, in regard to its purpose, was indeed very functional.

During November 1893 the main waterworks sub-committee met

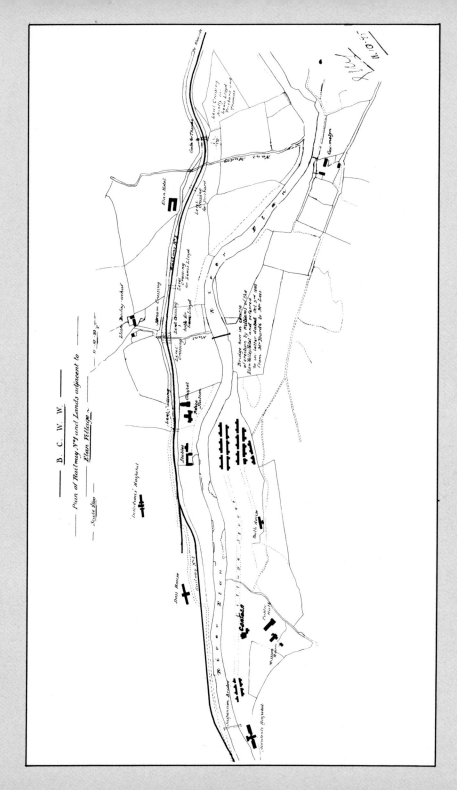

Plan of Railway No. 1 showing clearly the relevant positions of the village buildings.

at Rhayader, to inspect for themselves the village site and other sites in the Valley which had been proposed for temporary accommodation and other works. They were equipped with a proposed village plan (*see page 52*) as drawn by Mansergh, which showed the general siting of all the important proposed buildings, such as a hospital, public hall, reading rooms, canteen, bridge keeper's hut, school, shops and, of course, the hut accommodation.

After the inspection, the Water Committee reiterated that the course they had chosen was in the interest of the Water Department and that the subsequent work force would be of "superior class" especially if the accommodation was "of a high standard proposed". Most of the work would be carried out by men arranged in "gangs", and the absence of anyone of them through drunkenness or other cause would render the whole gang useless for a period of time, hence these men should be handpicked.

By September 1893 the work force employed was just 100 and the local inhabitants were already gaining benefit from the lucrative influx of "spenders". A local reporter summed up the situation:

> The Rhayader folk have a very high appreciation of the Birmingham scheme. Whatever it may do for Birmingham, it has done much for Rhayader. New buildings are springing up on every side. Brand new brick houses and shops stand shoulder to shoulder with ancient thatched cottages. The time-honoured "village shop" is now almost hidden by a modern-looking "drapery establishment", and the bootmaker of the village, with his hoary locks, and shoulders rounded with age, has in all probability to compete with the limited company, whose branch establishment has been opened at his threshold. White-haired and clean-aproned old grandmothers stand at their Jasmine-entwined doorways, gazing with astonishment at the butcher's cart as it dashes past, followed by the wine merchant's trap and the drapery delivery van – all spanking new and redolent of paint – and at the navvies as they saunter about the place, thronging the once almost neglected public-houses, and making the old town alive with their presence. These outward and visible signs of the advance of civilisation and the Birmingham Water Scheme may astonish the natives; but the proprietor of the hotels and the tradespeople, who on the tidal wave of Birmingham enterprise have developed great expectations, still regard Rhayader as a quiet place.

A new Elan Valley Hotel had been authorised on 26th August, 1893, and Mr Meredith from Wye won the contract with a bid of £2600. This project offered further rival work for the men arriving in the area as they also had the opportunity to join The Cambrian Railways Company (who were also employing men), for the enlargement of local station waiting rooms, a new station master's house and track alterations at the junction.

The Elan Valley Hotel licensee, Mr Cheese of Hay, applied for a beer licence in early 1894 and this was granted. All were invited to an official opening giving "free tap to all who attended".

During this period of time the local bobby, PC Morgan, was fully occupied dealing with increased robbery and drunkenness, and such reports appeared weekly in the local newspapers of the time. On a brighter note men were forming a good relationship with the local community, and, as early as 1st August, 1894, a football team from the navvies village called "The Rickerty Rackerty Crew" were playing local teams, and winning!

Navvies were often praised for their help in local situations, one such being reported on 14th July, 1894:

> *Narrow Escape.* – On Tuesday last, about noon as the Water Committee of the Birmingham Corporation were about to alight from the special train conveying them to the Elan Valley, a horse and cart belonging to David Lawrence, Bwlchoch, took fright apparently at the shrill whistle of the railway engine, and bolted down the road to the brink of a lofty embankment, and, failing to stop here, fell down, a distance of about 10 or 12 yards. Luckily, however, the horse fell on a mass of mould and marvellously escaped coming into contact with the large rocks which abound on each side. A body of navvies quickly came to the rescue, and succeeded in extricating the horse from its dangerous position, when it was found that no injuries had been sustained, and no damage done to the cart, although it had been overturned. The escape was most wonderful and that the horse pulled through the ordeal uninjured greatly surprised the onlookers.

The Navvies Mission supplied a temporary Rector to the area early in 1893 "for the well-being of the navvies' souls" but not until 17th February, 1894 did a permanent clergyman (Rev. Mr Harwood) take up post. He played a very important role in village life and also initiated a free library of books and periodicals for the men. Another facility soon installed was a permanent hairdresser who started work on 17th July, 1894.

As early as October 1893 Mr Hope Edwards of the Lion Hotel at Rhayader had applied for the "canteen sales rights" in the village. The sale of intoxicating liquor in this confined "workers village" obviously caused concern. The sub-committee considered the application by consulting a memorandum from Mr Walker, the contractor of the Manchester Ship Canal, and others. He clearly stated that on his site "no beer or spirits were allowed", and any offender would be instantly dismissed. The rule was to be enforced by officials such as foremen, timekeepers, watchmen and policemen. The Navvy Mission Society also were asked and suggested that the sale of beer (under strict regulation) would be better than secret drinking (which obviously took place). This was based upon an experiment of limited availability tried (with marked success) on the construction site of the Lyndley Wood Reservoir project for the Leeds Corporation Water Department.

The sub-committee took several days to discuss this point and came to the conclusion that, as the nearest Public House was over a mile away, the men would still walk to it, drink too much and cause problems, and the official Works Village police would have no control over them. They therefore decided to ask the Elan Supply Committee to apply for a license for the canteen and conduct its operation on the lines of the Lyndley project (modified to suit local needs). The first licensee was a Mr Frederick Lawrence on a salary of £4 10s. 0d. a week (free house, light and coal).

The next major problem was the housing of the men. The sub-committee ascertained from Mr Yourdi (and other sources) that the usual custom in workmen's settlements was for gangers to become "tenants" of the huts, providing accommodation for 8 and up to 20 lodgers, generally in one room and it was not uncommon, as stated before, to have two in a bed. Another ill result of the herding together of considerable numbers of men in one hut was the necessity for additional female labour in cooking and washing for the men and cleaning the house. This led in many cases to grave immorality. Where, as is general, the gangers were the tenants of the huts, their position tended to lead them to favour their own lodgers by keeping on inferior men, and discharging the better ones. Moreover, the ganger's wife usually made a profit out of her lodgers by selling food at enhanced prices, and the men (being dependent upon the ganger for their places) were not in a position to complain.

All this convinced the sub-committee that they should provide a separate cubicle for each man, and make the number of lodgers no greater than the hutkeeper's wife could herself attend to. Three types of huts were provided. Type One was to be a hut for the keeper and his wife and family plus eight lodgers, each having separate cubicles. This idea was another "first" in the history of accommodation in public works and was received with great satisfaction by the Navvy Mission Society. Type Two was a hut for a ganger and his family, providing a living room and three bedrooms with a scullery and W.C. This hut was not to be used for lodgers. Type Four was to be a superior hut, intended for one working ganger and his family with a sitting room, and three bedrooms, a scullery, pantry and W.C. These last type of huts were to be sited away from the other huts and not in the "proximity of the lower grades".

Most of the huts were constructed on site, by the resident work-

CITY OF BIRMINGHAM WATER DEPARTMENT

ELAN SUPPLY.

ELAN VALLEY WORKS.

RULES & REGULATIONS

RELATIVE TO

WORKMEN'S HUTS

Type 1. LODGERS'.

RULE 1.—The charge to be made by the hut-keeper for each lodger will be 2/6 per week, or 6d. per night for less than a week. For this, the hut-keeper must undertake to cook whatever may be reasonably required for breakfast, dinner, and supper, and must provide full attendance in all particulars, and, in the case of the weekly lodgers, the washing of the following garments:—

1 Shirt   1 pair Socks   1 pair Stockings   1 pair Trousers.

RULE 2.—Hut-keepers may supply the lodgers with food by mutual arrangement, but lodgers are at liberty to provide their own food, which shall be cooked without further charge.

RULE 3.—Each new occupant of a bed shall be provided with clean sheets, pillow and bolster slips, which shall be changed once a fortnight, or oftener if the Village Superintendent so directs.

RULE 4.—The hut shall be swept out and dusted daily, and regularly scrubbed with hot water and soft soap once a week, or oftener if the Village Superintendent so directs.

RULE 5.—No hut-keeper shall take more lodgers than the hut is arranged to accommodate, and each lodger shall be provided with a separate bed.

RULE 6.—No beer, porter, or other intoxicant shall be permitted in the hut beyond the quantity which each bona fide lodger is permitted to purchase at the Canteen for daily consumption.

RULE 7.—The only lamps permitted in the huts are the Defries patent or some other approved safety lamps with metal reservoirs and solid metal or glass bells hung over the funnels. The wooden ceiling over the lamps shall at all times be protected by tiles or sheet iron, with at least 1-inch of air space between the tiles or iron and the ceiling. These operations must always be carried out in the daytime, and never within the hut, but always in the separate lamp-room provided behind each hut. No oil whatever shall be stored within the hut, but only in the lamp-room at the back of the hut, and then only in the vessel provided for the purpose. Petroleum of the best quality only shall be used.

RULE 8.—The above rules may at any time be added to or varied by the Water Committee. Infringement of any of the above rules, or any other rules hereafter in force, will render the offender liable to notice to quit, and a second offence, after warning, will be followed by summary ejectment.

By order of the Water Committee.

G. N. YOURDI,
RESIDENT ENGINEER.

June 15th, 1894.

CITY OF BIRMINGHAM WATER DEPARTMENT

ELAN SUPPLY.

ELAN VALLEY WORKS.

RULES & REGULATIONS

RELATIVE TO

WORKMEN'S HUTS

Type 2. GANGERS'.

RULE 1.—Gangers shall under no circumstances receive workmen lodgers into their huts. If they desire to receive lodgers who are not workmen, they must apply for permission to the Village Superintendent, who will lay the case before the Resident Engineer, whose decision shall be final.

RULE 2.—The only lamps permitted in the huts are the Defries patent or some other approved safety lamps with metal reservoirs and solid metal or glass bells hung over the funnels. The wooden ceilings over the lamps shall at all times be protected by tiles or sheet iron, with at least 1-inch of air space between the tiles or iron and the ceiling. Under no circumstances shall lamps be cleaned or trimmed by artificial light. These operations shall always be carried out in the daytime, and never within the hut, but always in the separate lamp-room provided behind each hut. No oil whatever shall be stored within the hut, but only in the lamp-room at the back of the hut, and then only in approved, small, properly-closed vessels. Petroleum of the best quality only shall be used.

RULE 3.—The tenant undertakes that the sanitary arrangements connected with the hut shall be kept in a perfect state of cleanliness, and that he will permit no accumulation of dirt, filth, or refuse, about the premises. The hut and its appurtenances shall, at all reasonable times, be open to the inspection of the Village Superintendent, or any other official appointed for the purpose by the Corporation, with a view to see that the foregoing regulations, and any others which from time to time may be in force, are duly observed, and that the property of the Corporation is kept in a proper state of cleanliness and repair.

By order of the Water Committee.

G. N. YOURDI,
RESIDENT ENGINEER.

GEO. JONES & SON, PRINTERS, BIRMINGHAM.

June 15th, 1894.

BIRMINGHAM CORPORATION WATERWORKS.

ELAN SUPPLY.

RULES

OF THE

ELAN VILLAGE WORKMEN'S CLUB.

1.—All Employees of the Corporation are eligible for membership, and may become members, on application to the President or Secretary, and on agreeing to comply with the Rules.

2.—Each member is at liberty to introduce a friend, who for one week may enjoy the privileges of the Club. An extension of this time may be granted by the Committee.

3.—The officers of the Club are a President (who shall be the Corporation Missioner, ex-officio), and a Secretary, who shall be appointed by the Water Committee.

4.—A Committee of eight shall be chosen annually by the members from their number, to act with the President and Secretary in the management of the Club, particularly to assist in maintaining order, and in promoting amusements and recreation.

5.—Games, Newspapers, &c., and material for letter-writing will be provided. The Games will include Draughts, Halma, Dominoes, and Beanbags.

6.—A Bagatelle Table will be provided for the use of the members, at a charge of 1d. per game, or such other sum as the Club Committee may decide.

Approved by the Water Committee.

E. ANTONY LEES,
Secretary.

Council House, Birmingham,
21st December, 1904.

CITY OF BIRMINGHAM WATER DEPARTMENT.

ELAN SUPPLY.

ELAN VALLEY WORKS.

RULES & REGULATIONS

RELATIVE TO

WORKMEN'S HUTS

Type 4.   MARRIED WORKMEN'S.

RULE 1.—Tenants are not allowed to receive lodgers into their huts, except by special permission from the Resident Engineer, obtained on application through the Village Superintendent.

RULE 2.—The only lamps permitted in the huts are the Defries patent or some other approved safety lamps with metal reservoirs and solid metal or glass bells hung over the funnels. The wooden ceilings over the lamps shall at all times be protected by tiles or sheet iron, with at least 1-inch of air space between the tiles or iron and the ceiling. Under no circumstances shall lamps be cleaned or trimmed by artificial light. These operations shall always be carried out in the daytime, and never within the hut, but always in the separate lamp-room provided behind each hut. No oil whatever shall be stored within the hut, but only in the lamp-room at the back of the hut, and then only in approved, small, properly-closed vessels. Petroleum of the best quality only shall be used.

RULE 3.—The tenant undertakes that the sanitary arrangements connected with the hut shall be kept in a perfect state of cleanliness, and that he will permit no accumulation of dirt, filth, or refuse, about the premises. The hut and its appurtenances shall, at all reasonable times, be open to the inspection of the Village Superintendent, or any other official appointed for the purpose by the Corporation, with a view to see that the foregoing regulations, and any others which from time to time may be in force, are duly observed, and that the property of the Corporation is kept in a proper state of cleanliness and repair.

By order of the Water Committee.

G. N. YOURDI,
RESIDENT ENGINEER.

June 15th, 1904.

GEO. JONES & SON, TOWN HALL PRINTING OFFICES, 99&, SMITH STREET, BIRMINGHAM.

force under the watchful eye of Mr Yourdi. They were made of wood with brick and stone fireplaces and chimneys. The outside was of ¾ in. feather-edged boarding, fixed horizontally and overlapping with the inside which was lined with tongued and grooved ¾ in. match-boarding, arranged vertically. The space between the boards was 3 in. and filled with sawdust, whilst the roof was covered with a good felt over the boards, the whole being tarred with sand scattered over the roof.

At this early date of 1893 the accommodation proposed was to allow for an approximate population of around 1000 persons, being made up of 500 workers, plus their families, and other clerical workers.

One basic problem that arose with the construction of this village was, ironically, the supply of local water for drinking and sanitation. In the early days of the village this water supply came from a stream running down the eastern side of the valley, giving enough water for about 200 persons daily. Later this was succeeded by a piped water supply taken from a small reservoir held by a small dam at Nant-y-Gro*. The reservoir was fed by the Nant-y-Gro stream which joined the River Elan on its right, that is, south bank, about half a mile above the Caban Dam site (*marked E on plan at back*). Mr Mansergh proposed to construct a reservoir to hold about 500,000 gallons having its top water at about 875 feet O.D. The drainage area above this was about 450 acres and if its minimum yield, say the month of May, was adequate then this would amount to about 45,000 gallons a day. As little water was taken from this source for closets etc. Mr Mansergh was of the opinion that sufficient would be obtained (with the aid of storage) for Caban site works and domestic Elan village supplies. This was to be piped to all houses and also provide fire hydrants down all the streets.

The village sewerage system is worthy of a mention and the method proposed by Mr Mansergh for the drainage of the Elan village was described by him as follows:

> The sewer behind the houses on either side of the street will be a 13 in. stoneware pipe with a fall of 1 in 400 and vertical drops at intervals. A stream of water is to be kept running constantly through these pipes taken from the Elan river above, the inlet being controlled by a valve and by means of movable shutters acting as weirs. A sufficient depth of water will always be maintained under the closets. The closets for the men will consist of 12 in. pipes set or a vertical junction on the sewers, then a taper

---

* This Dam wall was used during World War Two, for tests on the strengths of explosives needed to blow holes in Dam walls. These tests were carried out secretly for the Bouncing Bombs trials and this, in an important and roundabout way, eventually helped destroy the German Dams in the Dam Busters raid by the RAF's 617 Squadron.

to 6 in. and a taper pan with a plumb back above. I propose this plan in order to avoid having any water apparatus liable to freeze out in the open. For the Hut-keeper's family a separate W.C. will be provided which will be flushed by the whole of the house waste water passing under it.

Above the outlet into the river at the low end of the Village I propose to put in a pair of grill chambers with iron screens simply for the purpose of extracting rags, paper and other solid matters which would show in the river. This will be doing more to sewerage than Rhayader or any other of the Villages on the river do (so far as I can ascertain), and we need not go to greater expense unless compelled. So far as our Village is concerned it will be the method least likely to create offence and the waste screened out will be buried.

For each hut of Type 1, I propose to put up three outside closets.

The road up to this village from Rhayader (three miles down-stream) was situated on the north bank of the River Elan, but the village was constructed on the south bank, on the gentle slope of the valley floor and at the foot of a beautifully wooded hillside. To avoid the use of a rough wooden bridge (originally the site of a ford and marked F on the plan) that existed over the River Elan at the lower end of the site, James Mansergh requested on 16th July, 1894 that he be allowed to purchase material for the construction of a suspension bridge near Aber Elan Ford. This was granted but not after a con-siderable fight with Mr Lloyd who requested a masonry bridge, and so, as can be seen from the photographs (*plates 16 and 17*), a hand-some bridge was erected at a total cost of £1009 0s. 8d.

This bridge, being the only approach to the village, Mansergh placed a guard house at the end, to be manned day and night so halting all unauthorised personnel (*see plate 18*). Thus all strangers, tramps, or genuine workmen in search of employment, were turned back and had to spend at least one night in the Corporation Barracks or "Doss House", which was situated on the north bank near the bridge (*see map*). Again, this bridge was essential for the men living in the village to gain access to the main workshops etc., on the northern bank.

The "Doss House" (*plates 19 and 20*) was built in order to protect the settled village population from the incursion of gangs of men from outside, who might well introduce smallpox and other infectious diseases. It was run as a "military style" organisation, and every applicant who was seeking work was compelled to strip and bathe in the evening and during the night his clothes were disinfected. In the early morning he was then thoroughly examined by the resident medical officer and, if all was well, the fortunate navvy was allowed to "cross the bridge" in search of work and lodgings within the village huts. These stringent rules ensured a clean and healthy state within this tightly packed community.

Plate 16: The first suspension bridge across the River Elan seen here in 1900, with Railway No. 1 seen on the left, the accident hospital on the right far bank and the village in the centre.   *Courtesy: Severn-Trent Water*

Plate 17: The bridge today, having twice been replaced during its lifetime. This third structure has now been condemned and a Bailey Bridge placed alongside to carry the traffic to the village.   *Author's Collection*

CITY OF BIRMINGHAM WATER DEPARTMENT.

ELAN SUPPLY.

ELAN VALLEY WORKS.

Rules for Bridge-Keeper, Elan Village.

1. To see that no person is allowed to pass the gates who is not a *bona fide* corporation official, hut-keeper, or lodger, or *bona fide* visitor to the huts desirous of seeing friends among the residents, and no tradesman without the necessary pass.

2. To examine each tradesman's van before allowing it to enter the village, with a view to intercept illicit commerce in intoxicants.

3. To open and close the gates when required for the passage of vehicles and foot-passengers.

4. To open the gates for the exit and entrance of the men for the first, second, and fourth quarters.

5. To close the bridge gates every evening at 10 o'clock, excepting Saturday, when the gates will be closed at 11 o'clock.

6. To obey the instructions of the Village Superintendent and of the Resident Engineer.

7. To observe any addition to, or variation of, these rules issued from time to time by the Water Committee.

By order of the Water Committee,

G. N. YOURDI,

Resident Engineer.

Plate 18: The "Guard House". The Elan village bridge keeper's hut, situated on the road into the village. Behind (*left*) is the Accident Hospital and the suspension bridge tower can be seen at the shoulder of the man on the cart (being searched).   *Courtesy: Severn-Trent Water*

The building contained 30 or 40 beds for these waifs and strays, with two baths and disinfecting chambers for clothes and was situated on the main road from Rhayader between the junction of Railway No. 1 and No. 2. It was interesting to note that a newspaper report of 14th October, 1893 stated that "every day large numbers of labourers arrive at Rhayader hoping for work. The work house (Doss House) had 186 in house at present". It must have been a tight squeeze!

Mr Yourdi submitted a written report to the Water Committee on another "Doss House" at Standedge for comparison and this has been included for interest.

"Doss" House

On my way from Standedge I paid a visit to the ship Canal Works at Latchford, and took the opportunity of visiting a Common Lodging or "Doss" House at Warrington, to which the Secretary of the Navvy Mission

Plates 19 and 20: These two photographs show the Doss House. *Plate 19:* The position of the Doss House between railways No. 1 and No. 2. This particular view shows the spur line rising to the Filter bed site being laid. *Plate 20* portrays the sparse interior of the Doss House with one stove, one light and no other facilities other than a bed.   *Courtesy: Severn-Trent Water*

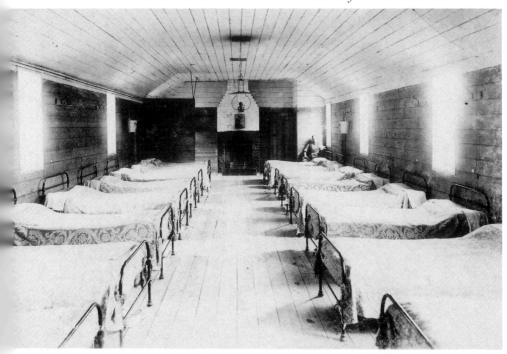

BIRMINGHAM CORPORATION WATERWORKS.

VACCINATION

NOTICE IS HEREBY GIVEN that the Corporation have made arrangements with **DR. GORDON RICHARDSON**, at the Accidents Hospital, in the Elan Village, to Vaccinate or Re-vaccinate, as the case may be (free of charge), all persons whose names are on the books of the Corporation.

All such persons who have been Vaccinated must call on the same day in the following week for inspection at the Accidents Hospital.

Days & Hours of attendance appointed for Vaccination:

Tuesdays and Fridays	-	1 p.m. to 2 p.m.
Sundays	-	10 a.m. to 12 noon.

By order of the Water Committee.

G. N. YOURDI,
RESIDENT ENGINEER.

March, 1896.

BIRMINGHAM CORPORATION WATERWORKS.

ELAN VALLEY WORKS.

DOSS HOUSE.
RULES FOR LODGERS.

(1.) The House is intended for the temporary accommodation of persons seeking employment on the Works of the Corporation.

(2.) No Applicant will be admitted unless he consents to have his clothes disinfected and to take a bath.

(3.) The price charged is 3d. each per night, which must be paid on entering. In exchange the Applicant will receive a numbered ticket, entitling him to a night's lodging, with use of clean night-shirt, bed, bed-clothes, and use of the common fire.

(4.) Lodgers are permitted to remain in the House one night only, unless, on the following day, they are successful in obtaining employment on the Works.

(5.) Men who obtain employment are required to remain in the Doss House a week before they will be permitted to take lodgings in the Elan Village, and must each obtain a "Workman's Doss House Ticket" from the time-keeper, and must show it to the care-taker at the Doss House, when applying for lodgings on the second and following nights.

(6.) Provisions can be obtained from the care-taker at the following prices:—

One pint of tea, with milk and sugar	-	-	1d.
Potatoes (per meal)	-	1d.	Two Red Herrings - 1d.
Bacon (per lb.)	-	8d.	Bloater (each) - 3½d.
Bread (per lb.)	-	1d.	Soup - 1d.

(7.) Lodgers are permitted to provide their own food and to use the common fire to cook it.

(8.) No one is permitted to bring intoxicating drink of any kind whatever into the House, and anyone infringing this rule will be at once turned out, and, if in employment on the Works, will be paid off, and will have no further chance of being engaged.

(9.) Lodgers must strictly observe the Rules, and must be quiet and orderly in their conduct. The care-taker is authorised to turn out anyone transgressing the Rules.

(10.) Lodgers are requested to help in the maintenance of order, and in the observance of the Rules.

By order of the Water Committee,

G. N. YOURDI,
RESIDENT ENGINEER.

February, 1895.

Geo. Jones & Son, Printers, Town Hall Printing Offices, 87-38, Edmund Street, Birmingham.

Society, in whose company I was, had the means of obtaining admission. The house, I was informed by him, was the most popular in the neighbourhood, and the landlady informed me that her accommodation was always fully occupied when the Works were in full swing. She had accommodation for 104 lodgers. The bedsteads and bedding were very similar in style to those furnished by the L & NW Railway at Standedge. In the common room was a large open fire and long tables and benches. Cooking utensils are provided by the landlord. The lodgers bring in and cook their own food; many of them are said to be excellent cooks.

The charge is 4d. per night; but the accommodation is of a superior order, and intended to attract and retain lodgers; not as would be the case with us, simply to provide temporary shelter for one night only. I think that probably it will be better for us to provide wooden beds, with rugs. The chief objection to the latter is that they retain vermin without their being apparent to the eye. Probably a charge of 2d. per night would be a fair one in our case.

One of the last buildings to be authorised was the main canteen which again is shown on the plan on page 52.

Whilst all this construction work was going on, Mr Yourdi was trying to build up his "superior work force", and requested help from his employers in Birmingham into establishing rates of pay and hours worked. He sent them a memorandum in December 1893, comparing local work rates to that of the site. This has been included as it indicates the pay and conditions of the area at the time and also shows the competition (already mentioned) that existed in the area.

The Cambrian Railways

Foreman of Gangs	21s. to 25s. per week
Labourers	18s. per week
Carpenters	4s. 4d. to 4s. 6d. per day
Masons	" " " "

Time worked 54 hours per week.

ADVANTAGES:
Constant work for the labourers. Free pass twice a year, and ticket to travel when required at ¼d. per mile. Some of the men live at level crossings at a rental of 1d. per week.

Elan Hotel – Llanfadog

Masons	6d. to 6½d. per hour
Carpenters	6d. per hour
Labourers	4d. per hour

Time worked per week 56½ hours.

Stone Quarries

Labourers getting stone	20s. per week

Time worked 54 hours per week.

Building Trade, Rhayader

Masons	5*d.* per hour
Bricklayers	" "
Carpenters	" "
Labourers	4*d.* & 4½*d.* per hour

Time worked 57½ hours per week.

The list which followed gave the rates for the dam construction workers, already working for the Corporation:

Quarry

Men drilling holes	5*d.* per hour
Men bearing bricks (as well as ordinary labourers)	4½*d.* per hour
Foreman or Ganger 36*s.* per week, wet & dry.	

Village & Offices

Masons, rough	6½*d.* per hour
Masons, fair	7*d.* per hour
Bricklayers	8*d.* per hour
Carpenters	6*d.* per hour
Carpenters in charge but who work as well	7*d.* per hour
Labourers, ordinary	4½*d.* per hour
Navvy	5*d.* per hour

Ordinary Navvy Ganger 30*s.* & 27*s.* per week, wet & dry.
Full time 55¼ hours per week. Men were allowed half an hour in the morning and the same at night to walk from and to Rhayader, pending completion of the huts now in progress.

Work begins on a Monday at 7 am.
Work stops on a Saturday at 1 pm.
Time thus made up:

Monday	9 hours
Tuesday	10 hours
Wednesday	10 hours
Thursday	10 hours
Friday	10 hours
Saturday	6½ hours
Full time	55½ hours

The accommodation huts themselves required to be furnished and Mr Yourdi based his suggestions again on a visit on 18th December, 1893 to the LNWR site works on the New Standedge Tunnel project, which was constructing a new bore through the Pennines. With 1500 men employed, the LNWR had provided similar "hut" accommodation to the Elan scheme and so it was appropriate to look at the furnishing of their accommodation. Mr Yourdi found that the LNWR had provided a double bed and bedding for the worker and his wife, single bed and linen for the children, single bed and linen for the lodgers, with a long table and benches in the living room for all. The bedding comprised of palliasses, flock mattress, pillow, sheets, blankets and a quilt. A fine touch was that the blankets had initials LNWR in large red letters sewn in, and the quilts the company's intricate coat of arms woven in. Mr Yourdi was told that by providing everything it made for uniformity and kept up standards and, above all, allowed the right of inspection at any time by the authorities – a clever move on their part.

Mr Yourdi obtained all the necessary addresses from the LNWR for supplies of bedsteads (single at 8s. each and doubles at 8s. 9d. each, less 5 per cent discount). The cost of mattresses was 7s. single and 10s. double; pillows cost 10d. each.

One landlady of a hut had told Mr Yourdi that "the oven was used to bake all the bread for her family and lodgers". This impressed him and he enquired as to their cost, but with the proviso that hot water boilers were attached (cost £2 13s. 6d.) to these oven/stoves to provide constant hot water for each hut.

The rent for accommodation at Standedge was analysed and a family had to pay 10s. per week entitling them to 5 cwt of coal, whilst each lodger paid 3s. 6d. per week (this sum providing tea, potatoes and the washing of one shirt and stockings (6d. extra for a trouser wash)). The Manchester Ship Canal by comparison, was charging 6s. per week, but without coal. Mr Yourdi gathered all this information together and recommended that the rent for a Type 2 hut should be 5s. (including 2 cwt of coal), a tactful compromise!

By late 1893, fourteen applications for retail shops had already been received from local inhabitants trying hard to "cash in" on the new-found trade. The applications were for general stores, grocers and provisions, drapers, barbers, confectioners, chemist, tobacconist, butcher and licensed victualler. The committee, however, decided not to build any shops but to allow the Rhayader traders to supply the village, with a proviso that land for shops should be reserved within the village should it be needed in the future. The land set apart for shops was on the south side of the main street, and eventually a Co-op stores was erected and opened in September 1895. This provided considerable relief to the villagers as there were many reports of excessive profiteering from the local suppliers.

An accident hospital was built (*see plate 21*) containing 16 beds initially, 10 for men and 6 for women or children, with resident quarters for the doctor and nurses. The first medical officer to be appointed by Dr Richardson (who was the local doctor to the village)

BIRMINGHAM CORPORATION WATERWORKS.

ELAN SUPPLY.

ELAN VALLEY WORKS.

ACCIDENTS HOSPITAL.

RULES.

1. The Hospital is intended only for the treatment of Accidents or Surgical Cases. The Employees of the Corporation and their families are alone entitled to be treated. Cases will be admitted to the Hospital, or treated as Out-patients, in the discretion of the Resident Medical Officer.

2. No Medical Cases shall be treated as Out-patients.

3. No person suffering from any Infectious Disease shall be admitted as an In-patient.

4. Friends of Patients are allowed to visit them on the following days:—

		P.M.		
WEDNESDAYS	-	6·30	to	7·30
SATURDAYS	-	2·0	to	4·0
SUNDAYS	-	2·0	to	4·0

No Patient is allowed to receive more than two visitors at the same time.

5. No smoking is allowed in the Hospital before 6 p.m., and only in the room provided for the purpose.

6. No stimulants, under any circumstances, are permitted to be brought into the Hospital by patients or visitors.

7. All articles brought into the Hospital by a Patient's friends or relations must be handed over to the Nurse in charge.

8. When in the Hospital, patients must behave in a quiet and orderly manner, and conform to the Rules of the Hospital. Any infringement of this Rule will render the patient liable to dismissal, at the discretion of the Resident Medical Officer.

By order of the the Water Committee,

E. ANTONY LEES,
Secretary.

Council House, Birmingham,
22nd February, 1896.

GEO. JONES & SON, TOWN HALL PRINTING OFFICES, 82-84, EDMUND STREET, BIRMINGHAM.

BIRMINGHAM CORPORATION WATERWORKS.

ELAN SUPPLY.

ELAN VALLEY WORKS.

RULES
FOR THE
ADMISSION OF IN-PATIENTS
AND FOR THE
TREATMENT OF OUT-PATIENTS
AT THE
ACCIDENTS HOSPITAL.

1.—The Hospital is intended only for the treatment of Accidents or Surgical Cases. The Employees of the Corporation and their families are alone entitled to be treated. Cases will be admitted to the Hospital or treated as Out-patients in the discretion of the Resident Medical Officer.

2.—No Medical Cases shall be treated as Out-patients.

3.—No person suffering from any Infectious Disease shall be admitted as an In-patient.

4.—When in the Hospital, patients must behave in a quiet and orderly manner, and conform to the Rules of the Hospital. Any infringement of this Rule will render the patient liable to dismissal, at the discretion of the Resident Medical Officer.

By order of the Water Committee,

E. ANTONY LEES,
Secretary.

Council House, Birmingham,
21st December, 1894.

GEO. JONES & SON, PRINTERS, 82-84, EDMUND STREET, BIRMINGHAM.

Plate 21: With a warm fire fighting off the cold of winter, the carpeted main ward in the general hospital, Elan village, looks very inviting. At 2.23, tea is simmering on the fire and the scene abounds with pot plants (February 1897).
Reproduced by permission of the Reference Library, Birmingham

was a Dr Barber of Aberdeen University, but his "habits" rendered him unsuitable and he was dismissed rapidly, with a Dr Clarke, MRCS, LRCP, from London taking his place. The head nurse, Mrs D.E. Parkes, who had 10 years experience in a children's hospital in Birmingham, was employed on a salary of £50 per annum, with one month's notice to be given on either side. From this salary she had to provide her own uniform. There was also a cook (£16 per year) and a house maid (£12 per year), both of whom arrived on 20th November, 1894, but it was reported that both these ladies left after only one month, due to the lack of patients and the total loneliness. During the early years two local nurses helped part time at night, but when the hospital was in "full swing" in the late 1890s, a further nurse, Miss Tarbolton, was employed at £40 per annum. With a smallpox epidemic having occurred in the vicinity in February 1890, the committee wisely decided to construct an Isolation Hospital for infectious diseases just in case. This was sited high on the hills overlooking the village (see pull-out map). The hospital was put to good use in September 1896 when a severe epidemic of typhoid fever spread through the work force. Medical care in these days had to be paid for and the Birmingham Water Committee established a weekly pay scheme to cover these costs. The accompanying rules tell all.

The men needed some form of banking facility, as the banks were in Rhayader and closed at the times the men were off work, so a branch of the Post Office was suggested (with Savings Bank facilities). The main site also now needed an office for the private telegraph wire and it seemed logical that this operator could also act for the Post Master and cover both jobs. Accordingly the Post Office* was opened on 1st October, 1894.

The main dam construction site and village construction moved swiftly on, and, by March 1894 (despite a very bad winter) the Elan sub-committee met to discuss the appointment of the first school mistress. After long discussion with local schools, and with the school master at Vyrnwy Reservoir, it was decided that she should be Welsh-speaking, but not necessarily able to teach Welsh. Although there were over 300 men on site, less than a quarter were Welsh, hardly any of these spoke Welsh in any case. None of the local schools were speaking Welsh either, so it was agreed that this qualification was not to be a stumbling block. Just as well, as the Committee only received one reply from a Miss Pitt, who had had good experience with navvy children in schools in the Severn Valley and the Manchester Ship Canal construction sites. She began employment in the new school (plates 22 and 23) on 24th April, 1894 (a quick decision due to the desperate plight of the growing numbers of village children) at £7 per month, but on a fortnight's notice.

The village needed public buildings for the welfare of the men and their families, and the first to be erected was a Mission and school rooms to hold about 200 persons. This would serve as a church on Sundays and act as a school during the week. A further public hall and reading room were constructed to hold entertainments, "penny readings", concerts and lantern slide shows etc., accommodating about 300 persons. Public baths and washhouses were built to attract

---

* Just out of interest, the Elan Visitors Centre received a lady visitor in 1986 who, as a child, remembers going to this Post Office with her mother to draw out money!

ELAN VALLEY SICK CLUB
RULES.

1.—The Club shall be called the "ELAN VALLEY SICK CLUB.' The membership shall be confined to the employees of the Birmingham Corporation engaged upon the Elan Valley Works . By arrangement with the Corporation, membership is compulsory upon all the workmen employed by the Corporation on the said Works, and the amount of the subscriptions payable by members to the Club will be deducted from the wages accruing due from time to time to them.

2.—The business of the Club shall be managed by a Committee, consisting of a President, Hon. Treasurer, Hon. Secretary, and nine members, to be elected at the Annual Meeting of the Club, to be held in the month of June in each year. The Resident Engineer of the Works, and the Secretary of the Water Department of the Corporation, are members of the Committee *ex-officio*. Vacancies among the elected members of the Committee will be filled by the vote of the members at the quarterly General Meetings.

3.—The subscriptions payable by members shall be 6d. per week for men, and 3d. per week for boys; workmen earning 4d. and upwards per hour being reckoned as men, and those earning less than 4d. per hour as boys. Members joining or leaving during a week will pay at the rate of 1d. per day for men, or ½d. per day for boys, for the odd days their names are on the books. By arrangement with the Corporation the subscriptions are collected by the Cashier of the Works, being deducted from the wages on pay-days. The amount so collected will be placed to the credit of the Club at the North and South Wales Bank in Rhayader, after which the Corporation will take no responsibility whatever for the appropriation of the money or for the management of the Club, or otherwise, and do not in any way guarantee the benefits offered.

4.—Members of the Club will, while resident on the Works, be entitled to free medical attendance by the Club Doctor for themselves, and for the resident members of their families. Members who, while employed on the Works, are unable, through sickness or accident to follow their employment, will be entitled to sick pay. An accident to entitle a member to sick pay must be incurred while following his employment on the Works, or if otherwise incurred, must be a *bona fide* accident from legitimate causes and not induced by the member's own negligence, misconduct, or fault. The decision of the Committee in such cases to be final.

5.—The Club Doctor, who must be a duly qualified practitioner, will be appointed by the Committee of the Club for the time being, who will also settle the amount of his remuneration and the duties to be performed, the appointment being terminable at three months' notice on either side. The Committee shall report the appointment to the members of the Club at the first General Meeting held after the date of such appointment.

6.—The Committee of the Club are empowered to make arrangements for the keeping of the books and the discharge of the clerical work of the Club, and to pay from the funds of the Club such remuneration as they think fit for such services. The cost of all stationery and other out-of-pocket expenses, when passed by the Committee, shall be paid out of the funds of the Club.

7.—Sick Pay will be at the rate of twelve shillings per week for men, and six shillings per week for boys (that is, at the rate of two shillings and one shilling per day respectively, excluding Sundays), for a period of thirteen weeks, and half these sums for a further period of thirteen weeks. In case a member fall ill before he has been a member for fourteen days, he shall be entitled to no benefit except medical attendance, but in case of disablement or death through accident during employment, full benefits shall commence at once.

8.—On the death of a member in benefit, the sum of £10 for a man and £5 for a boy shall be paid to his nearest relatives, or, in case of a member having no near relatives at hand, the Committee may elect to defray the expenses of the funeral. On the death of the wife of a member in benefit, the member shall be paid the sum of £5.

9.—Any member requiring the doctor's attendance for himself or any resident member of his family, must first obtain a certificate from the Secretary or Treasurer.

10.—Members desiring Sick Pay must obtain a certificate from the Club Doctor, or from a responsible person approved by the Committee. Such certificate must be presented to the Secretary, who will make an order upon the Treasurer for the amount payable. No member shall be entitled to Sick Pay until he has been three consecutive days upon the sick list. A member in receipt of Sick Pay shall be paid for the day on which he is certified by the doctor to be unfit for work, unless such certificate be granted later than noon, in which case his Sick Pay will commence on the following day. Sick Pay shall cease at the end of the day on which the writing-off certificate is dated. Claims for Sick Pay must be made weekly, and a fresh certificate obtained for each claim.

11.—Should any member who has been in receipt of Sick Pay declare off the funds, and within a period of thirteen weeks, for other cause than accident during employment, again go on the sick list, his second period of Sick Pay shall be considered to be continuous with the first period, and the weekly amount shall be determined accordingly.

12.—No member whose sickness arises from misconduct shall be entitled to Sick Pay, and any member, while in receipt of Sick Pay, found drinking excessively, or being out of doors beyond the hours of 5 p.m. in the months of November, December, January, and February; 6 p.m. in the months of March, April, September, and October; or 8 p.m. in the months of May, June, July, and August; or doing anything which may retard his recovery, or in any way imposing on the Club, shall be deprived of half his sick pay for a period of one week, and on a second offence, for a period of thirteen weeks.

13.—The Committee have power to appoint members of the Club to act as visitors to the sick, the duties of such visitors being to see that the rules of the Club are observed by those members who are on the sick list.

14.—The accounts of the Club shall be made up to the close of the last wages pay in August, November, February, and May respectively, all outstanding liabilities of the Club at the respective dates being taken into account. Of the funds in hand a sum shall be retained as a reserve fund, which, if the funds permit, shall amount to not less than two shillings for each man and one shilling for each boy; and any surplus remaining shall be divided among the members on the books at the time of closing the accounts of the quarter, in proportion to the amount of their subscriptions during the quarter. When the books are made up, but before dividends are paid, the accounts shall be audited by two auditors appointed by the members at the Quarterly or Annual Meetings. The accounts, when audited, shall be published by exhibition in the Public Hall of the Elan Village, where the copy of the last quarter's accounts shall remain until replaced by that for the following quarter. A copy of the accounts shall also be forwarded each quarter to the Secretary of the Department for presentation to the Water Committee.

15.—Any addition to, or alteration in, these rules may be made at any Quarterly or Annual Meeting. Notice of such proposed alteration or addition must be handed to the Honorary Secretary four clear weeks before the date of the last pay in the quarter; the notice to be prominently exhibited in the Public Hall for not less than three weeks before the said date.

16.—Any case not provided for in the rules of the Club for the time being, or any question arising as to the interpretation of the rules, shall be referred for settlement to two arbitrators, who shall be employees of the Corporation, one to be appointed by the member raising the point, and the other by the Committee. The arbitrators shall, before entering upon the consideration of the question referred to them, nominate an umpire, who must be a member or employee of the Corporation. In case of disagreement of the arbitrators, they shall call in the umpire, whose decision shall in all cases be final.

17.—The rules shall be printed, and copies may be obtained from the Honorary Secretary by the members at a cost of one penny per copy.

"superior classes of men as these had not been available on any other construction site of this nature". To bring together thousands of men for up to 10 years without provision for bathing, would, in the committee's eyes, be "unbearable". Thus the construction site housed 12 baths and 24 lavatories, the accompanying notices sum up their operation.

By March 1895, the village was fully established and some 56 Type 1 huts, 15 Type 2 and 40 Type 3 constructed, in addition to the public buildings already mentioned. At this time, approximately 1000 navvies and other tradesmen were housed within the village. This obviously called for further amenities including entertainment, sport, recreation etc. One such event was arranged to entertain the "women and children", and for £20 8s. 11d. a magic lantern show, a miscellaneous concert and an amateur dramatic performance (by the Engineering Staff) was held on 16th January, 1895.

The navvies also arranged many pianoforte concerts and recitals in local village halls and church rooms, under the watchful eye of Rev. Harwood. The village superintendent, Sergeant Payne (an experienced band master) had approval in 1898 to establish a Village Brass Band, which was a great success being partly paid for by the canteen profits!

The canteen was the centre of the nightly attractions and boasted about 100 to 150 men attending each evening, and this was found sufficient to keep the establishment in business.

The school was full to bursting, and it was estimated that by the summer of 1895, all the positions would be full, i.e. 78 boys, 40 girls and 50 infants. Miss Pitt was already being helped by an assistant, Miss Ethel Jones, together with part time help from mothers. It was suggested that a Head Master be appointed, so that his wife could help teach needlework and generally supervise. The following advert was placed:

> Wanted, immediately, Certificated Master (married) for the School of the Birmingham Corporation Waterworks, near Rhayader, Radnorshire. The Wife will be required to superintend the needlework, and to assist generally. Salary, £150 per annum. – Applications, with copy testimonials, to be sent to Mr E.A. Lees, Secretary, Water Department, 44 Broad Street, Birmingham.

In March 1895, just as this advert was placed, Miss Pitt handed in her notice (due to long illness), and so a complete change in school staffing had to be arranged.

By 1898 the total number of children accommodated was 218, comprised of 118 older children and 100 infants, making necessary further staff appointments and a large extension to the school, costing well

Plate 22: The school teachers posed outside the Elan village school in 1898.
Reproduced by permission of the Reference Library, Birmingham

Plate 23: Inside the village school, again in 1898. Note the ingenious desks/bench seats, with four ink well holes, at present folded down; this room was capable of accommodating up to 80 pupils.
Reproduced by permission of the Reference Library, Birmingham

BIRMINGHAM CORPORATION WATERWORKS.

PUBLIC HALL, ELAN VILLAGE

NOTICE.

SWEARING

AND

BAD LANGUAGE,

SPITTING

AND

WHISTLING

are strictly prohibited.

BY ORDER.

Sept. 24th, 1901.

CITY OF BIRMINGHAM WATER DEPARTMENT.

ELAN VILLAGE.

BATH & WASH-HOUSE

THE BATH AND WASH-HOUSE

WILL BE

OPENED ON MONDAY, AUGUST 12, 1895,

THE HOURS WILL BE--

FOR MEN:--

TUESDAYS   6 p.m. to 9 p.m.
FRIDAYS   6 p.m. to 9 p.m.
SATURDAYS 1 p.m. to 9 p.m.
SUNDAYS

FOR WOMEN:--WEDNESDAYS 2 p.m. to 5 p.m.

THE CHARGES WILL BE--

FOR A BATH—1st CLASS - - **3d.**
Including a Cake of Soap and the use of Two Towels.

FOR A BATH—2nd CLASS - - **2d.**
Including a Cake of Soap and the use of One Towel.

FOR LAVATORY - - - **1d.**
Including use of Soap and Towel.

By order of the Water Committee.

G. N. YOURDI,
RESIDENT ENGINEER.

31st JULY, 1895.

CITY OF BIRMINGHAM WATER DEPARTMENT.

ELAN SUPPLY.
ELAN VALLEY WORKS.

RULES FOR KEEPER OF THE CANTEEN
IN THE ELAN VILLAGE.

No. 1
Hours open.

(*a*) The Canteen will be opened every working-day in the week (Saturdays excepted) between the hours of 12 noon and 2 p.m., for one and a half hours only; and for the whole time in the evening between 5-30 and 9 o'clock.

Saturdays only.

(*b*) On Saturdays, the house will be opened from 1 to 4-30 and from 5-30 to 9 p.m.

Hours closed.

(*c*) The house will be closed every evening at 9 o'clock prompt.

Sundays.

(*d*) On Sundays the house will be closed all day.

No. 2
No women allowed in the bar.

Women will not be allowed in the bar at any time, under any pretext whatever.

No. 3
No boys in bar.

Men only over 18 years of age will be permitted in the bar.

No. 4
No women under 21 to fetch drink from Jug Department.

(*a*) No woman under the age of 21 years will be served with beer or porter at the jug department.

No boys under 16.

(*b*) No boy under the age of 16 years will be served with beer or porter at the jug department.

No. 5
No drinking in Jug Department.

No one will be allowed to remain in the jug department beyond the time necessary to obtain the liquor required, and no one will be allowed to drink in that department.

No. 6

No person shall be supplied with more than one quart of liquor at the morning hour.

No. 7

No person shall be allowed more than two quarts of liquor in the evening for consumption on the premises.

No. 8

No person who is in the slightest intoxicated shall be supplied with drink on any pretence whatever.

No. 9

All persons applying for liquor at the jug department must be duly registered inhabitants of the village, and no person shall be supplied who is not such.

No. 10

No hut-keeper shall be supplied with more than 1½ gallons of beer in any one evening, nor with more than two gallons for the mid-day meal from the jug department, except on Saturday evening, when a hut-keeper may purchase double the quantity.

No. 11

Only village residents shall be served at the bar, except on a written order signed by the Resident Engineer.

No. 12
No amusements in the house

Amusements in the house are strictly prohibited. No music, singing, juggling, reciting, gambling, card playing, playing dice, dominoes, draughts, marbles, shovel-penny, or any game either of skill or chance, will be permitted in the house.

No. 13
Disturbances.

In case of any disturbance or quarrel in the house, the parties will be immediately ejected. The Canteen-keeper and Village Superintendent have strict orders to turn out any disorderly person, and to close the house if order cannot be maintained.

No. 14

The above rules may at any time be added to or varied by the Water Committee.

BY ORDER OF THE WATER COMMITTEE,

G. N. YOURDI,
RESIDENT ENGINEER.

Plate 24: A very early 1894 view of the Recreation Hall, again poorly lit, but a reading desk, an oval style pool table, chess, dominoes, draughts and shove-halfpenny can all be seen in this view.

Reproduced by permission of the Reference Library, Birmingham

Plate 25: The main road in the "model village" Elan, showing the village sergeant on guard and a road engine standing alongside the only visible street light.   *Reproduced by permission of the Reference Library, Birmingham*

Plate 26: The wooden village was soon to be rebuilt permanently in stone and by 1909 was completed, many of the buildings remaining today. Here the Superintendent's House and Offices plus the Village Shop are shown.

Courtesy: Severn-Trent Water

over £200. The total number of men now employed was in excess of 1500.

After several small fires in this large village (all built in wood) the water committee decided to establish their own fire service. A village Fire Brigade was inaugurated on 13th March 1896, with one permanent officer and 5 volunteers, who earned an extra wage of 2d. per day for their 24 hour "on call"; two men patrolled each night around the area. The village by this time had electricity in all the main buildings and street lighting being powered from a generator situated near the base of the Caban Coch Dam, run by "water power". This system is still in use today at the village, with surplus power being transmitted to surrounding areas. Today the Elan Village (which is now constructed of stone; being completed in 1909 on the south side of the river) provides accommodation for the Severn-Trent employees and the total of eleven houses includes one for the school teacher, a house/shop (now converted to a guest house) and a house/office for the Superintendent. Between the two world wars, four houses were constructed on the north side of the river at Glan-yr-Afon and in connection with the construction of Claerwen Dam (which commenced in 1946) plus six bungalows erected behind the Elan Valley Hotel. One of these bungalows is included in the lease of the hotel as an annex. Most of the houses are let to Estate or Works employees although a few are occupied by retired employees or their widows.

Much more could be written about the original "model" village but it is hoped this chapter gives a good insight into Navvy life at Elan. It does show how Mr Yourdi tried to gain "one-upmanship" over rival Corporation Villages, by improving facilities in his village after touring the rival sites.

BIRMINGHAM CORPORATION WATERWORKS.

ELAN VILLAGE

NOTICE.

Bathers should not take a Hot Bath above 100 degrees Fahrenheit without Medical advice, and, in such cases, they are requested to see that the Bath Attendant regulates the temperature of the water by the Thermometer.

Bathers must not Trample upon or otherwise Damage, and unnecessarily Dirty the Towels, but, when they have finished Bathing, leave the Door open and deposit the Towels in the Basket placed in the Corridor adjoining.

Any person occupying a Bath Room for a longer period than 30 minutes, is liable to a second charge for admission.

Any person defacing the Mirrors, or otherwise wilfully damaging the Fittings and other articles provided for the public use will be Prosecuted.

A Ticket must be received in exchange for all money paid, which Ticket must be handed to the Attendant, in exchange for the soap and towel.

Purchasers of 3d. Tickets are entitled to two towels.

BY ORDER.

Sept. 24th, 1901.

Chapter Four

The Route Described

To travel the route of the Elan Valley Railway, it would be appropriate to commence our imaginary journey at the Cambrian Railway station of Rhayader, as this was the nearest main line station to the Elan junction. With again the help of the large foldout map at the back of this book and the illustrations, the would-be traveller can enjoy the beauty of this railway's route, sampling the experiences that the visitor would have enjoyed in the late 1890s.

One general point worthy of mention here is that the railway was constructed to run just above (about 13 ft) the intended final water level of the reservoirs and so the trackbed still appears alongside the reservoirs today. But at the time of the construction work, and with the reservoirs empty, the railway was high up the hillside, on a ledge perilously hugging the mountain side (*see plate 96*).

Rhayader station was situated between Brecon and Moat Lane on the single line Cambrian Railways and the 1923 station plan is shown on the next page. The Elan Valley Railway Junction was approximately 800 yds to the south through a tunnel (towards Brecon). Travelling from this station one passed through this straight single line tunnel, emerging immediately into a high sided, tree lined cutting.

From this cutting, the line doubled and the Elan Valley Railway Junction signal box could be seen ahead. This 40 lever Dutton-framed box was installed by the Cambrian Railway, opened in June 1894 and closed in January 1908. It is easy to see why Mr Mansergh would have rather enlarged the facilities at Rhayader Station than pay for all the doubling at the junction, as the station had good access and ample room for more sidings. But the Board of Trade then argued that freight trains arriving from Brecon would have had to stop in the tunnel (on the main running line) and back up the main line onto the Elan Valley line. They considered this a dangerous move and, with hindsight, were correct.

Branching off to the right, the main Corporation running line from this point was single throughout (with passing loops) and descended immediately a 1 in 40 gradient into the Elan Valley proper. Passing through the fairly large and important exchange sidings at Noyadd (*see plan page 84*) where "officially" all Cambrian locomotives stopped and the Corporation's engine took over, the line then swings round to the left on towards Aber-Caethon. After crossing a substantial single-arched stone bridge over a track, (*plate 32*) the line ran in close proximity to the main road, which had been re-routed in many places because of the railway construction work (*see plates 34 and 35*). The

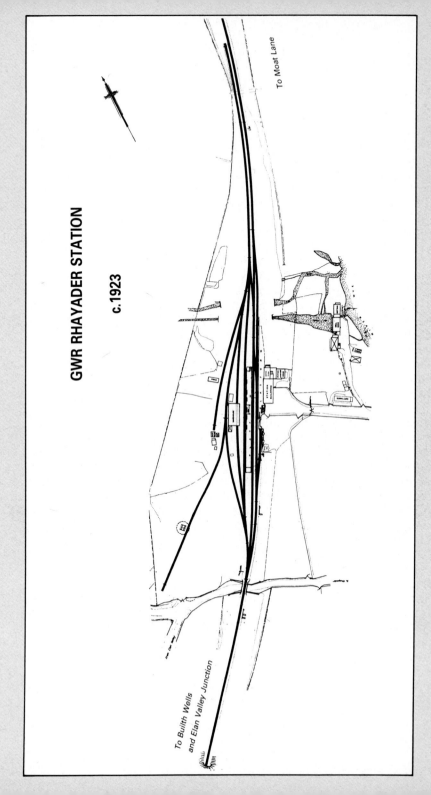

GWR RHAYADER STATION

c.1923

To Moat Lane

To Builth Wells
and Elan Valley Junction

Station Plan of Rhayader with the tunnel on the left. The Elan Valley Junction was at the other end of this tunnel.

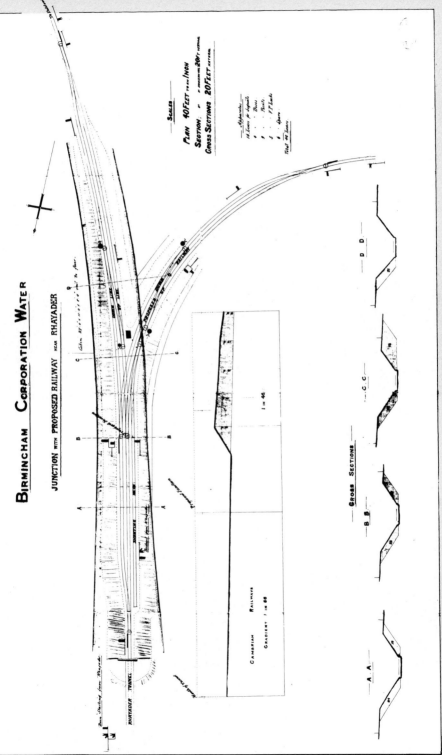

The final plan submitted by the Cambrian Railway to Mansergh, after the Board of Trade intervened and stipulated a "double junction".

Plate 27: Looking towards the north, Rhayader station, on the Cambrian Mid-Wales line, at the turn of the century, 1904.

LGRP, Courtesy David & Charles

Plate 28: A later view in the 1950s of Rhayader station, looking smart in the summer sunlight. *Oakwood Collection*

Plate 29: Looking south from Rhayader station towards the tunnel mouth (*centre left*) and the large goods shed in Rhayader yard. The station buildings are now council offices.   *Oakwood Collection*

Plate 30: The all important Tunnel Junction with the Elan Valley Railway Junction signal cabin commanding a good view of the double junction. The main line runs to the left and the Elan Valley BCWW line curves to the right. The tunnel is situated just behind the photographer.

LGRP, Courtesy David & Charles

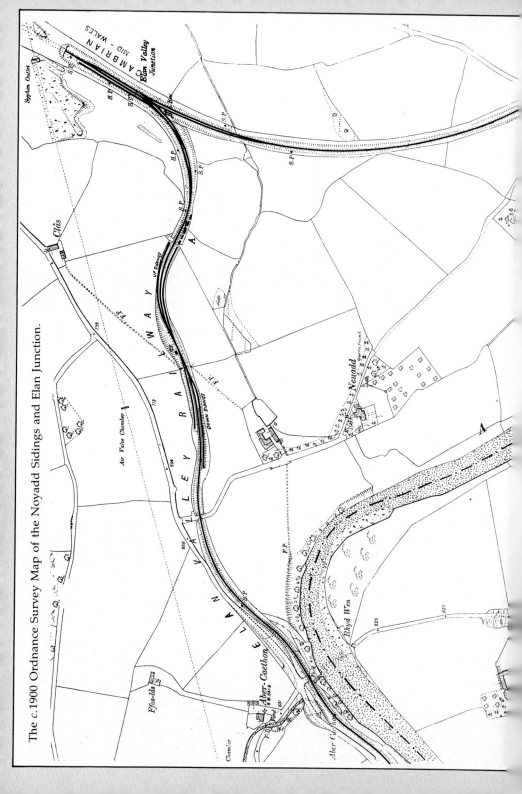

The c.1900 Ordnance Survey Map of the Noyadd Sidings and Elan Junction.

Plate 31: Elan Valley Railway Junction signal box containing a 40 lever frame manufactured by Dutton. The rebuilt 2–4–0T locomotive No. 57 named MAGLONA is allocated to the local shunting duties. The Elan Railway curves around behind the box with the home signals just visible by the box chimney.

Courtesy: Elan Valley Visitors' Centre

Plate 32: The overbridge (of substantial stone construction) at Aber-Caethon. The view in 1900 through the bridge shows the ford across the River Elan before a bridge was constructed over the river. This bridge was demolished in 1987. *Real Photographs*

Plate 33: A further view of the overbridge at Aber-Caethon but this time in April 1895, just after its construction. *Courtesy: Severn-Trent Water*

Plate 34: The railway alongside the road looking towards the Caban Coch Dam, mid-way between the junction and terminus of Railway No. 1. The Elan Valley Hotel can just be seen on the right in the trees.

Collection Mr C. Edwards, Rhayader

RHAYADER: THE ELAN VALLEY.

Plate 35: This interesting view shows the main No. 1 Railway coming up past the site of the new Baptist chapel, the police station (white single storey building) over the level crossing and on past the stables. Stables Junction is just out of the picture on the right.

Reproduced by permission of the Reference Library, Birmingham

scenery at this point is pleasant, the valley having gently sloping wooded hills on either side of the River Elan as it winds its way along the valley floor. Now reaching the lowest point, the main line of the railway traversed a further two miles passing through six level crossings before arriving at the junction of Railways No. 1 and No. 2, called Stables Junction (*see plates 35 and 36*). From this point Railway No. 1 dropped further into the valley serving the workshops, engine sheds and offices at the Caban site. The new suspension bridge over the River Elan was here and provided the main crossing point from the workshop site to the Elan Village. A vast network of spurs and sidings were within this area and are shown in *Diagram A* on the main foldout map at the back, but varied throughout the railway's life.

After Railway No. 1 was built and before the Caban Coch dam commenced, the railway entered the workshop site, turned sharp left over a wooden trestle bridge, (*plate 39*) straddling the River Elan to

Plate 36: Carrying on up the line from *Plate 35,* Stables Junction was reached where Railway No. 2 began and Railway No. 1 descended towards the Elan construction site. The photograph shows Railway No. 2 climbing up the valley side past the "Doss House" situated between the railways. The road had crossed the railway *(from left to right),* passed the Doss House and then turned over the level crossing *(centre)* to reach the village site.

Reproduced by permission of the Reference Library, Birmingham

*Plate 37: (opposite)*An interesting view taken in May 1902, of the Caban Coch Dam work site. Note the train in the far distance, travelling the main line from the next dam up-stream, near the passing loop of Abernant turnout. On the far right is the quarry site of Gigfran and below this can be seen the long engine shed. A horse box and explosives van, plus other wagons, are in the yard. The line and passing loops in the lower centre of the picture climb up to a spur behind the photographer, and then return along the hill to join up with the line at the top left hand side of the dam, these lines were reached by traffic passing over the trestle bridge *(centre)* from the main site on the right.

Reproduced by permission of the Reference Library, Birmingham

DAM UNDER CONSTRUCTION — FROM DOWNSTREAM FACE — MAY 1903

Plate 38: A general view of the Mason's Yard in October 1895 with the Goliath steam crane. The stone saw underneath the crane was driven by the stationary steam engine on the right.

Reproduced by permission of the Reference Library, Birmingham

the base of a quarry incline (*plate 40*). The standard line branched to the right around the hill and on towards the small dam site of Dol-y-Mynach (*plate 41*).

Railway No. 2 (the main line) climbed from the Stables Junction quite rapidly up to 133 ft above the River Elan bed, through steeper-sided hills, hugging the rock face. Just after leaving the Stables a further spur to the right climbed even steeper to a reverse spur into the filter bed construction site high up on the mountain side and *Plate 19* shows these three lines quite clearly with the one on the right being No. 1; the middle line, the mainline No. 2 and the new one on the left, up to the filter beds (*plate 46*).

---

* The short branch to the filter beds was used for the Royal visit in 1904 but today there is an interesting overhead monorail system which is still in use. Two electric locomotives with tramcar pickups and car controls, crawl along over the filter beds pulling the skips used in their maintenance.

Plate 39: A very important photograph of April 1895 showing the site of the workshops but this time looking back towards Rhayader. Note the village suspension bridge in the centre. The line is seen crossing the River Elan on a trestle bridge to the base of the incline and swinging round to the left of the picture, on towards the Dol-y-Mynach dam site. The photographer is standing at a point near the site of the Caban Coch Dam wall. No. 2 Railway (the mainline) can be seen high up on the rocks, to the right.

Courtesy: Severn-Trent Water

Plate 40: Another view of the Quarry incline in April 1895 showing the passing loop and double line at top and single line at the lower section (*diagram below*). The branch line to Dol-y-Mynach dam branches to the right around the base of the hill. The base of the Caban Coch dam had not been started when this photograph was taken. *Courtesy: Severn-Trent Water*

Plate 41: The site of the Dol-y-Mynach Dam showing the railway network
and construction taking place. *Courtesy: Severn-Trent Water*

Plate 42: The only view (poor quality) showing the railway (with train) along
the far bank under Craig Fawr and travelling the line to Dol-y-Mynach Dam
site. The Tan-y-foel sidings are in the foreground. *Author's Collection*

Plate 43: A very early view of the Caban Coch Dam site before construction was really established, showing the many lines going up the valley (both sides) to stone and mason's yards. The lines at higher levels are, on the left, Railway No. 2 (the main line), whilst the one on the right ran on to the Dol-y-Mynach Dam site. *Collection T. Ingram*

Plate 44: An unusual view from the hill behind the "new stone" village showing Caban Coch Dam (*left*), the filter beds (*right*) with the various railway levels clearly visible. *Collection Mr C. Edwards, Rhayader*

The filter beds were an added "works" to the scheme for the purpose of cleansing the water of an organism which had been discovered in it. This organism, which was of a vegetable growth, was not dangerous to the health of those people drinking the water, but it possessed the quality of developing very rapidly in iron pipes and conduits, and consequently, it was very necessary that means were taken to prevent it finding its way into the large iron pipes and constructions which conducted the water across country from Wales to Frankley. As stated, the original scheme did not comprise these filters, for at the time it was projected, the existence of the organism in question was not known, and the necessity for excluding it from the pipes was not recognised. Indeed it was not until three or four years later that a need for constructing the additional filters in the Elan Valley was realised, and in order to preserve the proper gradients of the pipeline it was necessary that the filters be constructed on a high plateau on the side of a huge rock eminence called the Foel Mountain. One side of the mountain had to be cut away in order to secure a plateau at the required level for the filters.

The main line (Railway No. 2) continued on up to a summit at the top of the proposed Caban Coch Dam wall to a point named Gigfran where one of the main quarries existed and *plates 47 and 48* show this area well. Several sidings off the main line were situated here.

Returning to the main line and to Railway No. 3, this started from the top of the Caban Dam (which although 120 ft above the Elan riverbed) was insignificant by comparison with the massive rocks and mountains around. The main line followed a fairly level path along the Radnorshire side of the valley at a uniform height of 13 ft above the intended top water level and on to the next dam site of Careg-Ddu Dam. Halfway along this section of line, the first passing loop was established being named the Abernant Turnout. Whilst travelling along this section it was possible to look down on the railway sidings at Tan-y-foel Yard (*see plates 43 and 49*). The line then curved round through 90 degrees to the right before reaching the Careg-Ddu site. Then curving through a further 90 degrees to the right, at this point was Careg-Ddu Junction. This was where the line dropped down steeply to the valley floor by a series of reverse spurs (*see diagram B on main map and plates 51, 54 and 55*) to the maze of sidings for the base of the dam construction.

There was a line also traversing the valley floor from this point, over a wooden bridge to the far side of the valley to the site of a stone-breaking plant and sand crusher which can be seen in *plate 51*.

Back at the junction, the main line continued for only a short way before the next passing loop was established named Cwm Elan Turn-

Plate 45: A view today with the railway trackbeds of No. 1 and No. 2 still visible, showing the incredible gradients. The filter beds are above the stone wall at top right, whilst the road on the left runs down to the Elan village and Visitors' Centre.   *Author*

Plate 46: A fine view of the filter bed site in 1902 from high up on the mountain side. The Elan village is on the left in the valley floor with railway No. 2 climbing hard up the middle of the photograph.

Courtesy: Severn-Trent Water

Plate 47: The top of the Caban Coch Dam in 1902 with the railway on the right and various sidings in the valley floor. The steam crane also is on a railway which ran from one side to another on the precarious track mounted around the Dam wall, as seen in the photograph. *Courtesy: Severn-Trent Water*

Plate 48: A later view of the Caban Coch Dam with the water in full spate. This view shows the many sidings, on both sides, with the river timber bridge crossing (*bottom left*). The main line runs long the right hand side, with the road beside; note just how full the sidings are.   *M. Christensen Collection*

Plate 49: A view from the Abernant Turnout in May 1902 and looking back towards the reservoir face of the Caban Coch Dam under construction. The many lines down to the Tan-y-foel yard can clearly be seen.

Courtesy: Severn-Trent Water

Caban Goch Reservoir and Careg-ddu Dam, Rhayader.

Plate 50: A composite picture postcard of the Caban Coch Reservoir with the Caban Coch Dam on the right and the Careg-Ddu Dam and bridge in the centre; the Baptist Chapel is to the left of the bridge. The original card produced in 1904 is over 10½ in. wide.

Collection Mr C. Edwards, Rhayader

Plate 51: This is the site of the base of the Careg-Ddu Dam and the school and church that were to be submerged are just out of picture on the right. The line running across the picture from right to left is a siding to the sand crusher plant whilst the mainline can be seen hugging the hill, just under the roadway.

Plate 52: The Careg-Ddu Dam from the left bank seen here in July 1904. Note the mainline across the bottom of the picture with the signal cabin controlling the point, to give access across the top of the dam. The new Baptist Church is clearly visible at the other end of the dam. *Courtesy: Severn-Trent Water*

Plate 53: A close-up view in 1986 of the Foel Tower, which is the "take-off" point for all the water. The important main line (Railway No. 3) track bed can be seen curving round the Foel, with fine wrought iron gates placed across the trackbed. The road is behind the second set of railings. *Author*

Plate 54: A view just around the Foel; the new Railway No. 3 on the left has just been laid, with another branch descending to the reverse spur and on to the construction site of Careg-Ddu Dam. The junction of these two lines was called Careg-Ddu Junction. *Courtesy: Severn-Trent Water*

Plate 55: This view is very important as, firstly, it shows Cwm Elan House just before the waters submerge the house. The reverse spur dropping away from the mainline shows clearly the three levels and acute gradients, but most of all the Cwm Elan Turnout can just be seen on the right controlled by a home signal. This is the only evidence of a signal post on the railway. *Courtesy: Severn-Trent Water*

out (*see plate 55 and plate 93*). These passing loops were places where the workmen alighted or were picked up on their way to or from the work sites and also where freight passed up and down the single line.

After this turnout, the main line meandered for a further 1½ miles, following closely the course of the River Elan amid splendid scenery.* Twisting curves and "S" shaped bends were in profusion (*see plate 57*) needing many check rails for safety, and extra wooden blocks fastened to the sleepers, to prevent rail movement. Two wooden bridges were used to cross streams, one at Llyn Clap shown in *plates 56, 57, 58, and 59*, and the other a minor stream (both bridges at the time of writing were still *in situ*). A third passing place was now encountered at Dol-Faenog Turnout and this consisted of a passing loop (*plate 60*) which was longer than the other two passing loops and used to hold wagons of stone travelling up the line to the top dams+. This was also the last passing place before the terminus of Railway No. 3.

Immediately after this passing loop came the Dol-Ffaenog Junction (*see plates 61 and 62*) which was the commencement of Railway No. 4 (the last section on the Elan Valley Railway), but before traversing this section, the end of Railway No. 3 came at the base of the Pen-y-Craig dam site. Here again a large series of sidings, sheds, and a bridge over the River Elan were sited (*diagram C on the main foldout map*) and can be clearly seen in *plate 63*, as can the route of the main line (Railway No. 4) striking out to the top of the great dam wall of Pen-y-Gareg (*plate 64*), which today holds back an area of 217 acres of reservoir water.

From here the line curves and winds up steepish gradients (at one point 1 in 36) to the terminus passing over a substantial stone and brick bridge (*see plate 65*) crossing the stream of Nant Hesgog then on into a shallow cutting, passing the site of the old Mission Hut (now demolished) which was used by the upper site construction workers for worship.

Further along the route, the railway had to be forced through a massive rock jutting out into the water, known locally as "The Devil's Gulch" and a deep vertical cutting had to be cut (*see plates 14, 15 and 66*). The railway was constructed on a sharp curve (more acute than had originally been planned) at this point and continued from here to the summit terminus along an embankment constructed on the

---

* Whilst travelling along this section of the line it was possible to catch a glimpse of the Nant Methan on the furthest slopes, the site of the Cwm Elan Lead Mines, which ceased operations in 1877.

+ As this one long loop was found insufficient storage, this was supplemented by a further set of loops at Dol-Falau. These were temporary and did not exist for long (*plate 60*).

Plate 56: A small but very well constructed bridge over a stream outlet just past the site of Cwm Elan turnout, still in place in 1986.   *Author's Collection*

Plate 57: The tight "S" curve at Llyn Clap with check rails throughout seen here in 1904. The magnificent bridge is still in place in 1987, and *Plates 58 and 59* show, respectively, the bridge from the reservoir waterside, and the detail construction of the bridge support, as seen today.

LRGP, Courtesy David and Charles

Plates 58 and 59: The sturdy stone bridge at Llyn Clap seen from the reservoir waterside and from the trackbed in 1986. Note the construction and support beams. *Author's Collection*

Plate 60: This 1986 composite photograph shows the site of temporary sidings on Railway 3 at Dol-Falau (*right by tree*) established in the days of the construction of the top dam. These were put in because the next and last passing loop at Dol-Faenog became inadequate to cope with the volume of traffic.

Author's Collection

Plates 61 and 62: Photographs taken on the Junctions of Railways No. 3 and No. 4 in 1986. *Plate 61* looks towards Caban Coch and the site of the Dol-Faenog turnout passing loop, and *Plate 62* shows the main No. 4 railway line trackbed passing through the trees centre (with picnic table on the track bed). The No. 3 line would have descended where the road is now (*left*) to the dam construction site.

Author's Collection

Plate 63: An interesting view of Pen-y-Gareg Dam under construction in July 1904. It shows the new road bridge being built and Railway No. 4 curving around the hillside and weaving past the dam *en route* to the top site. Note the spur coming off (near the construction workers' accommodation huts) and running around to the dam wall, allowing the large steam crane to operate. The maze of lines at the valley bottom is also of interest. The levels going up the far bank were originally railway lines when the dam first started, but now all the stone is in place, have been removed and used as roadways.

Reproduced by permission of the Reference Library, Birmingham

Plate 64: A view of Pen-y-Gareg Dam in July 1904 with Railway No. 4 running past the summit. Note the other line running up to the dam wall to feed the crane line along the dam wall face. *Courtesy: Severn-Trent Water*

Plate 65: The only bridge constructed on Railway No. 4 crossing the large stream of Nant Hesgog. The width would, in fact, have accommodated double track but Railway No. 4 was single throughout. Situated just up the line from Pen-y-Gareg Dam, it was a considerable undertaking for just a "construction" railway. Seen here in 1987. *Author's Collection*

Plate 66: "Devil's Gulch" as it was nicknamed by the navvies, looking down from the terminus. This old print shows the very tight curve and check rails. This small cutting held up construction of Railway No. 4 and the curve eventually ended up much tighter than first envisaged due to the rock structure. The cutting can still be walked today. *Courtesy "The Engineer"*

The gradient profile of Railway No. 4.

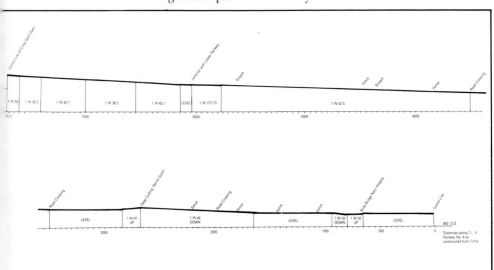

Plate 67: A view across Pen-y-Gareg Reservoir showing a composite photograph of Railway No. 4 from (*right*) the bridge, shown in *Plate 66* to "Devil's Gulch" (*left and arrowed*). The steady rising gradient can be clearly seen. *Author*

Plate 68: A further composite view of Railway No. 4 junction showing the two levels, with the beautifully curved Craig Goch Dam, on the left. *Author's Collection*

Rhayader, Pen-y-Gareg Reservoir.

Plate 69: Taken from the hill near the top dam of Craig Goch, this view looks back over the Pen-y-Gareg Reservoir. Railway No. 4 can be followed along the shore line from the "Devil's Gulch" peninsular to the junction, where the line of Railway No. 4 continued to the dam top and a spur descended to the valley floor.

Collection Mr C. Edwards, Rhayader

Plate 70: The terminus as it was known; the site of the Craig Goch Dam and end of Railway No. 4. A considerable railway network and buildings, including an engine shed, masons' yard and cement works, were established here due to the distance

slopes of the hillside, passing over the side-streams whose bridges (probably wooden) have long since disappeared. The lake reservoir is very wide at this point with wood and moorland on either side. (*See composite photographs in plates 67 and 68*). On reaching the terminus at the final Dam of Craig-Goch the railway had reached 1045 ft above sea level, a rise of over 270 ft from the junction; this reservoir, as previously stated, covers 217 acres.

At the busiest time of the railway's existence (around 1896–98) there was a reported track length of 33 miles, but with weekly changes to track layouts at each dam site, this figure is pure estimation. At the third and final dam site yet another large complex of railway tracks were assembled and again this is portrayed in *diagram D* on the main foldout map and *plate 70*.

The railway construction was reported to be of an exceptionally high quality throughout, using quality rail, sleepers and adequate spiking and up to the standard required of a passenger branch line. The solid rock cuttings and embankments were constructed to reduce to the minimum the severe gradients that otherwise would have prevailed. This high standard of workmanship was reported as being made possible because the Birmingham Water Corporation was prepared to employ and control its own work force, preventing "undesirables" being employed.

NOTICE.

BIRMINGHAM CORPORATION WATERWORKS.

NO UNAUTHORISED PERSONS ARE ALLOWED WITHIN THE FENCE OF THE CORPORATION RAILWAY.

BY ORDER.

Chapter Five

Locomotives of
the Birmingham Waterworks Company

On the 17th April, 1894 James Mansergh asked the Resident Engineer, Mr Yourdi, to investigate suppliers of steam locomotives. After consultation, Mr Mansergh was informed that the most suitable manufacturers currently available to tender were The Hunslet Engine Co., Manning Wardle & Co. and Peckett Bros of Bristol. The specification he required was submitted to each company and called for locomotives basically with 15 in. cylinders and with a 20 in. stroke. All three companies' quotations received, varied very little in their costings, but Mansergh recommended to the Board that the Manning Wardle specification and quote should be accepted. He urged the Board that their reply should be prompt, as a delivery date of ten weeks was being quoted at present and that Mr Yourdi required the locomotives "with all speed".

The relevant tender specifications are very interesting and are included in full.

TENDERS FOR TANK LOCOMOTIVE

Cylinders 15 in. diameter, 20 in. stroke, six wheels coupled, Standard gauge 4 ft 8½ in.

	Peckett & Sons Bristol	Manning Wardle & Co. Leeds	Hunslet Engine Co. Leeds
Diameter of wheels	3 ft 7 in.	3 ft 1 in.	3 ft 4 in.
Wheelbase	10 ft 6 in.	10 ft 6 in.	12 ft 0 in.
Boiler, diameter	3 ft 9½ in.	3 ft 9 in.	3 ft 9 in.
Boiler, length	12 ft 0 in. (includes fire box)	9 ft 0 in.	8 ft 7 in.
Copper fire box/plates	½ in. & ¾ in.	$\frac{7}{16}$ in. $\frac{5}{8}$ in. + ¾ in.	$\frac{7}{16}$ in. to ⅞ in.
Working pressure lb. per sq.inch	140	150	130
Capacity of tank	900 galls	700 galls	580 galls
Capacity of bunker	25 cwts	50 cube ft (about 35 cwt)	50 cube ft
Total heating surface	650 sq.ft	700 sq.ft	711½ sq.ft
Grate area	9¾ sq.ft	11 sq.ft	10¼ sq.ft
Weight loaded	30 tons	29 tons	29 tons
Weight empty	24 tons	–	23¼ tons
Price net	£1230 5s. 0d.	£1250	£1375

The Board replied in some detail to Mr Mansergh's proposals and also upheld the recommendation of the Manning Wardle quotation. The reply stated:

Dear Sir,

Birmingham Water, Elan Supply

We are duly in receipt of yours of the 13th inst., enclosing 3 tenders for locomotive engines, and have carefully examined them with the accompanying specification and sketches.

It is difficult without detailed drawings to make a complete comparison. We think, however, that the Hunslet Co's design is not suitable for the present purpose, because the wheelbase (12 ft instead of 10 ft 6 in.) would be too long for working on the curves likely to occur, and the inside cylinders and side tanks would cause much inconvenience in access to working parts of the engine.

The price also is considerably higher than the other two tenders. There is only a small difference in price between these, and we think that Messrs Manning Wardle's will be a cheaper engine than that of Messrs Peckett & Sons, considering that it has 50 sq.ft more heating surface (700 instead of 650) and $1\frac{1}{4}$ sq.ft more grate area (11 as against $9\frac{3}{4}$).

The axles are of Best Yorkshire Iron instead of steel; this is a more expensive material and we think it decidedly preferable in the case of a ballast engine, subject to frequent irregular and severe shocks. We also note that Messrs Manning Wardle offer to supply a 15 ton Screw Jack, which is not named in Messrs Peckett & Sons tender. These two engines are similar in wheel base and with outside cylinders. The design we think, is well suited to the present purpose.

We think the attention of the firm who receive the order should be specially directed to the importance of ample water space between the boiler tubes and the provision of plenty of wash-out plugs. We note that Messrs Manning Wardle & Co. offer to supply two injectors, if desired, in place of one pump and one injector, and we think that two injectors are preferable for the present purpose, as a pump can only be worked by running the engine, and in the present case, there may be a difficulty in getting the length of run wanted should there be anything the matter with the one injector.

The time for the execution of the work is not named in the memoranda sent to us.

With regard to Messrs Peckett & Sons works, we have had experience of these and have inspected locomotive work there some years ago. In comparison with Messrs Manning Wardle's works, we consider the latter have a superiority. We will, however, as requested, take an early opportunity of visiting Messrs Peckett & Sons works and report thereon.

We return the several documents herewith.
Yours very truly,
(Signed) by the Secretary

We presume that all materials used will be subjected to the usual tests.

The Board authorised the purchase of two locomotives from Manning Wardle (order No. 35100 dated 18th April 1894) at a cost of £1250 and No. 1286 ELAN (*plate 71*) and No. 1287 CLAERWEN (*plate 73*) were delivered on 28th July and 20th August of 1894 respectively.

The details and future owners of these two locomotives are listed below:

Works No.	Date Delivered	Wheel	Cylinders	Wheel Size	Gauge	Name	Owner & Subsequent Owner
1286	28.6.94 (date ordered April 1894)*	0–6–0ST	OC 15 in. x 20 in. (special)	3 ft 1 in.	Standard	ELAN	Birmingham Corpn Water Works, Elan.
						CARINGTON	To Holme & King Contr, Ince, Wigan 1906.
						CARINGTON‡	To Kettering Iron & Coal Co. Ltd, Kettering 1909.
						CARINGTON	To Luffenham Stone & Asphalt Co. Ltd, Rutland 1923. To Adams dealers, Newport 1941.
						VICTORY	To Royal Ordnance Factories, Ranskill Factory, Retford, Notts, loaned to Maltby Factory, Yorkshire –/48 & returned. Scrapped 1958.
1287	20.8.94 (date ordered April 1894)†	0–6–0ST	OC 15 in. x 20 in. (special)	3 ft 1 in.	Standard	CLAERWEN	Birmingham Corpn. Water-works, Elan.
						BANNER	To Holme & King Contr. Wigan 1906.
						BANNER	To T.W. Ward
						BANNER	To Greenway Bros, Widnes, Lancs 1909.

* Steamed
  at Boyne Engine Works, Leeds, 28th June, 1894.
† Steamed at Boyne Engine Works, Leeds, 6th July, 1894.
‡Named carried from November 1915

Plate 71: A fine study of the 0–6–0ST Manning Wardle ELAN (1894) here at the Caban Workshop site.

Reproduced by permission of the Reference Library, Birmingham

Plate 72: ELAN as sold to Kettering Iron and carrying its new name of CARINGTON sometime after 1915.

Frank Jones

Plate 73: Manning Wardle's official photograph of Works No. 1287 taken in 1894 before being named CLAERWEN and despatched thence to Rhayader.

Hunslet Locomotive Co. Ltd

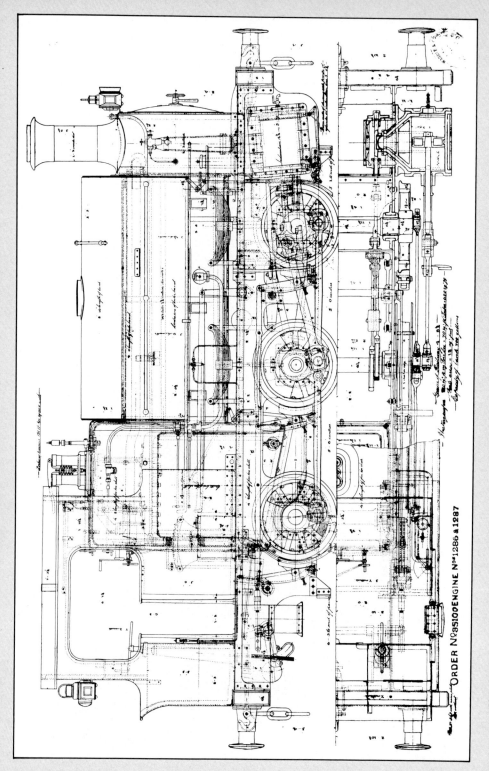

Works General Arrangement drawing of works Engines 1286 and 1287 for the Birmingham Waterworks Corporation.

The two locomotives themselves were described in the Engine books of the Manning Wardle Company as follows and were accompanied by the general arrangement drawing seen on opposite page.

No. 1286. Gauge 4 ft 8½ in. This is a special 15 in. x 20 in. outside cylinder Saddle Tank engine on six coupled wheels of 3 ft 1 in. diameter, wheelbase 10 ft 6 in. The working pressure is 150 lb. per sq.inch. All the plates are of mild steel. Boiler plates included. Boiler plates and tubes were tested. Also test piece taken from one of the axles for tensile and bending tests. Two injectors (no feed pump). Steam brake with our own brake valve and automatic drain cock (cylinder 7½ in. diameter). Trailing axle boxes of cast steel. Buffers class O but with 16 in. heads (diameter). Draw gear fitted with hook shackles and links having special volute spring behind the beam. Cross heads of steel for duplicate work and further particulars full list of drawings and tracings entered for this Order No. 35100. Railwashing cocks and gears supplied under Order 35546 dated July 7th 1894. Draw gear book same as 54233 supplied. Order No. 60318 March 15th 1907. Mild steel smokebox tube-plate with take holes 2 in. dia., supplied order No. 73352 July 16th 1915. Special brake adjusting nuts supplied July 26th 1923.
NAME: ELAN in brass plates 3¾ in. letters.

and

No. 1287. Gauge 4 ft 8½ in. same as No. 1286. One right hand trailing spring with buckles strengthened and thickness of plate altered (supplied order No. 58259 March 6th, 1905). Tyres 2⅝ in. thick supplied. Order No. 68928 August 3rd 1912. The wheels have had a loop shrunk on the skeleton and they are now 2 ft 10⅝ in. diameter. The tyres in future will have to be 2 ft 10⅝ in. inside dia. Tracking springs with buckle strengthened and thickness of plates altered supplied Order No. 71453 March 27th 1914. Case Iron chimney supplied Order No. 77992 May 24th 1918.
NAME: CLAERWEN in brass plate 3¾ in. letters.

Both these locomotives' weight distributions were as follows:

	Loading	Driving	Trailing
Empty	8T 10c 3q	9T 4c 0q	7T 13c 1q
Loaded 1 ton coal	10T 3c 2q	10T 9c 0q	9T 13c 2q

With an increasing workload, it was decided in 1894 that two more six-wheeled saddle tank locomotives were necessary. James Mansergh obtained two quotes from Manning Wardle (£1150 each) and The Hunslet Engine Co. Leeds (£1125 each). On 16th October, 1894 he wrote to the Water Committee asking them to select a tender.

By 16th November, 1894, the Birmingham Town clerk had duly sealed and signed the contracts for two Hunslet Clarke locomotives at a cost of £1125 each. It is a little surprising that the existing supplier

Plate 74: A fine study of CLAERWEN in full steam, taken at the Craig Goch worksite in 1902.   *Courtesy: Severn-Trent Water*

was not chosen (although slightly more expensive) but I presume that "price" won the day.

The specification for these locomotives, under order No. 16830, was identical to that shown in the accompanying page from the Hunslet Locomotive book:

Hunslet No. 618

This was an 0–6–0 saddle tank, with inside cylinders 13 in. x 18 in. and main wheels of 3 ft 1 in. diameter. It was tried in steam on 20th December, 1894 and despatched to the Birmingham Corporation, Rhayader on the same day. The nameplate was brass with the two words NANT GWYLLT (although recorded in the maker's records as NANTGWYLLT). Painted at the works in "Victorian" green, including the frames, springs etc., and with the usual lining (as detailed on

0-6-0 TYPE
SADDLE TANK ENGINE

Gauge of Railway	4 ft. 8½ in.
Size of Cylinders	13 in. dia. × 18 in. stroke
Dia. of Coupled Wheels	3 ft. 1 in.
Rigid Wheelbase (Engine)	10 ,, 6 ,,
Height from Rail to Top of Chimney	10 ,, 9 ,,
Extreme Width	7 ,, 7¼ ,,
Heating Surface—Small Tubes ... ... 442 sq. ft.	
,, ,, Firebox ... ... 48 ,,	
Total ... ... 490 ,,	490 sq. ft.
Grate Area	7·75 ,,
Working Pressure	140 lbs. per sq. in.
Tank Capacity	585 gallons
Fuel Space (Coal)	1 ton 0 cwts.
Weight Empty (Engine)	17 tons 14 ,,
,, in Working Order (Engine)	22 ,, 5 ,,
Total Weight on Coupled Wheels ... ...· ...	22 ,, 5 ,,
Maximum Axle Load	8 ,, 0 ,,
Tractive Effort at 75 per cent. of Boiler Pressure	8632 lbs.
Ratio Adhesive Weight ÷ Tractive Effort	5·7
Minimum Radius of Curve Engine will traverse with ease	220 ft.
Weight per Yard of Lightest Rail advisable	45 lbs.
Load Engine will haul on Level	455 tons
,, ,, ,, up Incline of 1 in 100	225 ,,
,, ,, ,, ,, ,, 1 in 50	130 ,,

(Similar Hunslet 618 and 619)

page 134). Inside the cab the paintwork was described as light brown. Buffer beams were vermillion with polished buffers (*plates 75 and 76*). It appears from the records that spares for this engine were being ordered by the BCWW up to May 1905.

The remaining history of this little engine appears to be as follows: Easton Gibb and Sons ordered spares between January 1907 until May 1912. The 1907 order was connected with contract work on the extension of the South Dock at Newport Monmouth (Alexandra Docks and Railway Company). The 1911 and 1912 spares orders were for the Gibb's contract at the Rosyth Naval Base.

In December 1916 spares were ordered for the engine by S. Pearson and Sons Ltd to be used in their construction of the munitions depot at Gretna for the Ministry of Munitions.

By 1919 (June) the Superintendent Civil Engineer (Special Construction) ordered spares for delivery to the locomotive, working at the Admiralty sidings at Rosyth in Fife, but it is not clear whether the order was placed by the Admiralty or the contractor.

In May 1922, the Cults Lime Works at Springfield in Fife put in a special order for locomotive spares, with follow-up orders as late as October 1930, April 1931 and February 1932.

From 1932 no further information is recorded but between the ownership in 1919 at Rosyth and Cults of 1922 (both Scottish), P. Baker of Cardiff is recorded in the Hunslet records as having acquired the locomotive on 31st March, 1919 and then a W. [or Mr] G. Watt bought the engine on 20th February, 1922. As Mr Baker acted as a dealer, he could have had No. 618 in his yard without actually owning it, and this could explain the entry in the Hunslet records. Mr Watt may have been a local dealer (to Cults) but this is purely guesswork.

Hunslet No. 619

This locomotive was to the same specification as No. 618, and was called METHAN (*plate 77*). The records show spares being ordered by the Birmingham Waterworks Corporation at intervals between 1897 and March 1905.

Further details again of this locomotive's life are given by the Hunslet records as follows: spares orders were received from Easton Gibb and Son in July 1910, December 1910 and June 1911 with a further order in May 1912, Easton Gibb's contract address being at The Rosyth Naval Base in Scotland. There is then a large gap in the dates until Shanks and McEwan Ltd started placing orders, and the following addresses for spares portray the contracts this locomotive worked on:

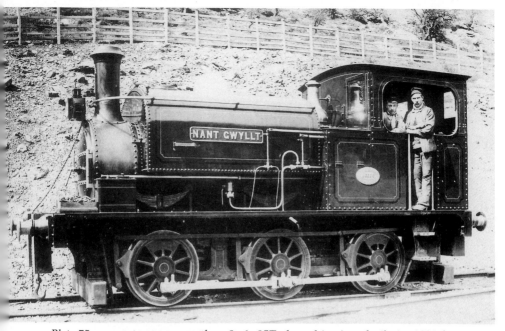

Plate 75: NANT GWYLLT, another 0–6–0ST, but this time built in 1894 by Hunslet Engine Co. (No. 618), posed at the Caban engine shed site, again in immaculate condition and showing the lining detail well.

Reproduced by permission of the Reference Library, Birmingham

Plate 76: Another view of NANT GWYLLT on the shed road at the Caban work-site. Note this time the two enormous lights fitted and the home made, wedge shaped box in front of the cab. A further addition of a shutter covering up half the cab opening (possibly for winter warmth).

Courtesy: Severn-Trent Water

Plate 77: A fine period photograph of locomotive METHAN, with crew, foreman and interested children (plus hoops). This locomotive was a 0–6–0ST built by Hunslet in 1894 (works No. 619). *Collection of Kevin Robertson*

For Mossend Contract: June 1927 and March 1928 and June 1928.
For No. 1 Dock Contracts, Shieldhall [Glasgow]: May 1929.
For the Mid-Notts Joint Railway Contract, Farnsfield, Notts: March 1931.
For Ambergate contract: August 1931.
For Whitemoor Yard contract [March]: November and December 1931.
For Corby: December 1933, February 1934, April 1936, April 1937 and
   September 1937.

From 1937 no further records appear but it is known from the Industrial Locomotive Society's records that No. 619 moved from Shanks & McEwan's Bromsgrove contract, to the Corby Works Extension contract for Stewarts and Lloyds Ltd, in 1933. At some date thereafter it moved on to the extension of the Islip Works contract (also for Stewart and Lloyds Ltd) but returning to Corby in 1942. It was later named LAUCHOPE when at Corby and Islip and was scrapped at Corby, probably in 1950.

The locomotive is shown by both ILS and IRS as "Rebuilt by Easton Gibb in 1911" and this tallies with the Hunslet record of an enquiry for a new copper firebox in 1911.

By the middle of 1895, with four locomotives working round-the-clock, Mr Mansergh again wrote to the Water Committee for an increase in locomotive stock and including the full tenders with his requisition, hoping to eliminate the length of time the committee took to reply. This minute is recorded as 19th July, 1895 and so desperate was the need for more steam power that the order was placed on 26th July, 1895 with Manning Wardle, Boyne Engine Works, Leeds. It is interesting to note that Mr Mansergh had requested the tenders to include the fitting of vacuum brakes as he envisaged the locomotives were to be used more for the passenger trains (mail trains as they were to be called) that were now becoming frequent on the line.

The tenders read as follows, with Mr Mansergh's comments following:

MANNING, WARDLE & Co., LEEDS.

For one Engine	£1380 0 0
For fitting Vacuum Brake	25 0 0
	1405 0 0
Reduction from price of Engine	13 0 0
	1392 0 0
Reduction from price for fitting brake	20 0 0
	£1372 0 0= £2744 for the two

THE HUNSLET ENGINE CO., LEEDS.

For one Engine	£1350 0 0
For fitting Vacuum Brake	7 0 0
Addition to price of Engine	15 0 0

£1372 0 0= £2744 for the two

It will be seen that the prices given by these two firms are exactly alike. Each of the firms has already supplied the Works with two locomotives, all of which have given entire satisfaction. I am of opinion, however, that the preference is to be given to Messrs Manning, Wardle & Co's Engines, and recommend the acceptance of their tender.

I recommend the acceptance of Manning & Wardle's tender.

(signed) JAS. MANSERGH.

The written specification from Manning Wardle, dated 20th July, 1895 is included and makes very interesting reading and gives the reader a rare chance to see a full works specification.

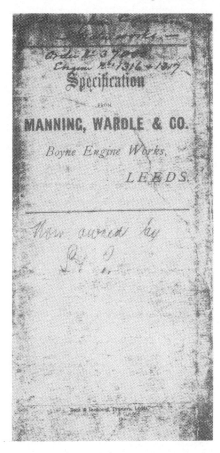

Specification

from

Manning, Wardle & Co.,

Boyne Engine Works,

Leeds.

July 22ⁿᵈ 1895

To *Birmingham Corporation.*

Order N° 37000. Eng. N° 1316 + 1317.

Delivery of Goods not to be binding during, or in consequence of strikes of workmen, accidents, or events of any kind causing an interruption of the work.

	FT.	IN.
GAUGE OF RAILWAY.	4 –	8½

General Description — The engine to be of the *inside* cylinder, *saddle* tank type, carried on *six* wheels *all* coupled together. The axle journals to be *inside* of the wheels, and in general appearance similar to enclosed *photo* No. 260.

Cylinders — The cylinders to be *15* inches diameter and *22* inches stroke, cast of strong close metal as hard as can be worked, and all joints truly surfaced by hand, fixed *inside* the frames with strong wrought-iron bolts turned so as to be a driven fit into rhymered holes through frames and cylinder flanges.

Frames — The pistons to be of cast-iron, similar to that used for the cylinders, and fitted with self-adjusting packing rings made of the *same*

Slide Valves — The slide valves to be either of best hard gun metal or of best hard cast-iron, at option of purchaser, accurately planed and scraped to a dead true face.

Motion — The eccentrics to be fitted with cast-iron hoops, with oil syphons cast on them, the eccentric rods, links and blocks, valve spindles, piston rods, cross heads, slide bars, connecting and coupling rods, to be made of best *steel* hammered iron (unless otherwise ordered), carefully fitted and thoroughly case-hardened in all wearing surfaces.

Pump and Injector — The pump to be of cast-iron, with gun metal glands, neck bush, valves and seats. The plunger to be of ———— and worked The injectors to be No. *8* size, fitted with all necessary steam, feed and overflow valves, or if preferred, two injectors can be put on instead of one pump and one injector. In either case the pump alone, or one injector, is capable of supplying the boiler with water. *to be fixed on each side of the engine*

Wheels and Axles — The wheel centres to be of *cast steel* fitted with Bessemer steel tyres 3 feet 6 inches diameter 2¼ inches thick and 5 inches wide. Distance from centre of leading to centre of trailing wheels *18* feet 6 inches. The axles to be of best Yorkshire iron, journals *hammered steel, journals 6¼ inches diameter, the leading and driving to be 6½ inches long, and the trailing 9 inches long.*

Axle Boxes and Horn Blocks

The axle boxes to be of best cast-~~iron~~ *steel (crossed out annotation)* with gun metal bearings, bored, planed, and fitted. The horn blocks to be of cast-iron, planed, and each carefully fitted to its own place on the frames. They will be held in position by wrought-iron bolts, turned so as to be a driven fit through both frames and horn blocks, all the holes being rhymered out with the blocks in position.

Springs

The springs are obtained from a high-class English firm, and made of the best spring steel.

Compensating Beam

A compensating beam to be fixed on each side of the engine, the ends to be connected with the *leading & driving springs*.

Frames

The frame plates to be of the " Best Mild Steel," rolled in one piece **1** inch thick, and extending the length of the engine, each pair of frame plates to be bolted together during planing, slotting, and drilling, to ensure perfect accuracy. When fixed on the engine they will be firmly braced together by strong transverse stays, all the bolts to be a driven fit into rhymered holes.

Buffer Beams, Buffers, and Draw Gear

The buffer beams to be of best oak **6** inches thick, fitted with cast-iron caps at each end and plated with wrought-iron on both sides. Unless otherwise ordered the engine will be fitted with ordinary spring buffers, having wrought-iron cases and plungers, and chain and hook draw gear fixed in centre. But the buffing and draw gear can be made of any required pattern to suit rolling stock. *The engine will also be fitted block buffers for tipping waggons*

Rail Guards

Wrought-iron rail guards to be fixed at each end of engine.

Barrel 8'- 6" long by 3'- 10" diar outer fire box 3'- 9" long, 3'- 11½ wide, & 2'- 3½

Boiler

The boiler and outer fire-box to be of best ~~Yorkshire Iron or~~ Best Mild Steel *deep below barrel* (at option of purchaser), barrel plates **7/16** inch thick, outer fire-box plates **1/2** inch thick, all the edges of the plates to be planed, and every joint carefully caulked both inside and outside of the boiler, and all flat surfaces protected with longitudinal or transverse stays. *& all longitudinal joints to be double rivetted.*

Dome

A dome to be securely rivetted to the boiler, & covered with a neat polished brass casing.

Fire box

31- 1" long, 3-3½ wide, & 4'- 10 deep inside
The fire-box to be of best selected copper, the thickness of plates **7/16** inch, tube plate **3/4** inch, and round mouthpiece **5/8** inch, all the rivets to be of copper. The inner and outer fire-boxes to be stayed together through water spaces with copper stays **1** inch diameter, about 4 inches centres, screwed into both boxes and rivetted over at both ends. The crown to be supported with strong wrought iron roof bars.

Foundation ring and mouthpiece

The foundation ring and mouthpiece to be solid forgings of best hammered iron, planed or slotted where required for joints.

Tubes

The tubes to be of solid drawn brass (best quality) **1 7/8** inches external diameter, No. 12 w.g. at firebox, and 14 w.g. at smoke-box end.

Safety Valves

The boiler to be fitted with a pair of **3** inches safety valves, with Salter's spring balances, graduated so that each pound on the balance indicates one pound pressure in the boiler, balances to be ferruled so that the working pressure in the boiler will be **150** lbs. per square inch.

Heating Surface

Heating surface in fire-box above fire bars **70** square feet, in the tubes ~~673~~ square feet. Total ~~743~~ square feet. *Grate area ~~~~ sq. ft. 12⅓*

Tank

A tank of neat pattern to be placed *above the* boiler, capable of holding ~~~~ *900* gallons.

Foot-plating

A " foot-plate " or platform of wrought-iron plates ¼ inch thick, to be fitted round back of fire-box shell, and extend along each side of engine. The whole to be supported by strong brackets bolted to frames.

Coke-box

A large coke-box to be placed upon the foot-plate *having a capacity* ~~to contain a proportionate quantity of fuel.~~ *of not less than 55 cubic ft.*

Sand boxes Two sand boxes to be placed *on the footplate in front of leading wheels, & two behind trailing wheels* with pipes extending down nearly to the rails. The handles for working sand valves to be within easy reach of driver.

Brake A powerful ~~screw brake~~ *steam + hand brake* to be worked from driver's foot-plate, and act upon *all the* wheels. The brake-blocks to be of *cast iron*.

Steam Jet A steam jet to be fixed in smoke-box and worked from driver's foot-plate.

Pipes All the steam, feed, steam jet, and pet pipes to be of best copper, solid drawn.

Cab *A neat cab of steel plates, fitted with plate glass circular windows, made to open both back and front to be fitted over the drivers footplate for his protection*

Lubricators ~~Two~~ Roscoe's Patent Lubricator to be fixed near the smoke-box, having copper pipe and unions connecting with steam pipe of cylinders.

Lamps One each head, tail, hand, and gauge lamps to be supplied, and suitable brackets for same fixed on the engine.

Screw Jack A *15* tons traversing screw-jack will be supplied with the engine.

Painting The engine is to receive not less than two coats of plain colours in oils, rubbed down, finished in *live* green (or any other colour at the option of purchaser), lined out and varnished.

General The engine to be fitted with water gauge, trial cocks, ~~pet cock for testing pump~~, whistle, steam-pressure gauge, washing-out plugs, or mudhole doors, fixed in convenient parts of fire-box shell and ~~both above and~~ below tubes in smoke-box, steam chest cock, tallow cocks, and ~~blow off cock~~ *a each washing cock will be fixed on each side of the engine with pipes leading to front of leading* ~~After~~ the boiler has been tested by hydraulic pressure to *200* lbs. and in steam to ~~300~~ lbs. per square inch, it is to be lagged with wood, covered with sheet-iron, and finished with neat polished brass mouldings.

The whole of the material and workmanship to be the best of their respective kinds. The motion details to be thoroughly case-hardened in all working parts, and syphon lubrication provided where necessary.

All screw threads to be Whitworth's Standards.

Name plate *a brass name plate to fixed on each side of engine*

Tools The following tools to be supplied with the engine :—A set of firing tools and crowbar, a lock-up tool box (to be fixed in a convenient place on the engine), containing a set of case-hardened screw keys, one copper *one lead* and one hand hammer, two chisels, oil cans (large and small), tallow kettle and hand brush.

SUMMARY.

	FT.	INS.
Gauge of Railway	4	8½
Diameter of Cylinders	1	3
Length of Stroke		*1—10*
Diameter of Wheels	3	6
Length of Wheel Base...		*10—6*

Capacity of Water Tank, *900* ~~450~~ gallons

Heating Surface	In the Fire-box	70
	In the Tubes	*673*
	Total	*743* ~~770~~ square ft.

{Weight of engine when empty about 26½ tons
" fully loaded - 34¼.   }
32½

ORDER Nº 37000 ENGINE Nºˢ 1316 & 1317

Manning Wardle No. 1316

The works record sheet shows the following and allows again an in-depth study of the specification to these locomotives. It was built to standard gauge but as a "special" 15 in. x 22 in. inside cylinder design saddle tank engine on six coupled wheels (cast steel) of 3 ft 6 in. diameter and a 10 ft 6 in. wheelbase. The water tanks carried 900 gallons, the boiler was fitted with a dome, working pressure being 150 lb. per sq. inch. Copper fire box plates were ½ in. thick, tube plates ¹³⁄₁₆ in. and tubes were 1⅞ in. outside diameter. All the axles, piston rods and valve spindle buckles were of the best hammered steel. The trailing axle box had ½ in. play in the journals, ¼ in. each side, and the leading axle ⅛ in. (¹⁄₁₆ in. each side). The flanges of the driving tyres were ⅝ in. thick and the coupling rods were fitted with universal joints. All the axle boxes were of cast steel as also the trailing axle boxes but the leading and driving keeps were cast iron.

The buffer beams were fitted with special block buffers and spring buffers as a "class K", the draw gear was fitted with springs behind the beams, like "class O" trailing springs, having a contractors hook. The trailing hook had a chain attached to it, fastened inside the cab for uncoupling; this engine had also a dropping bar at the front end and a transverse stay between rail guards at the back end.

The brake was worked by steam having a brake cylinder of 14 in. diameter. The steam brake valve and drain cocks for the brake cylinder were of Manning Wardle make. This engine was also fitted with a vacuum brake for braking the full train which was supplied by the Birmingham Corporation and fitted on to the engine by M.W. The cylinders were ordinary "class O" fitted with round studs in all the covers and a full set of cylinder cocks. Railwashers were fitted on the tank. Injectors No. 8 (special) were provided with feed valves screwed into the injectors, all the oil cups were special, with self-closing covers. The cross heads were also fitted with oil cups for lubricating the bottom slide bars. Oil cups were also fitted on the back of the smokebox tubeplate for lubricating piston and valve spindle rods. An oil box was positioned inside the cab for lubricating the trailing axleboxes.

In April 1900 a new set of connecting rod brasses, with recessed white metal bearings, was supplied. A cast iron chimney was supplied on 13th February, 1925. The name plate when supplied was brass with 3¾ in. letters forming the word CALETTWR (*see plate 78*).

Manning Wardle No. 1317 was identical to No. 1316 except for the name RHIWNANT (*plate 79*) and appears to have had new brass tubes in March 1903.

Plate 78: Seen here at Corby and numbered 34, but retaining its BCWW's name CALETTWR, this locomotive was built by Manning Wardle in 1895, to Works No. 1316.   *R.T. Russell Collection, National Railway Museum*

Plate 79: The Works photograph of RHIWNANT, a Manning Wardle 0-6-0 (No. 1317) built in 1895. Note the block of wood across the locomotive to protect the wheels from falling stones on the line.   *Hunslet Locomotive Co. Ltd*

Plate 80: The locomotive RHIWNANT again but this time at Corby Works and numbered 35, but lacking the nameplate.   *John Edgington*

Both Nos. 1316 and 1317 were obtained in 1912 from Thos. W. Ward Ltd by the Lloyds Ironstone Co. Ltd, Corby, Northants. It appears that No. 1316 was loaned to Glendon East Quarries, by then owned by Stewart and Lloyds Minerals Ltd, from 1950 and returned in November 1951, being finally scrapped in August 1966. The other locomotive No. 1317 lost its name at Corby (*plate 80*) and again was loaned out to Glendon East Quarries from August 1956 until September 1956. It then went into private ownership of Mr P. Elms and moved, in October 1969, to The Foxfield Light Railway where it can still be seen today.

The weight of these two locomotives was as follows:

Leading axle	Driving Axle	Trailing Axle	
9T 9c 0q	9T 9c 0q	8T 16c 1q	Unloaded
11T 0c 3q	12T 1c 1q	10T 12c 2q	14 cwt of coal

The Birmingham Waterworks railway locomotive stock had now become six.

A standard livery was now emerging for the Corporation's railway locomotives, and, although other reports have described a "dark green" livery, it is clear from the Manning Wardle specification on page 129 that an overall light olive had been adopted for their locomotives and Hunslet a "Victorian green", both colours being very similar.

It is possible that the conflicting reports of the livery could have arisen, as the photographs of METHAN, MARCHNANT and NANT GWYLTT show a darker green panel edged with lining, with the overall engine colour a lighter "Victorian" green. The lining was in black edged either side with two fine yellow lines and then a further white line, (*see figure below*).

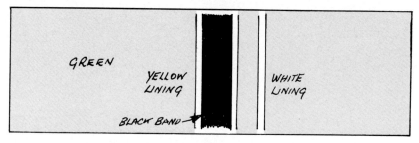

All the locomotives carried brass nameplates and polished work plates. Buffer beams were bright red with polished buffers, a fine sight when on shed on Sundays!

With six locomotives on site, the original engine shed on the Caban Lower workshop sidings was inadequate and on 18th October, 1895, Mr Mansergh requested authority to construct an extension to the engine shed, to be carried out by the workmen on site at an estimated cost of £110.

It is appropriate here to include the specification drawing of the original 132 ft locomotive shed which had an estimated cost of £300. The construction was wood framed with wooden side planks with continuous double windows along the top, tiled roof with a 1 ft 3in. raised, open, coping strip to allow the smoke to escape. This shed can be seen in *plate 12.*

The actual cost of the original shed was £228 1s. 7d. being £71 18s. 5d. below estimate.

No further need for locomotive power was evident until 16th March, 1898 when Mr Mansergh wrote to the Water-Committee as follows:

Two further locomotives are required for use at the Elan Valley Works – one 18 in. for shunting, coaling and other odd jobs at the Caban, as well as

BIRMINGHAM CORPORATION WATER.

PROPOSED LOCOMOTIVE SHED.

ESTIMATED COST £300.

ELEVATION.

132'-0"
OVERALL

4'-0"

4'-0"

for a spare engine, now that the present ones are getting the worse for wear and require more attention in the shed; and one 10 in. for running the traffic between Gigfran Quarry and Dol-faenog Junction, which is to become the depot for all material for Pen-y-Gareg and Graig Goch.

The Cardiff Corporation have two suitable locos. which they will be prepared to dispose of in a few months time, but they asked more than I was prepared to recommend the Committee to pay, and they would not come down in their price.

Four of the principal Railway Co's have been approached, but none of them have anything suitable to offer. Mr T.W. Ward's stocks at Sheffield and Warrington have been inspected; but there is nothing suitable to be had there.

Quotations are herewith submitted for new locos. from Messrs Manning Wardle & Co. and the Hunslet Engine Co., both of which firms have already supplied locos. to the Works. Messrs Manning Wardle & Co's price is the lower for the 10 in. engine and The Hunslet Engine Co., for the 18 in.

Before any order is given, the Resident Engineer wishes to communicate with the firms as to some alterations and modifications which may affect the prices.

I have talked over this matter with Mr Yourdi on several occasions, and am satisfied that we ought to have these two new locomotives if we are to make sure of avoiding delays due to possible breakdowns.

The following resolution was entered into the Minute book dated the 18th March, 1898:

Resolved –
No. 3863. That the tender of Messrs Manning Wardle & Co. for a 10 in. locomotive at £850, and that of the Hunslet Engine Co. for an 18 in. at £1,065 be accepted, subject in each case to certain modifications; any consequent alteration of price to be subject to the approval of the Chairman.

The first of the two locomotives to arrive was the diminutive 0–4–0 COEL from Messrs Manning Wardle. The order number for this locomotive was 41700, and the maker's No. 1405. This entry was dated only one day after the above resolution had been passed. Obviously no time was wasted by the Town Clerk's office in ordering the locomotive. The stated time of delivery was 4 months; with the first steaming on 25th July, the locomotive was sent away to Rhayader early in August 1895, only a week later than the quoted time, quite an achievement. It is interesting that Mr Yourdi did not however report this locomotive's arrival until 11th October, 1898, and at a cost of £931 0s. 0d. so presumably this cost had been agreed by the Chairman of the Water Committee as this was in excess of the quotation.

The works specification for maker's No. 1405 was as follows:

Manning Wardle No. 1405

This locomotive again was standard gauge with 10 in. x 16 in. outside cylinders built to an ordinary "class F" design except for the following alterations and additions. A special cab was ordered, special frame ends and buffer beams with dropping bars at each end but no railguards and a special whistle. This engine was fitted with Hopkinson's small size water gauges and M.W. No. 5 injector. Steam brakes were also fitted and steam brake valve. Special boiler mountings were provided, with a whistle fixed on top of the cab, block buffers fitted for earth wagons and ordinary "class H" buffers. Special draw gear was supplied with slip hook. Slide blocks were lined with white metal on the faces. Railwashing cocks and pipes were placed on each side of the engine. There were special footstep stay to frames and special coke boxes. With this engine M.W. commenced a new kind of cast steel brake pillar bracket and cast steel footsteps. The engine was fitted also with the latest type of brake hangers. The records show it was later supplied with a mild steel smokebox tube plate in May 1922.

The brass nameplate had the word COEL, with the "C" in 3½ in. letters and "OEL" in 2½ in. letters (*see plate 94*).

The dimensions for the "class F" locomotive were as follows:

Wheelbase	4 ft 9 in.	Thickness of bufferbeams	5 in.
Overhang – leading	5 ft 3 in.	Boiler diameter	2 ft 7 in.
Overhang – trailing	5 ft 2 in.	Boiler length	7 ft 11 in.
		Grate area	5.5 sq.ft.
Heating surface – tubes	267 sq.ft	Water capacity	350 gallons
Heating surface – firebox	32.5 sq.ft	Boiler centre line to rail level	4 ft 6 in.

No. 1405 was not weighed but (based on other class Fs) it would be about 12½ tons empty and about 15 tons in working order.

The locomotive was sold to Thos. W. Ward Ltd in 1906 and immediately purchased for use on the Earl of Dudley's Round Oak Works Ltd Railway at Brierley Hill, Staffs. It was finally scrapped in March 1934.

The last of the Birmingham Waterworks locomotives to arrive was MARCHNANT supplied from The Hunslet Works and based on a standard "sales" design but with 3 ft 1 in. instead of the 3 ft 2½ in. wheels, that the sales sheet illustrated. The order number for this locomotive was 21150 and the maker's No. 687. First tried in steam on 18th October, 1898, she was sent to Rhayader the next day. Mr Yourdi reported that this locomotive had arrived and was in service by 8th December, 1898, but this again may have been belated advice.

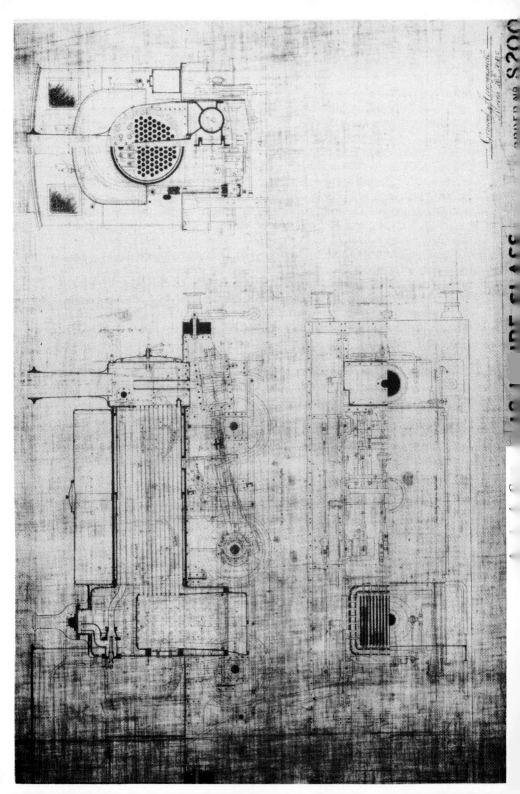

0-6-0 TYPE

SADDLE TANK ENGINE

Gauge of Railway		4 ft. 8½ in.
Size of Cylinders		12 in. dia. × 18 in. stroke
Dia. of Coupled Wheels		3 ft. 2½ in.
Rigid Wheelbase (Engine)		10 ,, 6 ,,
Height from Rail to Top of Chimney		10 ,, 9¼ ,,
Extreme Width		7 ,, 7¼ ,,
Heating Surface—Small Tubes	356 sq. ft.	
,, ,, Firebox	45 ,,	
Total	401 ,,	401 sq. ft.
Grate Area		7·375 ,,
Working Pressure		140 lbs. per sq. in.
Tank Capacity		500 gallons
Fuel Space (Coal)		1 ton 0 cwts.
Weight Empty (Engine)		18 tons 10 ,
,, in Working Order (Engine)		23 ,, 0 ,,
Total Weight on Coupled Wheels		23 ,, 0 ,,
Maximum Axle Load		8 ,, 0 ,,
Tractive Effort at 75 per cent. of Boiler Pressure		7069 lbs.
Minimum Radius of Curve Engine will traverse with ease		220 ft.
Weight per Yard of Lightest Rail advisable		40 lbs.
Load Engine will haul on Level		370 tons
,, ,, ,, up Incline of 1 in 100		180 ,,
,, ,, ,, ,, ,, 1 in 50		100 ,,

This specification was similar to HE687 except that 3′ 1″ dia. wheels were supplied.

Plate 81: Cambrian 0-4-0 locomotive No. 22, which was normally used on the Van Branch, but often pressed into use on the Elan Valley Railway by the Cambrian Railway.   *R.W. Kidner Collection*

A note from The Hunslet company appeared with the letter from Mr Yourdi and read as follows:

This class of Engine is a favourite one with Contractors, Colliery Proprietors etc. for whose description of work it is particularly suited, though they are also used for a variety of purposes. They all have the cylinders bolted together and to the inside of the frames. The advantages which they possess over the outside cylinder class are, steadier running, compactness of mechanism, and less strain on the frames due to the transverse centres of the cylinders being brought closer together, and the force being transmitted to the axle between the bearings, instead of outside. All the moving parts being inside the frames except the coupling rods, there is less danger also, of injury to the Engine by striking obstructions near the outside of the rails, such as are common on railways during construction.

They are good steam raisers. They have flush topped boilers with steam domes containing the regulator, and also raised manholes. The Engine has a raised firebox shell and manhole from the top of which the regulator draws the steam. Steam pipes, tubes, etc., ease of access through circular dished smoke box door. Four sand-boxes, delivering in front of the wheels at each end of the Engine. Hand screw brake acting on all six wheels; steam brake if required.

Any kind of buffing and draw gear that may be required. The water is carried in a Saddle Tank. Fuel in a box behind, filled from outside through a door in the back of the Cab. Driver's Cab with windows back and front, or for hot climates, awning open at the sides. If necessary, these Engines can be made to traverse quicker curves than those given in the tables by having flat tyres on the middle pair of wheels and by allowing the leading or trailing axle-boxes to slide transversely. Automatic Vacuum brake also can be fitted.

The records show that Hunslet 687 was painted the same as Hunslet 618. Spares were ordered by the Corporation at intervals from November 1898 to September 1906. A long gap then appears in the records, until January 1913, when Walsall Corporation Gas Works ordered a new boiler for the locomotive, with further orders in May 1918 and October 1930. It was finally scrapped at Walsall in 1939.

Despite the fact that eight "iron horses" were now stabled, it was sometimes necessary to request help from the Cambrian and there are several reports of their locomotives working the Elan Valley railway and recorded in the minute books. The favourite engine was No. 22 (*plate 81*), a little Manning Wardle 0–4–0 saddle tank (builder's No. 1523) which had been purchased by the Cambrian at a cost of £1100 (excluding vacuum brake). She was delivered to the Cambrian on 30th July, 1901, having 3 ft diameter wheels, 5 ft 4 in. wheelbase, 12 in. x 18 in. outside cylinders and weighed 19 tons 10 cwt.

She was an ideal engine for use on the Birmingham Waterworks line and was first put to use at Elan Valley Junction and Noyadd exchange sidings by the Cambrian, but, as previously stated, worked many excursions right up the Elan Valley "main line". In later life it ran on the Van Branch ceasing its Cambrian service in September 1914 and being purchased by Messrs Armytage & Jones of Sheffield on behalf of the Government in May 1916, and sent to Prees Heath camp near Whitchurch (Salop). It became Air Ministry Works No. 128 and, in 1933, was sold to the White Moss Coal Co. Upholland, near Wigan, and worked at Skelmersdale colliery.

To conclude this chapter on the locomotives that were owned by the Birmingham Waterworks, a report has been included dated 21st May, 1897 by Mr Yourdi on the quality of coal used. This shows how keen the company were to ensure top quality supplies of coal were purchased for these little locomotives and how they went about choosing the appropriate suppliers.

I beg to submit herewith schedule of prices tendered for steam coal, together with the original tenders.

Steam Coal

Sample trucks of steam coal have been obtained as under:

No. of Tender	Name of Tenderer	Description of coal	Colliery	Price per ton
64	J.A. Jebb, B'ham	Best double screened smokeless	Cripnant	11s. 0d. No. 1
63	B. Bowen, Bishops Castle	Best South Wales anthracite	Swansea	12s. 10d. No. 2
26	Lancaster Speer & Co. Cardiff	Russells New Black Vein Large	Cwmtillery & Rose Heyworth	13s. 3d. No. 3
33	Westminster Brymbo C&C Co. Wrexham	Best Westminster	Westminster	13s. 6d. No. 4
58	Powells Tillery Steam Coal Co. Cardiff	Large	Tillery Abertillery	13s. 9d. No. 5
10	Ebbw Vale SI & C Co. Cardiff	Large	Wann Lloyd & Marine Pits	14s. 9d. No. 6
6	G. Williams & Co. Newport Mon.	Dowlais Merthyr Large	Vochriw	15s.2½d. No. 7
25	T. Boston & Son, Birmingham	Dowlais Merthyr Large		15s. 3d. No. 8
2	Fred Martin, B'ham		Nixons Navigation	17s. 3d. No. 9

Each of the six locomotives received one day's supply from each truck, and each driver was required to give his opinion of the steaming qualities of the different lots.

The reports of the several drivers are as follows:

LOCO. CALETTWR The driver states he has found none of the samples so good as that he has been accustomed to burn. The best he considers is No. 8, which is a fair steaming coal but not economical. No. 9 a good coal, but too "rapid" with the strong blast. No. 2 was so bad that he could not use it with a heavy load.

LOCO. CLAERWEN The driver found all the samples inferior to that he has been supplied with during the past year. No. 8 and No. 9 are the only two he thinks at all suitable but he would use considerably more of these than his usual allowance. The rest are bad, and with some it would be impossible to keep up steam.

LOCO. METHAN The driver does not think the best of the samples approach anywhere near the last year's coal. No. 4 he found very soft, smoky and quick burning.

LOCO. NANT GWILLT The driver considers the coal used last year a better steaming coal and more economical than any of the samples. None of the lots were good, and some extremely bad.

LOCO. ELAN The driver prefers last year's coal to the best of the samples, and has not a good opinion of any of the latter.

LOCO. RHIWNANT The driver was not able to get through the day on the allowance, and he had to take additional coal. He estimates that he would require 6 cwt a day more if he burnt coal similar to the best of the samples.

It will be seen that the only coals which obtained anything like a favourable report were those supplied by Messrs G. Williams & Co., of Newport, Mon., and Mr F. Martin of Birmingham, and it was stated that these were not economical, and that if either of the coals were adopted, a considerably larger quantity would be required to do the necessary work. The prices quoted for these coals respectively are 15s. 2½d. and 17s. 3d. per ton.

The present contractors to the Corporation for Steam Coal are the Old Radnor Coal, Lime & General Supply Co. of Kington. The coal supplied is described as "Best Large Dowlais-Merthyr". The current price is 15s. 1d. and their present tender is 15s. 7d. or a rise of 6d. per ton, which reckoned on the quantity obtained during the last twelve months would make a difference to the Corporation of about £88. The two best samples, viz: Messrs G. Williams & Co's, and Mr Fred Martin's compare, as regards price, as under with the Old Radnor Co.

G. Williams & Co.   15s. 2½d. per ton, a saving of 3½d. per ton or roughly speaking, £52 in the year

F. Martin   17s.3d. per ton, a loss of 1s. 8d. per ton, or roughly speaking £300 in the year.

A similar coal to that offered by Mr F. Martin is offered by Messrs T. Boston & Son at 17s. 9d. per ton, a loss of roughly speaking, £390 in the year.

From this report it was resolved to continue with their present contractors, the Old Radnor Co. at the new price of 15s. 7d. per ton from 1st June, 1897, for one year.

All the photographs included in this book show the locomotives clean and well kept throughout their life with the Corporation, and they certainly reflected great credit on the Elan Valley Railway staff. At least seven of the locomotives appear to have been sold to Thomas W. Ward Ltd in 1906, but actual dates of the sale are vague. An auction sale of the 8th–10th May, 1907 included one standard gauge Hunslet 0–6–0ST with 12 in. x 18 in. cylinders and steam brake, this was probably Hunslet 687 MARCHNANT. So ended the motive power of this fascinating and hard working railway.

SUMMARY OF LOCOMOTIVES

Locomotives of the Birmingham Corporation Water Department, Elan Valley, Rhayader

All these locomotives took their names from streams that flow into the reservoirs. Gauge 4 ft 8½ in. (Standard).

Name	Type	Cyls	Bldr	Bldr No.	Date	Supplied
ELAN	0–6–0ST	OC	MW	1286	1894	New
CLAERWEN	0–6–0ST	OC	MW	1287	1894	New
NANT GWYLLT	0–6–0ST	IC	HE	618	1894	New
METHAN	0–6–0ST	IC	HE	619	1894	New
CALETTWR	0–6–0ST	IC	MW	1316	1895	New
RHIWNANT	0–6–0ST	IC	MW	1317	1895	New
MARCHNANT	0–6–0ST	IC	HE	687	1898	New
COEL	0–4–0ST	OC	MW	1405	1898	New

Chapter Six

Coaching and Goods Stock

COACHING STOCK

As the dam construction work increased and the railway's material-carrying role was expanded, most of the workmen were conveyed in open trucks to the work sites. After many complaints from the men, particularly during the early part of the winter in December 1894, it was decided that passenger coaches were needed. In January 1895, Mr Mansergh wrote requesting permission to purchase six second-hand passenger coaches to take the men to and from their work at the Caban site, and later for similar purposes when the subsequent dams were built.

With his request he included a letter from the Great Western Railway Co., which read as follows:

Great Western Railway
Locomotive & Carriage Department
Engineer's Office,
Swindon

7th Decr., 1894

Dear Sir,

Third Class Coaches

In reply to yours of 3rd inst, below I give you the dimensions of six coaches we have here, also the price at which I should be prepared to recommend my Directors to dispose of them:

GWR Number	Length		Width		Height		Seating Capacity	Price
	ft	in.	ft	in.	ft	in.		
1099	23	0	7	6	6	9	40	£56
951	21	0	7	6	6	6	40	£54
2303	21	0	7	6	6	9	30	£50
2312	21	0	7	6	6	9	30	£50
2323	21	0	7	6	6	9	30	£50
2377	21	0	7	6	6	9	30	£50

The terms of sale would be net cash before delivery, the price in each case to cover delivery free on Great Western Railway not beyond.

The coaches are fitted with the automatic vacuum brake apparatus which it is not proposed to remove.

Yours truly,

(signed) Wm Dean
per C.J.F.

It is interesting to note the GWR needed cash *before* delivery, nothing was on credit in those days!

With this information to hand it appears that a Mr Charters from Birmingham Waterworks Corporation was sent to inspect the stock at Swindon in February 1895 and asked the GWR to write a report on the vehicles he had chosen from the "withdrawn stockpile" at Swindon Works. It is again interesting to note that only two of the original stock offered, had been selected by Mr Charters:

Great Western Railway,
Locomotive & Carriage Department,
Engineer's Office, Swindon

February 8th, 1895

Dear Sir,

Third Class Coaches

With reference to yours of the 6th inst., Mr Charters to-day inspected the coaches we have for disposal, and, as requested by him, I give you particulars of eight which he selected, also the price at which I should be prepared to recommend my Directors to dispose of them, with or without the vacuum brake apparatus, and short-coupled or fitted with long buffers, as may be required:

GWR Number	Length ft in.	Seating capacity	Price including Vacuum Brake Apparatus	Price without Vacuum Brake Apparatus
456	21 0	40	£52	£40
846	21 0	40	£50	£45
472	21 0	40	£50	£45
437	21 0	40	£50	£45
488	21 0	40	£50	£45
2366	21 0	30	£52	£47
2377	21 0	30	£50	£45
2312	21 0	30	£50	£45

All the coaches are 7 ft 6 in. wide by 6 ft 6 in. high, and have a wheel base of 12 ft. The axles are 6 ft 4 in. long between centres of journals, and the sizes of the journals vary from 8 in. by 3¼ in. to 8 in. by 3½ in.

The price quoted for No. 2366 includes the trimmings at present in the coach, and in the case of No. 456 the price is inclusive of the hand brake. The terms of sale would be net cash before delivery, the price in each case to cover delivery free on Great Western Railway.

Yours truly,
(signed) William Dean

This letter and the following report by Mr Williams was sent to the

Committee in Birmingham for their consideration and hopefully subsequent approval.

Notes of Gt. Western Railway Third Class Coaches, seen at Swindon on Friday February 8th, 1895.

Coaches No. 456, 846, 472, 437 and 488 are at present made into a short-coupled train, but will be supplied with long buffers and couplings if required; they are all fitted with the automatic vacuum brake; No. 456 is also provided with hand brake. These five coaches have iron and wood frames. The seating capacity of No. 456 is at present 35.

Numbers 2377 and 2312, though the same overall length as the above, have only three compartments each, to seat 10 a side. These coaches have wood frames, and are fitted with long buffers and automatic vacuum brake.

Number 2366 is a saloon coach with two compartments, each to seat 14, and arranged as here sketched.

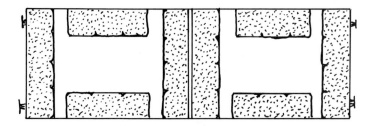

This coach has wood frame, and is fitted with long buffers and automatic vacuum brake. The price for this includes leaving in the present trimmings.

The coaches are all 21 feet long, and are carried on four wheels, the wheel base being 12 feet. The couplings, wheels and axles are all of the GWRy stock type, consisting of screw coupling and two safety chains, wrought iron or steel axles, the wheels being of the solid wood pattern with iron rim and steel tyre.

The short-coupled train is, at present, connected with links, and, with the exception of rear coach, viz: that provided with hand-brake, have only spring-buffers at one end, which abut against the ends of the frames of the next coach.

The prices given in annexed quotation (except No. 2366) include removing present trimmings, painting inside and out, and putting everything in complete running order. The price does not include lamps.

Six of these coaches were purchased and arrived at Rhayader from Swindon on 11th March, 1895, the only clue to which six were chosen (from the eight inspected) is that Mr Yourdi stated "5 cost £50 and one £52".

GWR
SECOND CLASS CARRIAGE

Historical Details of the eight coaches available for purchase
prepared by J.N. Slinn (HMRS)

GW No. when sold	Ex First	Ex Composite	Ex Second	Built	Condemned by GWR
	Date	Date	Date	Date	Date
437			Lot 31 Oct. 1870	Railway Carriage Co. Feb. 1862	Dec. 1894
456			Lot 80 Dec. 1870	Brown Marshalls Nov. 1861	Nov. 1894
470			Lot 29 June 1872	Brown Marshalls Oct. 1861	Dec. 1894
488			Lot 94 April 1872	Brown Marshalls Nov. 1861	Dec. 1894
846			Lot 4 Sept. 1873	G.W. Saltney Dec. 1864	Dec. 1894
2366	Lot 127 April 1890	Lot 127 Nov. 1868	–	J. Wright Dec. 1861	Aug. 1894
2377	Lot 80 March 1878		Lot 177 Sept 1890	Brown Marshalls Oct. 1861	Aug. 1894
2312	Lot 95 March 1878		Lot 191 April 1889	Brown Marshalls Jan. 1862	July 1894

Note: The 2nd class coaches had 4 compartments; the firsts and composite coaches had 3 compartments.

Soon this stock was found insufficient for the growing army of men working on the dam sites and as early as 18th June, 1895 Mr Mansergh submitted a request for six further second-hand coaches, offered by the GWR at £50 apiece, free by rail to Hereford only.

In an attempt to influence the committee's decision, Mr Mansergh added as a postscript:

The using of these trains will probably diminish materially the necessity of building huts on the Watershed.

The request was agreed but Mr Mansergh's anticipated saving on building accommodation probably did not materialise because the weather conditions were so bad it is evident that many huts were built at the dam sites to house the men thus avoiding, as quoted, "waiting for men" due to snow etc.

The vehicles appear to have arrived at the end of August 1895 as Mr Yourdi reported then as follows:

I beg to report that the six second-hand coaches have been purchased from the Great Western Railway Company, at a cost of £300, being the amount

Plate 82: High up, hugging the hillside, the "Mail" train approaches Gigfran quarry, at the point nearest the top of the Caban Coch Dam wall on Railway No. 3. The train comprises of ex-GWR coaching stock as described in the text.

Reproduced by permission of the Reference Library, Birmingham

Plate 83: Photograph of the type of stock acquired by the BCWW. Seen here in GWR days, before the BCWW purchased coaches like these from the scrap yard at Swindon.   *J.N. Slinn Collection*

Plate 84: The Cambrian coaches used on the Royal train of July 1904 showing an old four wheeled 1st and 2nd class composite No. 34 (*left*) which was purchased from Ashbury's in February 1861 for £387. The next coach is a full 1st class coach No. 9 (built 1889), gas lit and only seating 12 persons. This coach was taken into GWR service as No. 9218. The remaining two coaches are unidentified but are 1st class and brake 3rd, respectively. Similar coaches were purchased by the BCWW from the Cambrian and worked the Elan Valley. The coaches had been repainted for this occasion in the white and green livery of the Cambrian Railway.   *LGRP, Courtesy David & Charles*

authorised. As none of the Coaches quoted for were supplied with brakes, the Great Western Railway Company agreed to fit a hand brake to one of the Coaches at a cost of £3, which has been done, bringing the total amount expended to £303.

With the Cambrian Railways close at hand, and possessing many unwanted "early" vehicles it is likely that further passenger stock was purchased from them. The following list was compiled by the late Eric Mountford from the Cambrian records:

Four Wheel Composite Carriages (see plate 84)
Cambrian Nos. 77 and 80, both built by the Metropolitan C&W Co. July 1864 and were sold to Birmingham Corporation, Rhayader, in November 1902.

Four Wheel Third Class Carriages
Cambrian No. 26 (Ashbury Carriage Co. 7/1860) and No. 28 (built by the Cambrian Railways Co. also 7/1860) are both listed as "painted for use of workmen at Rhayader". Neither was given as sold, and in December 1906 both were shown as "used by the Engineer's dept as a Ballast vehicle" (presumably riding vehicles for platelayers in Ballast trains).

Cambrian No. 18 (Ashbury 12/1860) was also given as "Sold" – without further details. As it was replaced in May 1903, it is possible it was sold to Birmingham Corporation for Rhayader also, but this is not certain. However, the dates do seem to correspond with the sale of Cambrian Composite No. 77 and 80 above.

It is certain that the railway possessed at least seventeen coaches, twelve from the Great Western and five from the Cambrian but it is possible that, at the height of construction, with over 5000 men working, even more were purchased or borrowed.

The livery of the coaching stock was reported to have been dark chocolate, without any lining or lettering and lit by oil lamps, with black underframes and buffing gear; but the records show that the Cambrian stock (as sold) were painted all-over crimson-red before being delivered to the BCWW but may have been repainted, when necessary, in the dark chocolate. From *Plate 97* it appears that the coaches did carry lettering on the sides, and each coach number was about 10 inches in height, painted yellow and black shaded.

WAGONS etc.

To detail all the many types of wagons used on the Birmingham Waterworks Railway would be a huge undertaking because of the many second-hand wagons they purchased particularly around the turn of the century. But a look at some of the early purchases does give the reader an idea of the variety of stock utilised in the early days of the railway's operation.

The first entry is of a request by James Mansergh for wagons, dated 12th June, 1894.

I am sending on the tenders which Mr Yourdi has received for end and side tip wagons. As these tenders have been invited, I take it the Committee will feel bound to accept the lowest, viz: that of the Bristol Wagon Co., and my opinion would be that it would be worth while to pay the 38s. extra, and have oak in place of elm. The number at present required will be six of each kind.

Arranged in order from the lowest

Firm and Wood	Date	Side Tip	End Tip
Elm	1894	£ s. d.	£ s. s.
The Bristol Wagon Co. Bristol	May 25	21 10 0	20 17 0
The Oldbury R'way Car. Co. Oldbury	May 26	21 15 0	21 7 0
W. Glover & Son Ltd, Warwick	May 24	22 15 0	22 15 0
Midland R'way Car. Co, Birmingham	May 25	24 0 0	22 0 0
Turner Bros, Newtown	April 17	31 10 0	30 0 0
Oak			
Bristol Wagon Co.	May 25	23 10 0	21 15 0
Midland R'way Car. Co.	May 25	26 5 0	24 0 0
W. Glover & Son Ltd	May 24	27 10 0	– – –
Turner Bros	April 17	33 0 0	32 10 0

The committee agreed to purchase 6 side-tip and 6 end-tip wagons from the Bristol Wagon Co. and a similar wagon to these can be seen in *Plates 85 and 86.* It is interesting to note that whilst researching this book, the following wagon plate (*same size as reproduction*) was found

near the Caban Coch Dam, on the side of the old track bed and it is
pleasing to speculate that it came from one of these first wagons.

The following month a further 13 second-hand, 3½ cu.yard end-tip
wagons, offered by Joseph Buggins & Co. Birmingham were requi-
sitioned. The price asked was £11 each, delivered to Rhayader. Each
wagon was made of English oak with wrought iron wheels, steel
tyres and axles; following inspection at Henley-in-Arden the trucks
were purchased.

More wagons were bought in April 1895:

From the Bristol Wagon Co.

4 x 3 yard Side Tip Wagons at £23 10s. 0d. each	£94 0s. 0d.
4 x 3 yard End Tip Wagons at £21 15s. 0d. each	£87 0s. 0d.

From the Wigan Wagon Co.

46 x 4 yard Side Tip Wagons at £19 10s. 0d. each	£897 0s. 0d.

From the Oldbury Wagon Co.

20 x 3 yard Side Tip Wagons at £22 5s. 0d.	£445 0s. 0d.
	£1523 0s. 0d.

Later the same month another large purchase was made when no
less than fifty 4 cu.yard side-tip wagons of English Oak were
ordered. There were six tenders for this order ranging from £1350 to
£1550. The Engineer was instructed to purchase the 50 wagons from
the Ashbury Railway Carriage and Wagon Company of Openshaw,
Manchester for the sum of £1350 (delivered).

An even bigger order was placed for 100 x 4 cu.yd side-tipping
wagons in July 1895 with the Ashbury Railway Carriage and Iron
Company Ltd at a total cost of £2,577 10s. 0d. and a further 36 in
October 1895. The specification for these was altered slightly to "the
sides, back, tailboard, floor and rockers are to be of English Elm
instead of Oak and to incorporate two dodgers".

In October 1895 Mr Yourdi reported that he had successfully
purchased a second-hand horse box, at a cost of £25 delivered, from
the LNWR. This was to be used to convey horses to the dam sites.
Previously these had been walked from the stables, near the junction
of Railway No. 1 and No. 2 but, on arriving at the required sites, the
horses were "tired and often late". So the Engineer had the bright
idea of conveying these animals by rail to the appropriate place of
work.

By August 1896 slightly larger wagons were required for the distribution of cement, coal and general stores to the various work sites.
Just at that time the Cardiff Corporation advertised for tenders for 50
wagons of the type required and the BCWW tendered £22 10s. 0d. for

Plate 85: This shows a locomotive at the top dam site of Craig Goch with an assortment of wagons, with an enlargement below of a side-tip wagon typical of the ones used (in quantity) in the construction of the dams on the BCWW Railway. *Courtesy: Severn-Trent Water*

16 of them. This was accepted and the foreman wagon fettler was sent to select the wagons.

By 1897 Mr Mansergh had decided not to purchase any further "tip" wagons but to build them in the workshops at Caban site.

He put in the following report for material to build 100 wagons:

It is proposed to build 50 tip wagons and 50 stone bogies in the company works, and quotations have been obtained for the necessary timber, wheels, and axles.

The tip wagons are required for the distribution of material from the Crusher Yard, and the stone bogies for the conveyance of "plums" from the quarries to the dams.

The timber required (elm) worked out to the lowest quotation, amounts to the following:

For Tip Wagons	£251 12s. 2d.
For Stone Bogies	£177 18s. 11d.
	£429 11s. 1d.

Plate 86: Locomotive CLAERWEN, the Manning Wardle 0–6–0 at the terminus of Railway No. 4 in 1904, bringing material to make a new platform, on which the King alighted to see the Craig Goch Dam. This photograph shows one of the types of side-tip wagons used on the railway. *Real Photographs*

Plate 87: A marvellous period scene at the "topping-out" ceremony, with the plaque carrying the inscription, just being lowered; note the livery of the two-plank open wagons of the BCWWR and the photographer, photographing the photographer!

Reproduced by permission of the Reference Library, Birmingham

Plate 88: Taken at the Careg-Ddu Dam, one wonders at the safety conditions in force when these wagons, fully loaded (or overloaded) travelled along the precarious track mounted over the tops of the brick arches. The wagons would have been loose coupled and look at those curves! Note the wagons have individual numbers and the unusual feature of carrying the ladder on the side for the personnel to mount and dismount.

Reproduced by permission of the Reference Library, Birmingham

Wheels and Axles

200 sets of two wheels and one axle are required.

Hadfield's Steel Foundry Co. Sheffield –
£5 13s. 9d. per set = £1,137 10s. 0d. less 2½%.

Patent Shaft & Axletree Co., Wednesbury –
£5 17s. 6d. per set = £1,175   0s. 0d. less 2½%.

Henry Bessemer & Co., Sheffield –   £7 5s. 0d. per set = £1,450 0s. 0d. net

So the scene was set for mass production of these vehicles. Later in 1897 a further 550 sets of wheels and axles were ordered for new wagons and stone bogies to be made on the works site, plus some to be used for repairs to the older vehicles.

Plate 89: The main trench at the start of the construction work on the top dam site of Craig Goch, as seen from the right bank in February 1897. Note the five levels of railway operation with locomotive NANT GWYLTT in view, and the numerous types of wagons being used. Each wagon in this photograph has a serial number on its side, being about 6 in. high in serif lettering and painted in black. *Reproduced by permission of the Reference Library, Birmingham*

By this time, as can be seen from *plate 89*, wagons of the end- and side-tip variety, were in abundance around the sites and, apart from the purchase of materials, no more wagons of this type were bought from an outside supplier.

In June 1898, four more permanent way ballast wagons were purchased at £22 10s. 0d. each (delivered) from The Bute Works Supply Co. Cardiff (again selected from 10 they had for sale). James Mansergh told Mr Yourdi to inspect these vehicles very thoroughly as; "this price seems very low for sound trucks and we do not want to risk accident".

Lastly from the minutes, it seems that 4 small box vans (*see plate 100*), a Mid-Wales brake (*see plate 94*), 2 explosive wagons and 8 more open wagons were purchased during the main building programme of the dams. The records do not record much of railway interest after 1898, so it is not certain what further wagons were acquired, but the Elan Valley certainly had its share of "home-made" side- and end-tip wagons and a good variety of second hand "company" rolling stock!

STEAM CRANES AND HAND CRANES

One of the largest items of railway stock required by the Corporation (other than wagons) appears to have been the cranes. Many different types were obtained and the following record has been compiled from the requisition orders submitted by Mr Mansergh (and approved) and portrays the enormous variety of lifting machinery used during the dam's construction.

As early as March 1894 three locomotive cranes were purchased, namely:

Thos. Smith, one ten ton	£790 0s. 0d.
Thos. Smith, one five ton	£495 0s. 0d.
Ransomes, one five ton	£662 10s. 0d.

these being recommended by Mr Mansergh out of the five companies who quoted. Mr Mansergh's report continued:

> For the second five-ton crane I should like to go to Messrs Ransomes & Rapier, although their price is considerably higher than Mr Smith's. I do this partly because their crane can be sent off within a few days of your giving the order; but mainly because it has an exceptionally long reach jib, which would be of great use for some of the work we have to do.
>
> I know there is some advantage in having on a job only cranes of similar design and similar motions, but, on the starting of such a work as we have in hand, I think it is desirable that we should be in a position to inform ourselves by actual experience of the capabilities of several sorts of lifting tackle.
>
> Mr Smith's 5 ton crane has a jib 18 feet long, and Messrs Ransome's a jib of 40 feet.

The duty of their crane, tested on a 4 ft 8½ in. road, to lift at right angles to the rails, is given as follows:

At 16 ft radius   6 tons
At 18 ft radius   5 tons
At 22 ft radius   4 tons
At 28 ft radius   3 tons
At 40 ft radius   2 tons

The safe working loads, whilst travelling or swinging round, are:

At 16 ft radius   5 tons
At 18 ft radius   4 tons
At 22 ft radius   3 tons
At 28 ft radius   2 tons
At 40 ft radius   1½ tons

A crane of this class is, manifestly, a most useful tool to have upon a job, and I have no doubt Mr Yourdi will be glad to get it.

Soon there was a need for a 10 ton overhead travelling Goliath steam crane for use in the Masons' Yard (*see plate 38*) and eight companies were asked to tender. Five immediately responded, the remaining three took several months to submit quotes, the final list submitted by Mr Mansergh reading as follows:

List of Tenders for 10 ton steam overhead Goliath Crane

Messrs J. & H. Wilson & Sons, Liverpool	£480 0s. 0d.
Messrs Isles, Ltd, Stanningley, nr Leeds	£485 0s. 0d.
Messrs J. Booth & Bros, Rodley, nr Leeds	£495 0s. 0d.
Messrs J. Jessop & Co., Leicester	£530 0s. 0d.
Messrs Appleby, 22 Walbrook, London	£552 10s. 0d.
Mr H.J. Coles, Southwark, London	£555 0s. 0d.
Mr Thos. Smith, Rodley, Leeds	£600 0s. 0d.
Messrs Stothert & Pitt, Bath	£600 0s. 0d.
Messrs Ransomes & Rapier, Ipswich	£685 0s. 0d.

The lowest tender here was accepted and so H. Wilson & Sons from Liverpool supplied the crane.

From then on cranes were being purchased almost monthly and the following are just a few of the types in use:

6 x 4 ton hand powered derrick cranes from Messrs Isles Ltd @ £390 0s. 0d.

1 x 10 ton steam loco crane from Booth Bros in July 1895 @ £825 0s. 0d.

3 x hydraulic overhead travelling cranes to lift the cement from the railway wagons into the cooling bins

1 x 5 ton hand powered, break-down bogie crane from Ransomes and Rapier, Ipswich, April 1895 @ £345 0s. 0d.

One full report on a requisition in April 1895 is included to show why, how and where some of these cranes were used:

Plate 90: One of the enormous steam cranes seen here working the quarry. The BCWW had many and varied steam cranes on the site working, most being of standard gauge and self-propelled, but this one has a portable track of 12 ft gauge.   *Reproduced by permission of the Reference Library, Birmingham*

Plate 91: One of the many standard, self-propelled steam cranes.
Courtesy: Severn-Trent Water

Plate 92: A 5 ton travelling hand crane used on the BCWW (sold to the Cambrian Railways in 1905). This crane was built by Messrs Ransome and Rapier and when sold became No. 14 on the Cambrian stock. It was passed into GWR service and is believed to have been operational well into the 1960s.
Courtesy the late E. Mountford, A.G. Ellis Collection

Eight 5-ton Locomotive Steam Cranes

Authority is asked to purchase eight 5-tons locomotive steam cranes – four with jibs 24 ft long and four with 42 ft jibs – which are now required for carrying on the works.

The probable distribution of the cranes will be as follows:

Careg-ddu Dam, 2 long jibbed cranes

Pen-y-gareg Reservoir – 1 long and two short jibbed cranes

Allt Goch Reservoir – 1 long and 1 short jibbed crane

Caban Reservoir – 1 short jibbed crane

They will, however, during the progress of the Works, be transferred from place to place, and later on more cranes will be required.

Delivery of four of the cranes is wanted without delay, and I therefore recommend that you purchase two 24 ft jib cranes from Smith of Rodley, if he will do them for £560 each. I say £560 because he tenders £565 for one and £555 each for four. I also recommend that you purchase two of the 42 ft jib cranes from Messrs Ransomes & Rapier at £682 each.

I also recommend you purchase from Stothert & Pitts their amended design for two 42 ft jib cranes which can be obtained from them at £600 each and one 24 ft jib at £560; and a third 24 ft jib from Smiths of Rodley at £560. This completes the requisition for the eight cranes.

This order finally totalled £4760 when delivered.

Later in 1895, two further 10 ton steam derrick cranes were purchased from Messrs Isles Limited, Stanningley, Leeds for the sum of £575 0s. 0d. each and two 3 ton quick-speeded locomotive steam cranes (one to work in the Masons Yard and one the Stone Crushing Yard) from Messrs Booth Bros at £395 0s. 0d. each.

During the next few years many further cranes were purchased and were working all over the sites (*see Plates 89, 90 and 91*). Costs had risen considerably as the purchase of six 5 ton locomotive steam cranes from Ransomes & Rapier Ltd cost £922 each in January 1898; some £240 increase since 1895!

The total number of cranes and their incredible variety will never be known but from photographic evidence and the records in the minute books, there were well over sixty-five at the peak of the construction work.

Chapter Seven

Operation of the Railway

In June 1894 the signal box at Elan Valley Railway Junction, on the Cambrian main line, was officially opened, so bringing the main BCWW No. 1 railway line into operation. During the early days an arrangement was made with the Cambrian Railways to move all the BCWW traffic (which was reported to be 2040 tons by mid-1894) by Cambrian Railways' locomotives and stock to the Caban Workshop site. For this arrangement to work it was necessary to give the Cambrian the control of the line during the hours appointed. This, of course, interfered with the Corporation's own freedom to make movements and conduct important engineering operations. After lengthy discussions the two parties finalised a short-lived agreement, "that the Cambrian supply a full and necessary service to Caban Coch from Rhayader Sidings and use of wagons for 24 hours only", for a fee of £700 per annum. The agreement also had conditions that a 4 mph speed limit would be in force and that a tank engine would have to be used as the curves into the existing two sidings were of 3½ chains radius on this part of the railway. A letter from the Cambrian Railways Engineer requested a new "Bogie Tank" of 4–4–0 wheel arrangement especially for this working and continues, "this locomotive would come in handy for the Mid-Wales section of the Cambrian"; needless to say his efforts did not produce the "new" locomotive hoped for.

The reason for this agreement can be found in the 1894 track plan of the junction on page 81. The double line and junction put in resulted in the BCWW branch being on a curve and falling gradient of 1 in 60 (with a part at 1 in 40) and the thought of changing stock and locomotives on these gradients was quite impossible.

NOYADD SIDINGS (see plan on page 84)

Mr Mansergh seemed to accept this situation until December 1894 when he visited the site of the Elan Junction, with Cambrian officials. Following this visit he recommended a further purchase of land at Noyadd (26¼ perches at a cost of £24 12s. 2d.). This land was relatively level and about 400 yds down the line from the junction. Here he suggested that four further "level" exchange sidings could be constructed. The BCWW locomotives could then run the empty return wagons into the neck of the junction using the existing head shunt and then drop them back into the new down sidings, without fouling the main Cambrian running lines.

The Cambrian locomotives could also bring in the new loaded

wagons on the Elan line and reverse these wagons into one of the two up sidings, and then couple up to the empties in the down sidings before leaving. One problem that arose just after the start of operations was that if the Cambrian train came from the Brecon direction it had to reverse in to the Elan Valley Railway and so would be trapped in the siding at A (*on the plan page 84*) until the BCWW locomotive removed the loaded wagons. It was proposed that a crossover be put in at point A so that the Cambrian locomotive could be released. This siding was at least 170 yards long and able to handle 25 wagons.

The Cambrian agreed to these proposals so the BCWW bought the land and built the sidings for about £900; the four Noyadd Exchange sidings were ready for use on 12th August, 1895, a great relief to both parties.

This arrangement meant a resident shunting engine was needed at the junction each day for ½ day's work and *plate 31* shows the ground staff and one of these engines. The question of the costs of the operation generated vast amounts of correspondence and on 16th December, 1895, the Cambrian finally agreed to all the details and a contract was signed, but not until after several interesting letters were exchanged, one of which is included below.

The letter of the 31st August, 1895 from Mr Yourdi to Alfred Aslett, Cambrian Railways, Oswestry clearly states,

> . . . that hand signalling was recommended for these sidings by the Cambrian and he (Yourdi) suggested the working timetable.
>
> The 5.30 pm and 6.00 pm trains from the south and the 9.05 am, 11.25 am and the 8.35 pm trains from the north to be at the Noyadd Sidings at 7 pm the day following arrival. The 7.45 am from the south to be in place at Noyadd Sidings at 8.15 am the same day. This will allow 64 minutes between this time and the arrival of the 9.19 am passenger train.
>
> All the goods trains being disposed of and put into the sidings by 8.15 am; the Corporation engine with its empties will be due there at 8.30, when the line should be clear, the Cambrian engine standing on the Corporation main line and protected by the stop signal. All wagons being in place, the Corporation engine will clear out by 9 am.
>
> But for the 7.45 am train, the traffic could be delivered at the Noyadd Sidings by 7 am. The Corporation engine could be there at 7.45 and get clear away by 8.15, thus making a saving of 45 minutes. You will observe that I have taken the winter timetables as the winter is now coming on.
>
> Whatever signals may be adopted the fact remains that the line is a time-protected one, that is to say we shall have to work to a timetable.
>
> Of course a distant signal will have to be placed on the eminence, where it can be seen by the Corporation engine driver, so that he may be made to

stop at Llan-rhyd-wen, just before Abercaethon bridge, particularly at the foot of the 1 in 40 gradient.

The Cambrian's reply on 9th October agreed that the exchange sidings at Noyadd "be used on and after Monday next" but using the staff signalling system until its use could be discussed with Mr Denniss, General Manager of the Cambrian, in the near future.

The Cambrian General Manager's office wrote to the local manager, Mr Alfred Aslett, the following letter discussing in detail the signalling at the four sidings:

Messrs Dutton, Ellis, Fowler and myself saw Mr Yourdi from BCWWR yesterday at the Noyadd Sidings and Mr Yourdi would not agree to the whole four sidings being connected to the Elan Junction signalbox frame, but it was proposed to slot the Elan Junction starting signal with the shunting neck, which should be kept open to the main line and also a stop signal put on the present distant signal post, slotted with that and the first-named starting signal.

The other three sidings to be worked by hand points and have throw-off scotches, these would then only necessitate a ground frame of three levers, also this signal to be locked with Annett's Key in both directions and the key to form a staff so that when the signal was lowered and the staff/token taken out, it could not be put up again, nor the other signal lowered until the token/staff was replaced. The staff would be taken by the man in charge of the sidings to the Cambrian driver at Elan Junction (a distance of 260 yds) and the driver must not go past the starting signal, whether up or down, without it.

It would have been a good thing if the scotches of the three sidings could have been worked on and off from the signal box, there would then be no danger of them being forgotten. Mr Dutton will be sending a detailed description of the scheme and costs.

Dutton and Co. sent the following letter:

The Cambrian then issued a set of instructions dated 30th October, 1895 for the working, as follows:

CAMBRIAN RAILWAYS

INSTRUCTIONS TO BE OBSERVED IN WORKING TRAFFIC BETWEEN ELAN JUNCTION (SITUATED ON CAMBRIAN LINE) AND NOYADD SIDINGS (SITUATED ON BIRMINGHAM CORPORATION LINE)

---

1. The Line between Elan Junction Starting Signal and Noyadd Sidings must be worked by train Staff. The Staff to be painted red and lettered "Noyadd Sidings".
2. Only one engine, or two engines coupled together, to be at Noyadd Sidings at the same time.

Description of the Signals and Interlocking for B.C.W.W. Elan Valley Sidings.

Train from Water Works —

Nº 5 works Down Signal and puts square lock on 1 normal. This lock remains on until key **D** has been taken out, put back and turned.

The driver must not shunt without the key, which will be lettered as follows

SHUNTING KEY
TO BE LEFT AT
ELAN SIDS

D →

DUTTON & CO. LIMITED
DRAWING OFFICE
15 OCT 95
RAILWAY SIGNAL WORKS, WORCESTER

Elan Valley Sidings

Scheme discussed on the ground

Two Staff Keys —

One to be used between the Junction and sidings to lock the Safety points so that they shall stand for the neck when a train comes down from the Junction with the staff.

Objections

This Key must be kept in Junction Cabin, and would have to be obtained by some means before the points could be set for an up train. Distance there and back 800 yards.

The other key to be used between the Sidings and the Water Works. This key to be kept in the Locking apparatus at the sidings, and to be released by setting the safety points for the straight line.

Objections

The Signalman would have to send to the Junction for one key to unlock the points that release the second key. That key must then be conveyed to the Up Train where it may be waiting.

A copy of the actual document supplied by Dutton's.

3. No engine or train must pass the starting signal at Elan Junction until it has been lowered, and the Driver has received the Noyadd Sidings Staff from the Corporation signalman, who, after putting the points at the Siding right and releasing the starting signal at Elan Junction, will proceed to the Junction with the Staff, and hand it to the Driver who must keep it in his possession until he returns from the sidings to Elan Junction.

4. No Corporation engine or train must foul the Noyadd Sidings until the Driver is instructed by the man in charge, and then not until he has received the Noyadd Sidings Train Staff.

5. The Cambrian Guard, so far as the Cambrian Train is concerned, must do all the shunting work, and the man in charge of the Sidings will hold over and attend to all the points.

6. The Corporation wil be responsible for their Signalman carrying out the above instructions. The Corporation will also be responsible for the safe working of traffic to and from the Sidings, as well as the locking of all stop blocks and points.

   The Train Staff must be in the possession of the Corporation Signalman when not in use.

7. The Cambrian Trains to work between Rhayader and Noyadd Sidings as under.

Down Trains					Up Trains				
	1	3	5	7		2	4	6	8
	am	am	am	am		am	am	am	am
Rhayader dep.	7.20	8.05	8.40	–	Noyadd Sid. dep.	7.40	8.23	9.00	9.30
Elan Junction dep.	7.25	8.10	8.45	9.22	Elan Junction dep.	7.48	8.26	9.03	9.33
Noyadd Sidings arr.	7.28	8.13	8.48	9.25	Rhayader arr.	7.53	8.31	–	9.38

The running times of the Corporation engine between Caban and Noyadd Sidings will be as under:

Caban	dep.	7.30 am	8.50 am	Noyadd Sid.	dep.	8.10 am	9.20 am
Noyadd Sid.	arr.	7.50 am	9.10 am	Caban	arr.	8.25 am	9.40 am

The Cambrian engine, after putting the traffic off No. 5 train into the Sidings at Noyadd, will run back to Elan Junction and wait there until the Corporation engine has put off and picked up its traffic and left for Caban. The Cambrian engine will then return to Noyadd Siding to pick up the traffic put off by the Corporation engine.

8. In the event of the traffic being too heavy for the Cambrian Company to deliver to the Sidings by the three trains arranged, notice will be given by Inspector Fowler to the Station Master at Rhayader, the Signalman at Elan Junction and Mr Yourdi, and arrangements made for working the traffic forward.

MAIN LINE OPERATION

The main line appears during its working life to have been operated by a token system from line side huts at different points on the railway, as seen in *plate 93* and on the "one engine in steam" principle. It did not appear to run to any particular timetable except for

Plate 93: Cwm Elan turnout with a ballast train headed by the locomotive ELAN, running past the set of six ex-GWR coaches. White roofs and well painted bodies are evident on this rake of coaches. Note the points and the signalman in the hut on the left.

Reproduced by permission of the Reference Library, Birmingham

the "mail train" discussed in a later section of this chapter.

Several accidents were reported mainly in the local newspaper and one, on the 10th May, 1894, was considered "of a serious nature". Apparently a short train of 26 waggons (note the spelling) fully loaded with ballast and timber "and of extreme weight", was being conveyed to the Caban Coch site from Stables Junction. These being pushed, the couplings broke and several wagons careered wildly down the gradient towards the main "shops" and construction site. Just a quarter of a mile from the buildings they hit a "dobbin" wagon which was mounted and then overturned the runaway wagons. Four wagons were destroyed.

Working of Birmingham Corporation Traffic to and from Noyadd Siding on the Corporation Railway.

The above Traffic will be worked as under:—

DOWN.	a.m.	UP.	a.m.
Rhayader ....dep	6 40	Noyadd ....dep	7 0
Noyadd ....arr	6 50	Rhayader...........arr	7 10

Rhayader must arrange for traffic to be taken to Noyadd Siding in accordance with the following instructions:—

Traffic may be placed in the Noyadd Sidings by the Cambrian Company's Engine at any time between 8 0 a.m. and 12 0 noon and 2 0 p.m. and 4 0 p.m., but no Cambrian Company's Engine or train will be allowed in the Sidings between 7 0 and 8 0 a.m. or between 12 0 noon and 2 0 p.m. without an advice being previously sent to the Corporation Signalman at Caban by the Signalman at Elan Junction.

No Corporation Engine will run to Noyadd Sidings between 8 0 a.m. and 12 0 noon, nor between 2 0 and 4 0 p.m. without previous advice by Telephone being sent by the Corporation Signalman at Caban to the Signalman at Elan Junction.

The Guard in charge of either Cambrian Company's or Corporation trains will be responsible for the proper locking of the stop blocks and points after having been in the Sidings.

The load from Rhayader to Noyadd must not consist of more than six Mineral Wagons and Van, or eight Mixed and Van; and from Noyadd to Rhayader of twelve empties.

The Sidings will be worked by fixed and hand Signals only.

Only one Engine and train or two Engines and train coupled, must be allowed to work at the Sidings at the same time. The Corporation Signalman will be held responsible for seeing that this instruction is strictly carried out.

Notice of Accidents.

The person in charge of the Station nearest to which an accident occurs must immediately telegraph the fullest particulars available to the Engineer, Locomotive Superintendent, and Traffic Superintendent; and, as soon as these telegrams have been sent off, he must send a similar one to the District Inspector, who must also telegraph to the Traffic Superintendent, informing him what steps he is taking to clear the Line; he should also promptly send a full report.

All accidents, whether to Goods or Passenger trains, or during shunting operations, must be reported as above; also any personal injury, whether to Company's Servants or the Public.

This instruction does not set aside the requirements of Rule No. 115 in the Company's Book of Rules and Regulations, which must in all cases be observed.

In all cases of *serious* Accident, particulars must also be promptly telegraphed to me.

C. S. DENNISS,

Oswestry, *Sept. 30th, 1903.*   Secretary and General Manager.

The 1903 Working Timetable published by The Cambrian Railway for the operation of the Noyadd sidings.

RHAYADER.	Up and Down Main Line	1
	From Moat Lane end of Yard to and from Goods Shed	2 & 1 Crow
	From Moat Lane end of Yard to Up Line	3
	From Brecon end of Yard to Goods Shed	2
	From Brecon end of Yard to Up Line...	2 & 2 Crows
	For Carriage Dock	1 & 1 Crew
	For Cross-over Road	4 Short
RHAYADER JUNCTION.	Up and Down Main Line	1
	To and from Branch Line	3
	For Branch Cross-over	6 Short
	To and from Neck	2
	For Main Line Cross-over	4
DOLDOWLOD.	Up and Down Main Line	1
	For Cross-over Road	3
	From Down Line to or from Neck	4
	., ,, Back Siding	5
	From Neck to and from Back Siding	} 1 Whistle 2 Crows

Cambrian Whistle Codes

Rhayader Junction—Birmingham Water Works Line.

The speed of all down trains must on approaching the Junction of above line be reduced to 10 miles per hour.

All Down trains for the above Branch Line must be brought to a stand at the Down Home Signal before the latter is lowered or points put over, and before proceeding with Goods trains all wagon brakes must be pinned down.

Many similar incidents must have taken place within the railway's life, due to the arduous nature of the loads and conditions it was worked under, but the records do not contain any except the following. This was submitted because of an insurance claim put into the BCWW by the LNWR. Note it is very similar to the incident just described.

Resident Engineer's Office,
Elan Valley,
Rhayader.
3rd February, 1896.

Dear Sir,

Runaway on Railway No. 2

On the 20th ult., a runaway of a serious character took place on Railway No. 2, as you have already been informed. There was no loss of life, fortunately, though it resulted in considerable damage to the Corporation's rolling stock, as well as to three trucks belonging to the LNWR Co., and to one especially, which was broken up completely, the ironwork being all that is left of any value.

The route engine *Calettwr* on its return journey from Pen-y-gareg, at or about 1.40 pm with 10 empty end-tip wagons coupled on behind, and an empty LNW wagon in front, found the Railway blocked opposite Tybach, by a set of 12 side-tip wagons – 10 full and 2 empty – which the men on the Road Diversion working at the same place had just finished filling. The empties belonged to the Quarry gang, and were waiting to be returned. The full set belonged to the *Claerwen* but as this engine was detained at the Caban, the *Calettwr* had the earth wagons coupled on in front of the LNW truck and started to move forward. On approaching the Gigfran, the roperunner put in three sprags to assist the engine in descending the 1 in 33 gradient. The set, however, had not proceeded far, when the coupling of the LNW truck snapped, the sprags following suit, soon after, and away went the set down the gradient. At the Stables Junction three LNW trucks were being emptied of rails and into these the runaway set dashed, with the following result:

LNW truck No. 218 completely destroyed
LNW truck No. 60,068 slightly damaged
LNW truck No. 60,069 slightly damaged
BCWW Side Tip wagons –
   2 completely wrecked excepting the ironwork.
   2 frames badly broken; bodies uninjured.
   1 frame damaged.
   1 bumper broken as well as one side.
   1 ironwork in body damaged only.
   4 uninjured.
   1 rocker broken.

The lad at the level crossings acted with the greatest presence of mind, as he promptly closed the gates against vehicular traffic and warned the men unloading at the stables.

The accident was brought about through the rope-runner attempting to let down the full wagons with the engine behind, a practice which they are very fond of doing when behind time and no-one is about. In this particular case the *Calettwr* should have slipped its set into the Gifran Sidings, if clear, or waited for the *Claerwen* on the level at Abernant turnout to come and take its set away.

The estimated damage is put down at £120. It is, however, difficult to say exactly, as no bill has as yet come in from the LNWR Co.

Both the Driver and the Roperunner of the *Calettwr* have the reputation of being the most careful in the Valley. They are both, nevertheless, very much to blame in attempting the feat, in spite of the fact that their orders were to get to the Caban Yard as quickly as possible, but not with the full set in front.

Yours very truly,
(signed) G.N. Yourdi

The Water Committee wished to fine the driver heavily if not dismiss him, but Mr Yourdi claimed that this driver was one of the best and in any case there was no laid down procedure for dealing with accidents and therefore he could not fine him! In the end the incident seems to have been dealt with by a "stern" letter.

By 1905 the BCWW were contemplating withdrawing and selling their locomotives and approached the Cambrian to see if they would operate the entire line.

Mr Denniss reported on the results of a meeting with the BCWW on 16th August, 1905:

> Mr Denniss stated that the Company would be willing to provide an engine for shunting purposes, etc, at a charge of 7s. 6d. per hour with a minimum of £1 per trip.
>
> Mr Denniss would advise Mr Lees what fixed time would be charged for the running of the engine on the Cambrian to and from its stable.
>
> The question of providing a shunter or guard for dealing with the traffic was considered and Mr Denniss stated that if this service was required some addition would have to be made to the above charge and he promised to advise Mr Lees what this would be.
>
> Mr Lees enquired whether the Company would be willing to undertake the maintenance of the permanent way, and Mr Denniss promised that this should be considered and that he would inform Mr Lees what the charge would be if the Company could undertake the work.
>
> The question of the abolition of the signal box was also discussed and Mr Denniss stated that before this could be done the sanction of the Board of Trade would have to be obtained, and he promised to have a scheme prepared and submitted to the Board of Trade and to advise Mr Lees of any arrangement to be proposed.

An internal report was made (in October 1905) by the Cambrian's Engineer on the state of the Elan Valley Railway, in case they should take over the operation of the line.

> It appears that the traffic to be expected is extremely light, probably not requiring more than one journey per month, and it would therefore be quite unnecessary to retain the present Elan Valley Railway Junction signal box and connection with the Cambrian Railways. I enclose a plan showing the present arrangements at the Junction, and what portions I should recommend be retained. An ordinary siding tablet frame would be substituted for the signal box. I estimate the cost of making the alteration would be £120, and the credit to be allowed for the materials recovered £350.
>
> There is, in my opinion, no reason why the Cambrian Railways should not work the railway, but do not know if the ordinary engines could be used, as the curves are very sharp, and there are gradients of 1 in 33. The road, however, is amply strong enough to carry any of the engines now working on the Mid Wales.
>
> With regard to the question of maintenance: The road at present is in a very good condition. The rails are 68 lb. flat-bottomed, fastened to the sleepers with clips and fang-bolts. The sleepers appear to be quite sound, but have been laid for 12 years (the line was made in 1893). The ballast is

Plate 94: A fine study of the 0–4–0ST COEL, which was supposedly manufactured "with all speed" from standard parts from stores, to Yourdi's specification. Note the screw jack on the front of the engine and extra coal on the tank side. The Resident Engineer, Mr G.N. Yourdi, stands in his striped suit (*on the right*) obviously enjoying conversation with his employees.

Reproduced by permission of the Reference Library, Birmingham

Plate 95: The locomotive NANT GWYLTT, with the 4 wheeled BCWW brake van in tow in 1904. The large lettering on the brake van is in two colours with shading. *LGRP Collection, Courtesy David & Charles*

excellent of broken stone throughout. The fencing is indifferent. There are three bridges, two of which are timber cattle creeps, and the other one a brick arch over a public road; all in good condition. The total length of the line it is suggested that we should maintain is 5¼ miles.

Basing my figures on the cost of maintaining one mile of the Cambrian Railways, and allowing for the difference in the weight of the materials, I estimate the cost of maintaining the Water Works line in first class condition, would be about £100 per mile per year, or £525 per year for the whole line. This allows for renewing the rails every 25 years and the sleepers every 15 years.

I am not disposed to recommend the Cambrian Company to undertake this maintainance, as I think the trouble involved in doing so would in no way be compensated for by any small profit which might be made, and do not see that any advantage would accrue to the Company.

I am strongly of opinion that the Birmingham Corporation could maintain it much cheaper with their own men. There is bound to be a considerable staff kept at the reservoirs which might include a few platelayers with very little extra expense.

(Signed) G.C. McDonald
Engineer

After the sale of the BCWW locomotives in 1906 it appears that the line was operated unofficially by the Cambrian for a time, but in July 1907 the Cambrian's Engineer's office decided to inspect the line and made the following report:

Dear Sir,

BIRMINGHAM WATERWORKS SIDING AT ELAN JUNCTION

We made an inspection of this Siding on Friday last, and found the road is in excellent condition, but with several curves of six chains radius.

We took a four wheeled coupled tank engine of the old "Seaham" class over it, which has a wheel base of 12 ft 3 in. and no difficulty was experienced. It is proposed that the Cambrian Company should work the line up to the first dam, Caban Coch, and the yard and sidings at that place.

The Birmingham Corporation Engineers were present, and appeared quite satisfied with the engine; in fact, some years ago, this class of engine worked over the road frequently. We do not, therefore, think that the clause as to a 10 ft 6 in. wheel base, proposed by the Birmingham Corporation, is necessary, but it would not be advisable to work the line with an engine having a much greater wheel base than the 12 ft 3 in. which we tried.

If the small type of engine they propose had to be employed, it would necessitate keeping an engine specially for this particular work, and probably the purchase of an additional engine, as the whole of these small engines are already fully employed on our own branch lines, and they would not, of course, be available for banking or other purposes.

The traffic over the Elan Valley line, after the material for sale has been cleared off, will not amount, so far as we can learn, to more than about two wagons per week.

The engine will have to run light either from Llanidloes or Builth, unless loading can be found for it, the distance being 14 miles in each direction in the former case, and 13 miles in the latter.

A tank engine of the "Seaham" class is at present kept at Builth, which does the shunting at the latter place, and the Corporation work at Rhayader, but if it were not for the work on the Elan Valley line, another class of engine which could be utilised for other purposes as well might be substituted. It is necessary, therefore, to keep a tank engine on section solely on account of the Elan Valley traffic, and this point should be taken into account when the question as to what the Birmingham Corporation should be charged for its use is considered.

Yours faithfully,

(Signed) Herbert E. Jones
Locomotive Superintendent
(Signed) G.C. McDonald
Engineer

Although the Elan Valley Junction signal box and track layout was considered redundant in 1905, it was not until January 1908 that the Cambrian wrote the following letter to the Board of Trade:

I beg to notify the Department that it is intended to dismantle the Elan Valley double Junction near Rhayader, and convert it into a siding connection off the main line which will be worked and locked by a double frame as shewn on the accompanying plan.

The present Signal Cabin, Signals, etc. will be removed and one tablet section between Doldowlod and Rhayader will be substituted for the two existing tablet sections, viz. from Doldowlod to Elan Junction and Elan Junction to Rhayader.

I have to request that you will be kind enough to accept this as the statutory notice required by the Regulation of Railways Act, 1871, and shall be glad to receive the authority of the Department to bring into operation the new arrangement on the usual conditions.

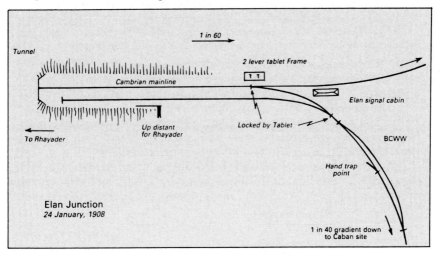

Elan Junction
24 January, 1908

This was agreed and the resultant changes carried out and inspected on 27th June, 1908, approval being given.

During March 1908, the Water Committee challenged an invoice received from the Cambrian regarding charges for engines crews and an internal Cambrian memo mentions the rates of pay for the crews at this date, interesting in itself:

Dear Sir,

Elan Valley Railway, Working Agreement

In reply to your letter of the 6th inst. There is one driver and one fireman in charge of the Engine that works up the Elan Valley line, but the rate of wages paid to such men vary. The maximum rate for a driver is 7s. 0d. per day, and the minimum 5s. 0d. and for firemen 4s. 0d. maximum and 3s. 0d. minimum, and although as a rule the men placed in charge of the Engine working this branch are those paid at one of the lower rates, still we may, as a matter of convenience, employ at times men who are in receipt of the maximum rates.

Yours truly,
C. Denniss

The end for the railway came in 1916 when the Cambrian carried out a survey (in August) and found that the line was "out of repair". They asked to meet the Corporation to discuss work necessary to keep the line fit for traffic. The Water Committee represented by Mr Lees said that it was probable that further reservoirs would be constructed in twelve years time,

. . . and that if the line would cost a considerable amount to repair, the Corporation would have to consider whether it would not be best to pick up the rails at once, and sell them at the present high prices; and then when the new reservoirs have to be made, purchase materials and reconstruct the railway.

If this were done, it would probably be proposed that the Company should take traffic to and from the Noyadd Sidings as was done when the Water Works were being constructed, and the traffic would be conveyed by road motor-lorry between the Water Works and the sidings.

The Corporation Committee report continued to the effect that the rails were in excellent condition and were well maintained in "line" and "level". They showed little wear and had many years of useful life. The sleepers were less satisfactory and many in a state of decay, but ballast was in excellent condition. A suggestion was made that if 500 sleepers were replaced now and 1000 per year over a five year period it would bring the line into "tip-top" condition.

But if the Committee decided to sell the rail as scrap materials then the price was excellent at this time, being £9 10s. for rails (50 per cent more than the normal price of rail). The monies invested should with interest, cover the estimated cost of relaying the track in 15 years time, and (the report went on) leave enough to purchase a lorry.

An Estimate is given for your guidance (assuming that the rails have worn only 3 lb. a yard).

Credit from Old Materials			*Cost of relaying with New Materials*	
306 tons of rails @ £9 10s.		£2,907	320 tons rails @ £6 10s.	£2,080
3,000 serviceable sleepers @ 1s.		150	(1½ tons fish bolts) (13½ tons fang bolts) @ £15	225
20 tons scrap @ £7 10s.		150	10 tons fishplates @ £8 10s.	85
		£3,207	5,700 sleepers @ 5s. 6d.	1,567
			Running out and laying 5,280 yards @ 1s. 6d.	396
				£4,353
Deduct Labour dismantling 5280 L. yards @ 6d. =	132			
Cost of motor lorry say =	800	932		
		£2,275	Balance	150
£2,275 @ 4½% compound interest for 15 years would produce		£4,403		£4,403

The above prices are based on those recently realised for similar materials

The above prices are based on 1913 figures

So the decision to close the railway was taken, leaving just the simple siding from the Elan junction to Noyadd Sidings in place and the Cambrian were informed of this on 14th October, 1916. It appears that apart from two coal wagons, the only other form of traffic was chalk for the filter beds. The Cambrian now looked at the new method of working required in delivering all remaining traffic to Noyadd Sidings from which the Corporation would then transport by road to the various sites.

October 27th 1916

Visited Noyadd Siding today in company with the Permanent Way Inspector.

1. The distance from Rhayader Station to the Siding is about ¾ mile. The gradient on the Cambrian main line on the Doldowlod side of the Elan Junction is about 1 in 60, and so it is inadvisable to allow a goods train to remain there whilst the siding is being shunted. And a train left on the main line travelling from Rhayader southwards would be partly in Rhayader Tunnel whilst the siding was being shunted, and that is also an objection.

2. It appears that the only safe way is to propel wagons direct from Rhayader Station into the siding.

3. There is a sharp curve in the siding, but the Inspector was of opinion that the siding could be worked over by a bogie engine, but not by a 6 wheeled coupled engine.

4. Hitherto the traffic has been taken up to Caban near the Reservoir once a month, and the average tonnage for that period is about 50 tons, representing about 6 or 7 covered vans. This is chalk, and comes from Dunstable via Welshpool.

5. Coal comes from the South, but this only averages about 5 tons per month, and is therefore unimportant.

6. Wagons can only be propelled into the siding. The siding appears to have been originally laid so that wagons could be hauled in as well as propelled, but the position is now that only wagons propelled can be dealt with.

7. The high road from Rhayader Station to Noyadd Sidings has a very steep incline and a curve, and I should imagine that it would be dangerous and difficult to haul the chalk by tractive power over this part of the road. I mention this in order to show their difficulty, and which we should bear in mind when negotiating terms for the rail charges.

8. The Inspector pointed out that the company's siding at the entrance to the Elan Railway had not been used for 9 years. I mention this in view of the Railway Executive Committee's enquiry with regard to taking up disused sidings.

9. The Rhayader Agent informed me that the remaining rails were being sent from the Elan Line to John Ward, Limited, Government Contractor, Sheffield, so that the material is probably being used for Government work.

By January 1917 the Cambrian were still trying to establish a goods contract with the Water Committee and the "No. 31 goods" was the allocated train carrying out the run from Rhayader to Noyadd sidings, and back taking over 40 minutes within the single line section. They even carried out an engine test using the largest type of goods engine on the Mid-Wales section, on 15th January, 1917:

I tested a six coupled good engine down this line as far as the Noyadd

Siding on Monday last. It went round the curves without any difficulty, and I think there will be no trouble with the little traffic there is, in working it with the ordinary train engines.

The engine I tested was the largest type of goods engine in use on the Mid Wales.

But the service was in its death throes. Only six journeys of 25 minutes each were made between 23rd February, 1917 and 14th May, 1917 as most of the traffic now was on the road. The siding became inoperative and was lifted sometime later, but no definite date can be found.

CEMENT TRAFFIC

The undertaking needed enormous amounts of cement to construct the dams and very early in the negotiations it became apparent that Mr Aslett, the General Manager of the Cambrian Railways attached great importance to the conveyance of the cement by sea to Aberdovey (a port on Cardigan Bay belonging to the Cambrian Railways Company) and thence to the Birmingham works, by rail. The Committee obtained quotations for the conveyance of cement from various sources, and by various routes. They, moreover, requested the Engineer to report from what district he considered it most desirable the cement should be obtained. Mr Mansergh stated that, in his opinion, the cement used should undoubtedly be one of the makes produced at Works on the Thames, or Medway, and such being the case, the cheapest mode of conveyance to the works was by sea to Aberdovey, and thence by the Cambrian Railways.

Competitive quotations were obtained for the sea portion of the route, the lowest of which was 5s. per ton. The ordinary rate from Aberdovey to Rhayader by rail was 13s. 4d., but successive reductions were made in the Cambrian Railway Company's quotation, and the Committee, in a general settlement of the points between the Corporation and the Cambrian Company secured a rate of 6s. 3d. per ton. This included all port dues at Aberdovey, transfer of the goods from the ship to the railway wagons, and free return of all empties to Aberdovey but by a preferred route and all consignments to carry an appropriate label (*see page 227*). The Committee then informed the Cambrian Railways Company that it was the intention of the Corporation that the bulk of the cement would go to Aberdovey, on the understanding that proper facilities for the traffic were provided by the Cambrian Railways Company, but that the Corporation were unable to enter into any absolute undertaking.

PASSENGER AND MAIL TRAINS

In the early days of the dam projects, the local workforce pressed for passenger or workmen's trains on the company's line and a report in the local newspaper as early as the 16th September, 1893, read:

WORKMEN'S TRAINS TO RHAYADER

On Tuesday last a numerous deputation attended at the railway station, Llanidloes, to meet Mr Aslett, manager of the Cambrian Company, for the purpose of presenting a petition to the Company, with reference to the establishment of workmen's trains between Llanidloes and Rhayader. Mr Aslett, who was unable to attend, sent Mr F. Morgan in his stead, who received the deputation in the waiting room. The deputation consisted of Messrs K. Davies (Mayor), J.D. Davies (town clerk), Samuel Ikin, J.H. Mills, Evan Evans, Evan Williams, C.E. Pryce, G.M. Benbow, J. Sibbald, Daniel Higgs, Edward Hamer, Edmund Hamer, Richard Bunford, Richard Evans &c.. The petition was read by Mr J.D. Davies, who had kindly drawn it up at very short notice, and was as follows:

"TO THE DIRECTORS AND SECRETARY AND MANAGER OF
THE CAMBRIAN RAILWAYS COMPANY

The Petition of the undersigned representative Tradesmen and others connected with the Borough Town of Llanidloes, in the County of Montgomery, sheweth (1) that your Petitioners respectfully ask you to arrange to run workmen's trains to and fro between Llanidloes and Rhayader during the construction of the work at the latter place for supplying the City of Birmingham with water. (2) That Llanidloes, owing to the proximity to Rhayader, and also to the fact that there are a large number of vacant dwelling houses and cottages in the town eligible and convenient for the accommodation of workmen, and that a large number of experienced workmen and excavators now in South Wales and elsewhere have their families resident in Llanidloes, is undoubtedly a most convenient residence for workmen adapted for the work to be performed at the waterworks, and that it would be a great convenience both to the workmen and their employers that convenient workmen's trains should be run to and fro between Llanidloes and Rhayader. (3) That the accommodation in Llanidloes for working men with families and also for lodgers is practically unlimited. (4) That very little, if any, alteration as regards the timing of the trains in the morning from Llanidloes and in the evening from Rhayader would be necessary. Your Petitioners therefore humbly pray that you will be pleased to grant their petition."

The petition was signed by the Mayor and upwards of 300 of the principal inhabitants of the town – Mr Morgan said that he had simply been sent to make a few inquiries, and did not expect to meet any deputation at all, but he should have great pleasure in presenting the petition to Mr Aslett, and to give him any further information that the deputation could give him. After the matter had been well discussed in its various aspects, the deputation withdrew upon the understanding that the matter would be brought under the immediate notice of the manager, who would no doubt communicate further with the promoters of the petition.

The response was immediate and the following statement appeared one week later:

CAMBRIAN RAILWAYS
WORKMEN'S TRAINS GRANTED BETWEEN
LLANIDLOES AND RHAYADER

We are pleased to be able to announce that the petition got up at Llanidloes in favour of the above object has been successful, and that the Company has agreed to run workmen's trains daily between Llanidloes and Rhayader during the progress of the new waterworks at the latter place, at 3s. per week, or 6d. per day; weekend tickets (Saturday to Monday) will also be issued; both of which will be a great boon to those employed at the work whose homes are at Llanidloes. The petition Committee (with Mr J.D. Davies, town clerk) are entitled to a word of congratulation on the success attending their efforts to secure cheap workmen's trains.

This, of course, only brought the workmen to Rhayader and they still had to journey from this station to their place of work, so naturally the question of workmen's trains on the Corporation line was soon raised. The first request was made by Mr Yourdi in May 1894 but no reply was made until February 1895, when the Corporation pointed out that the Board of Trade had not passed the line for passenger traffic, and that their Act prevented the taking of tolls for passenger or goods carried.

So for the time being, the workmen walked to the Caban workshop site from Rhayader, but by September 1896, the Mayor Llanidloes had taken up their cause and submitted the following letter:

Llanidloes, September 14/96.

Dear Sir,

I have been asked by the workmen resident in our town and neighbourhood, who work at the Elan Valley Waterworks, to write you asking you to be kind enough to run a train from Rhayader to the Works on Monday mornings. They say that they lose half a day by having to walk to their work, which is about seven miles from Rhayader Station. If you can see your way to do this they will consider it a great kindness. They tell me that the train takes the workmen from the Corporation Village, and want you to send the same train down to meet the train they arrive on Monday morning about 6 am (*see timetable*).

They have asked me to write I suppose owing to the position I hold of Mayor of the town.

Trusting to receive a favourable reply,
    I remain,
                Yours faithfully,
                (signed) Alfred J Morris

By November 1896 the Water Committee had asked the Engineer, Mr Yourdi, to make a full report on the matter and this is recorded in

Moat Lane, Builth Wells, Brecon, etc.

Miles.	DOWN.	WEEK DAYS. a m (Mondays only.)	H a m	a m (Fridays only.)	a m	a m	noon (Runs during June only.)	p m	p m	p m	p m	p m (Mondays only.)	H p m	p m	p m	p m	p m	p m	p m	p m	SU a m
—	**Moat Lane Junction** ... dep	...	5 5	...	...	10 15		...	1235	...	...		3 10	...	...	4 40	...	8 25	9 20	...	7 50
2	Llandinam ... ... "	...	*	...	...	10 20		...	1240	...	...		*	...	...	4 47	...	8 30	*	...	7 55
4¾	Dolwen	...	*	...	...	10 27		...	1247	...	...		*	...	...	4 53	...	8 38	*	...	8 1
7½	**LLANIDLOES** arr	...	**5 25**	...	...	**10 35**		...	**1255**	...	...		**3 30**	...	...	**5 0**	...	**8 45**	**9 40**	...	**8 7**
	dep	*5 15*	**5 27**	...	...	**10 38**		...	...	...	...		**3 35**	...	...	**5 5**	...			...	**8 10**
10¾	Tylwch ... ... "	...	5 35	...	...	10 46		...	...	...	...		3 41	...	...	5 15	...	...	...	...	8 18
14¾	Pantydwr ... ... "	...	5 45	...	...	10 56		...	...	...	...		3 49	...	...	5 25	...	...	...	...	8 27
16	St. Harmons ... ... "	...	*	...	...	11 1		...	...	...	...		*	...	...	*	...	...	...	...	*
21½	Rhayader ... ... "	*5 45*	6 2		...	11 15		...	...	...	...		4 4	...	...	5 45	...	...	...	...	8 43
24¾	Doldowlod ... ... "		6 9		...	11 22		...	...	...	...		4 11	...	...	5 53	...	...	...	...	8 51
28¾	Newbridge-on-Wye ... ... "		6 18		...	11 33		...	...	...	...		4 19	...	...	6 3	...	...	...	...	9 0
32¾	**Builth Road** ... ... arr		6 27		...	11 42		...	...	...	...		4 26	...	...	6 13	...	...	...	...	9 7
	dep		6 29		9 35	11 45		1225	...	1 5	...	*4 15*	4 30	...	...	6 15	...	...	...	...	9 8
34¼	**BUILTH WELLS** arr		**6 33**		**9 39**	**11 50**		**1230**	...	**1 10**	...	*4 20*	**4 34**	...	...	**6 20**	...	...	...	...	**9 12**
	dep		**6 35**		**9 40**		*12 0*	...	...	**1 12**	...		**4 38**	...	...	**6 30**	...	...	...	...	**9 16**
38¼	Aberedw ... ... "		*		*	...	...	...	...	1 21	...	...	*	...	...	*	...	...	...	...	*
41	Erwood ... ... "		6 50		9 55	...	...	...	...	1 27	...	...	4 51	...	...	6 45	...	...	...	...	9 32
45¼	Boughrood ... ... "		7 2		10 5	...	...	...	...	1 37	...	...	4 59	...	...	6 57	...	...	...	...	9 43
48	**Three Cocks Junct** arr		7 7		10 12	...	*1230*	...	...	1 43	...	...	5 5	...	...	7 5	...	...	...	...	9 51
	dep		7 9	*1015*	10 29	...	*1232*	...	...	1 52	...	...	5 7	...	...	7 7	...	...	...	...	9 53
50½	Talgarth ... ... "		7 14	*1020*	10 35	...	*1237*	...	...	1 58	...	...	5 12	...	...	7 12	...	...	...	...	9 58
53	Trefeinon ... ... "		*		Frids	...	...	...	...	*	...	...	...	...	...	*	...	...	...	...	*
56	**Talyllyn Junction** .. arr		7 27	...	10 46	...	*1250*	...	...	2 10	...	...	5 23	...	...	7 25	...	...	...	...	1011
	dep		7 35	...	10 58	...	*1255*	...	...	2 15	...	...	5 28	...	...	7 30	...	...	...	...	1013
60	**BRECON** ... ... arr		**7 45**	...	**11 8**	...	*1 5*	...	...	**2 25**	...	...	**5 38**	...	...	**7 40**	...	...	...	...	**1023**

Moat Lane, Builth Wells, Brecon, etc.

Miles.	UP.	WEEK DAYS. a m	a m	a m	a m	a m	a m	a m	a m	a m	p m	p m (Saturdays only.)	p m	p m	p m	p m (Mondays only)	p m	p m (Runs during June only.)	p m	H p m	SUN p m
	BRECON ... ... dep.	...	**7 25**	...	...	...	...	...	**1040**	...	...		...	**1 20**	...	...	...	*4 15*	...	**5 35**	**5 30**
4	**Talyllyn Jc.** ... ... arr.	...	7 35	...	...	...	...	...	1050	...	...		...	1 30	...	...	...	*4 25*	...	5 45	5 40
	dep.	...	7 40	...	...	...	...	...	11 0	...	...		...	1 33	...	...	...	*4 35*	...	5 46	5 41
7	Trefeinon ... ... "	...	*	...	...	...	...	...	*	...	...		...	*	...	...	...	*	...	*	*
9¼	Talgarth ... ... "	...	7 54	...	...	...	...	...	1113	...	...		...	1 46	...	...	...	*4 48*	...	5 57	5 54
11¾	**Three Cocks Junction** ... ... arr.	...	7 59	...	...	...	...	...	1118	...	...		...	1 51	...	...	...	*4 53*	...	6 2	5 59
	dep.	...	8 0	...	...	...	...	...	1120	...	...		...	1 55	...	...	...	*5 5*	...	6 3	6 0
14½	Boughrood ... ... "	...	8 8	...	...	...	...	...	1128	...	...		...	2 1	...	...	...	*5 12*	...	6 9	6 6
18¾	Erwood ... ... "	...	8 17	...	...	...	...	...	1135	...	...		...	2 9	...	...	...	*5 22*	...	6 17	6 15
21½	Aberedw ... ... "	...	*	...	...	...	...	...	*	...	...		...	*	...	...	...	*	...	*	*
25½	**BUILTH WELLS** arr.	...	**8 32**	...	...	...	...	...	**1150**	...	...		...	**2 22**	...	...	...	*5 35*	...	**6 30**	**6 30**
	dep	...	**8 36**	...	**8 45**	...	...	...	**1155**	...	**1240**		...	**2 27**	...	*3 45*	...		...	**6 34**	**6 32**
27	**Builth Road** ... ... arr.	...	8 40	...	8 50	...	...	...	12 0	...	1245		...	2 31	...	*3 50*	...		...	6 38	6 35
	dep	...	8 41	...	...	...	...	...		...	1 5		...	2 35	...		...		...	6 40	6 36
31	Newbridge-on-Wye ... "	...	8 49	...	...	...	...	...	...	...	1 13		...	2 44	...		...		...	6 47	6 43
35	Doldowlod ... ... "	...	8 57	...	...	...	...	...	...	...	1 21		...	2 51	...		...		...	*	*
38¼	Rhayader ... ... "	...	9 8	...	...	...	...	...	...	...	1 30	*2 15*	...	3 5	...		...		...	7 6	7 2
43¾	St. Harmons ... ... "	...	*	...	...	...	...	...	...	...	*	...	...	*	...		...		...	*	*
45	Pantydwr ... ... "	...	9 21	...	...	...	...	...	...	...	1 43	...	...	3 17	...		...		...	*	7 15
49	Tylwch ... ... "	...	9 31	...	...	...	...	...	...	...	1 53	...	...	3 28	...		...		...	7 29	7 25
52¼	**LLANIDLOES** ... ... arr.	...	**9 37**	...	...	...	...	...	...	...	**2 0**	*2 50*	...	**3 34**	...		...		...	**7 35**	**7 31**
	dep.	**6 35**	**9 42**	...	...	...	**1150**	...	...	...	**2 5**		...	**3 37**	...		...		...	**7 40**	**7 35**
55	Dolwen ... ... "	6 40	9 48	...	...	...	1155	...	...	...	2 11	...	...	3 43	...		...		...	7 46	7 41
57¾	Llandinam ... ... "	6 45	9 55	...	...	...	12 4	...	...	...	2 18	...	...	3 50	...		...		...	7 55	7 50
60	**Moat Lane Jc.** ... ... arr.	6 53	10 0	...	...	...	1210	...	...	...	2 25	...	...	3 55	...	...	...		...	8 0	7 55

FOR NOTES SEE PAGE 9.

full, although rather lengthy, as it gives the reader a detailed account of the situation:

> In accordance with the above resolution I have had prepared the enclosed tables, for the purpose of ascertaining how much time and its equivalent in money was lost by those employed on the Works but who live or have their homes at Llanidloes, and on whose behalf the Mayor of that town has petitioned the Elan Supply Committee to run a special train on Monday mornings only from Rhayader to the Works, thus enabling the men to be here in time to start punctually the first quarter.
>
> A timekeeper was instructed to take the name and number of each man at Rhayader Station as he entered the train on Saturday 17th October. On Monday 19th, idem, the same timekeeper obtained the same information on the arrival of the Workmen's Train from Llanidloes. In this way the Llanidloes men were traced through the books.
>
> The number of men and boys – all told – according to the return furnished, who live at Llanidloes, going there on the Saturday and returning on the Monday, number 84. This figure has been further corroborated by the Stationmaster at Rhayader.
>
> The above are spread over the different works as follows:

> 47 at and about the Caban, Quarries and Masons' yard
> 6 at Careg-ddu
> 11 at Craig Goch
> 20 at Pen-y-gareg
> ___
> 84

> From Pay 139 to 163, or during a period of six months, it is found that, taking the 84 as a whole:

45, as a rule, make full time on Mondays	9 hours
22, as a rule, lose the first quarter, i.e. make	7½ hours
17, as a rule, lose half an hour, i.e. make	8½ hours

> The average loss sustained by each of the 84 men was something under one hour on each Monday, being an average equivalent to a monetary loss of, say, 4*d*.

Caban

> Total number of individuals working 47. Of these:

30 make, as a rule, full time on Mondays	9 hours
8 lose, as a rule, the first quarter, i.e. make	7½ hours
9 lose, as a rule, half an hour, i.e. make	8½ hours
47	

the average loss sustained by each being about ¾ of an hour on each Monday, being an average equivalent to a monetary loss of, say, 3½*d*.

Careg-ddu

Total number of individuals working 6. Of these:

3, as a rule, make full time on Mondays	9 hours
2, as a rule, lose the first quarter, i.e. make	7½ hours
1, as a rule, loses half an hour, i.e. makes	8½ hours
6	

the average loss sustained by each being about an hour on each Monday, being an average equivalent to a monetary loss, of say, 3½d.

Pen-y-Gareg

Total number of individuals working 20. Of these:

6, as a rule, make full time on Mondays	9 hours
7, as a rule, lose the first quarter, i.e. make	7½ hours
7, as a rule, lose half an hour, i.e. make	8½ hours
20	

the average loss sustained by each being about an hour on each Monday, being an average equivalent to a monetary loss of, say, 5d.

Craig Goch

Total number of individuals working 11. Of these:

6, as a rule, make full time on Mondays	9 hours
5, as a rule, lose the first quarter, i.e. make	7½ hours
11	

the average loss sustained by each being about an hour on each Monday, being an average equivalent to a monetary loss of, say, 5½d.

Taking a general view of the 84, as a rule 45 sustain no loss, 17 lose half an hour, and 22 an hour and half.

The time for starting work in the Valley all the year round on Mondays is 7 am. The Workmen's Train is timed, I believe, to reach Rhayader at 6 am. The distance from Rhayader Station to, say, the Caban Office is 3½ miles.

The object of the men in asking to be brought up by train from Rhayader is to avoid a drenching in case it be wet, save themselves the walk, and last but not least to make sure of not losing time.

A suggestion has been thrown out that the Committee shall run a train to the Elan Junction, and there meet the Cambrian train from Llanidloes. This, however, is so surrounded with difficulties that, for the present, it must be thrown out of count and be passed over altogether and the advisability of running a train to Abercaethon, near the distant signal post *only* considered.

The working hours observed in the Valley during the *Summer season* are as follows:

Mondays	⎱	
Tuesdays	⎰7 to 8.30; 9 to 1; 2 to 5.30	
Wednesdays	⎰	
Thursdays and Fridays	⎰6 to 8.30; 9 to 1; 2 to 5.30	
Saturdays	6 to 8.30; 9 to 1	Total 55½ hours

Winter Season

Mondays	⎱	
Tuesdays	⎰	
Wednesdays	⎰7 to 8.30; 9 to 1; 1.30 to 5	
Thursdays	⎰	
and Fridays	⎰	
Saturdays	7 to 8.30; 9 to 1;	Total 50½ hours

All the locomotive drivers are paid from 6 am to 6 pm on all days of the week, excepting Saturdays, when the hours are from 6 am to 3 pm, overtime counting before or after these hours. The locomotives are out of the shed ¾ of an hour before starting time and leave for the higher reaches a quarter of an hour later, viz:

Summer Season
Out of the Shed 6.15 am Mondays
Out of the Shed 5.15 am, other days
Start for higher reaches 6.30 am Mondays
Start for higher reaches 5.30 am, other days

Winter Season
Out of the Shed 6.15 am each day
Start for higher reaches 6.30 am, each day

The men would have to walk from Rhayader to Abercaethon, and when the Cambrian train is up to time, would reach there at, say, 6.15 am, or in other words the Corporation engine would have to be there with two carriages at or about that time.

Now, as there are no turntables or turnouts at Abercaethon, the engine would have to push the carriages in front of it, and return engine foremost or go down engine foremost and push the carriages back, and it is here that one meets the first difficulty, as in both cases the great risk is run of derailment, in other words of the carriages leaving the rails. The first method would be preferable, as the carriages would be empty, and there would be no risk to life and limb, unless the engine were pulled over. It would, however, be otherwise if the same method were followed with the carriages full. The worst part of the line for such tactics is, of course, the curve at Llanfadog.

To get over this difficulty there are four course open, viz:

(1) to run forward to the Elan Junction and change over

(2) provide a turntable at Abercaethon

(3) provide a turnout consisting of 200 rails, about 2 pairs of points and crossings, and 100 sleepers and purchase the necessary land.

(4) take two engines – one in front and one behind.

On arrival at the Corporation Stables, the men would have to debark, that is to say, those working at the Caban and Craig Goch, the former walking forward to their work and the latter changing over into the Craig Goch train, which would have to be there waiting, and the Village men for Pen-y-gareg would walk up to Railway No. 2, and there wait to be picked up, as many that are late frequently do now, or prefer to do so.

All the four methods of getting the engine in front may be objected to, the first on account of having to run to the Elan Junction, when the question would at once be raised, that if the engine could run there why not pick the men up, the second and third on the score of expenditure, and the fourth that a second engine cannot very well be spared.

But apart from all these objections, is it absolutely necessary that the Works should be put to all this trouble, not to say additional anxiety, for the sake of bringing up 84 men on a Monday morning? I think not. Were it, however, absolutely necessary to run a train, as it was thought at one time would have to be done when work started on Contract No. 3, I should be the first to suggest it.

I am, Gentlemen,

Your obedient Servant,

(signed) G.N. Yourdi

The mayor was informed accordingly of the negative reply.

During all this time a passenger train was being run every working day and the men were being conveyed by the "mail" train (*see plate 96*) from the suspension bridge at Elan up to Stables Junction, reverse and then up the valley, being dropped off at their respective stations till all had reached their posts. Then, the train, which was made up of old passenger stock, returned empty to the suspension bridge, there to find all the children of the village waiting to be conveyed down the valley to the school at Rhayader (three miles away) but stopping at Noyadd Sidings. Similarly in the evening, the converse operation took place, the train going down to Noyadd Sidings for the scholars, and then proceeding up the valley from the suspension bridge, light, to return later with the workmen after "knocking off" time.

Finally, when the Elan village school was set up, this train service was changed again and left Noyadd Crossing (about one mile from Rhayader station) around 6.30 am. This then formed the much wanted workmen's service to take the men who lived in Llanidloes and Rhayader to their work up the valley. Returning, this train would bring the children of the workmen residing in the site huts on the upper dam sites to the school in the Elan village. Another service at 7.45 am was laid on for the conveyance of office clerks and officials

Plate 96: The "mail train" hugging the hillside just starting its descent to Stables Junction after passing the site of the top of the Caban Coch Dam.

Courtesy: Severn-Trent Water

Plate 97: Locomotive COEL with coach No. 13, confirming the BCWW did number their coaching stock. This train was reportedly photographed on the 7.45 am "staff" service from Noyadd sidings to the Caban Work site.

LGRP, Courtesy David & Charles

(residing in Rhayader) to the Caban and Elan village site (*see plate 97*). All these trains carried out trips in the reverse direction in the evening, so at the heyday of operation a heavy passenger schedule was maintained both in the morning and evening.

VISITS

The Cambrian did not take long to cash in and establish excursions to see the "mighty" works and in the local newspaper as early as June 1893 advertised:

CAMBRIAN RAILWAYS
COACH AND RAIL TRIPS
COMMENCING ON JUNE 1st 1893

Also to Nantgwyllt and Elan Valley (proposed Birmingham Waterworks Reservoir), on Every Week Day in June, 1893. Excursions by this trip take train to Rhayader, thence by Coach. For full particulars respecting these magnificent Rail and Coach Drives see Cambrian Company's Bills and Tourist Programmes

---

More detailed excursions were published in 1895:

This is a most delightful Excursion. Shortly after leaving Rhayader the scenery is of the loveliest description. It is at Nantgwyllt that the Birmingham Waterworks Reservoir is in course of construction.

TRIP TO NANTGWYLLT AND CWM ELAN (Birmingham Waterworks Reservoir.)

On every week Day in July, August, and September, CHEAP EXCURSION TICKETS, will be issued as under.

From	Times of Starting	Fares for D'ble Jn'y incl'd'g R'l & Coach.		From	Times of Starting	Fare for D'ble Jn'y, incl'd'g R'l & Coach.	
		1st Class	3rd Class			1st Class	3rd Class
	A M	s d	s d		A M	s d	s d
Wrexham	7 0			Tylwch	10 30	5 6	4 6
Bangor-or -Dee	7 13			Pantydwr	10 40	5 0	4 3
Overton-on-Dee	7 20	9 0	7 0	Doldowlod	8 4	4 6	4 0
Ellesmere	7 40			Newbridge	7 56	5 0	4 3
Whittington	7 53	8 6	6 6	Builth Road	7 48	5 6	4 6
Oswestry	8 5			Builth Wells	7 40	6 0	4 9
Llynclys	8 13			Aberedw	7 20	6 6	5 0
Llanymynech	8 20			Erwood	7 15		
Four Crosses	8 25	8 0	6 0	Boughrood	7 7	7 0	5 6
Pool Quay	8 35			Three Cocks	7 0	7 6	5 9
Buttington	8 40			Talgarth	6 54		
Welshpool	8 50			Talyllyn	6 41	8 0	6 0
Forden	8 59			Brecon	6 30		
Montgomery	9 4	7 6	9	Machynlleth	8 15	7 6	5 6
Abermule	9 12			Borth	7 35	7 6	5 6
Kerry	8 40			Aberystwyth	7 15	8 6	5 9
Newtown	9 26			Llandovery	11 25		6 0
Moat Lane	9 50	6 6	5 0	Llanwrtyd Wells	11 20		5 0
Llandinam	9 55			Llangamarch W'ls	11 26		4 9
Dolwen	10 2			Llandrindod Wells	12 5		4 5
Llanidloes	10 20	6 0	4 9				

Excursionists by this Trip take Train to RHAYADER, thence by Brake. The Brake will leave Rhayader at 11-50 a.m, and arrive at Nantgwyllt at 12-50 p.m, return from Nantgwyllt at 4-30 p.m in time for the 6-3 p.m Train for Builth Wells, Brecon, etc., and the 7-6 p.m Train for Pantydwr, Llanidloes, Newtown, Welshpool, Oswestry, Ellesmere, Wrexham, Machynlleth, Aberystwyth, etc, Vehicles will leave the Three Tuns Hotel, Bishop's Castle, for Montgomery Station in connection with this Excursion provided parties of not less than 4 in number travel at a through Return fare of 8s 3d.

Passengers from L. and N.W. Stations leave Rhayader by Coach at 1-30 p.m and arrive at Nantgwyllt at 2.30 p.m. Return from Nantgwyllt at 4-30 pm in time for the 6-3 pm train from Rhayader

Courtesy Mayland Books

Other visits were organised by various interested parties and one such was made by the Institute of Journalists from Cardiff in September 1897 proving that, when they wanted to, the Cambrian operated their stock and locomotives over the BCWW line. Part of the request read:

Cambrian Railways Company,
General Manager's Office
Oswestry.
2nd June, 1897

I should, however, be obliged if you would ask the Waterworks Committee to give their assent to a special train passing over the Corporation Railway to Caban Coch, subject to the certificate of this Company's Engineer that the line would be safe for such a train to pass over it.

The visit of the Journalists to the number of from 2/300 is proposed to be made on Monday, September 6th.

The Reception Committee at Cardiff desire the information with regard to the proposed trip to insert particulars in their guide book which will be published in a few days: therefore, if you could let me have the necessary assent in the course of a day or two I should be much obliged.

Permission was granted subject to the understanding that no responsibility in connection with this train was attached to the Birmingham Corporation in any way, and one wonders what engine and stock carried out this visit, alas no records are available!

Plate 98: Three ex-Cambrian coaches on a passing loop near the end of Railway No. 3, showing the crude water tower and temporary trestle bridge. Again the coach numbers can be seen in the top middle of the coach sides.
LGRP, Courtesy David & Charles

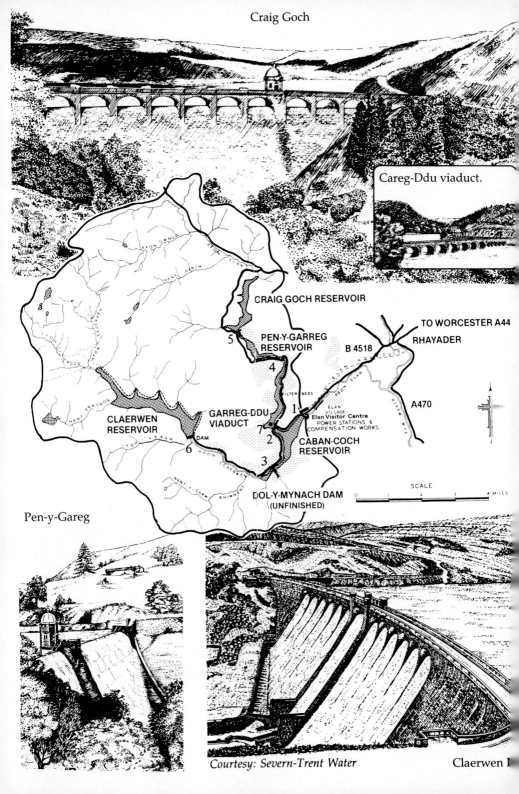

Craig Goch

Careg-Ddu viaduct.

CRAIG GOCH RESERVOIR

PEN-Y-GARREG RESERVOIR

5

4

B 4518

TO WORCESTER A44

RHAYADER

A470

FILTER BEDS

1

ELAN VILLAGE
Elan Visitor Centre
POWER STATIONS &
COMPENSATION WORKS

GARREG-DDU VIADUCT

7

2

3

CABAN-COCH RESERVOIR

CLAERWEN RESERVOIR

DAM

6

DOL-Y-MYNACH DAM
(UNFINISHED)

SCALE

0   1   2   3   4 MILES

Pen-y-Gareg

Courtesy: Severn-Trent Water

Claerwen

Chapter Eight

The Dams, Aqueduct and Pipeline

The whole purpose of this book is to record the construction, working and demise of the Elan Valley Railway, but one must not overlook the reason why the railway was built in the first place, namely to construct the dams and reservoirs of the BCWW. This work was once reported as being the "eighth wonder of the world" and if you can go to see the area and the massive dams, I think you would find it hard to disagree with this statement.

The complexity and engineering skills involved in this scheme were immense and I feel a pictorial tribute will illustrate this best. First, however, a copy of a full report to the Birmingham Water Committee published in June 1908, is included as this covers the whole project's progress over the 14 years of construction.

Impounding Reservoirs

The three impounding reservoirs at present constructed have been formed by the erection of masonry dams at Caban Coch, Pen-y-gareg, and Craig Goch. There are a subsidiary submerged dam at Careg-ddu, and the foundations of another dam at Dol-y mynach. Stone for all of these dams and for the other work in the Elan Valley was obtained from two quarries, opened on the same outcrop of conglomerate on opposite sides of the River Elan, adjoining the dam at Caban Coch, the names of the quarries being the Gigfran on the north or left bank, and the Cnwch on the south or right bank. The yield of the quarries was supplemented to a small extent, as regards facing and other dressed stone, by importations from quarries in similar measures at Builth and Pontypridd. The dams are all built of cyclopean rubble, embedded in five to one concrete, with a lining up-stream of four to one concrete, six feet thick, and are faced up-stream and down-stream with shaped stones arranged in snecked courses. The cement used was all obtained from works on the River Medway.

The dams and all of the other works in the Elan Valley were carried out under the supervision of Mr George Nicholas Yourdi MIntCE, as Resident Engineer.

On each of the impounding dams a tablet is fixed, giving the following particulars regarding the respective reservoirs:

Caban Coch Reservoir and Dam (No. 1 on accompanying map)
Total capacity, 8,000,000,000 gallons.
Top water area, 500 acres.
Top water level, 822 feet above Ordnance Datum.
Height of dam above river bed, 122 ft.
Depth of foundations below river bed, 25 ft.
Length of weir, 566 ft.
Thickness of dam at base, 122 ft 6 in.
Estimated quantity of masonry, 144,800 cub.yds.
Total area of watershed, 45,562 acres.

Pen-y-Gareg Reservoir and Dam(No. 4)
 Total capacity, 1,320,000,000 gallons.
 Top water area, 124 acres.
 Top water level, 945 ft above Ordnance Datum.
 Height of dam above river bed, 123 ft.
 Depth of foundations below river bed, 17 ft.
 Length of weir, 417 ft 6 in.
 Thickness of dam at base, 115 ft 4 in.
 Estimated quantity of masonry, 90,372 cub.yds.

Craig Goch Reservoir and Dam (No. 5)
 Total capacity, 2,000,000,000 gallons.
 Top water area, 217 acres.
 Top water level, 1,040 ft above Ordnance Datum.
 Height of dam above river bed, 120 ft.
 Depth of foundations below river bed, 17 ft.
 Length of weir, 417 ft 6 in.
 Thickness of dam at base, 115 ft 4 in.
 Estimated quantity of masonry, 90,372 cub.yds.

Compensation Water
 The amount of compensation water is fixed by the Act of Parliament at 27 million gallons per day. The board of Conservators Wye Fishery District have the right to require the Corporation to reserve 5 million gallons per day of the total for 21 days, and to discharge the same in 48 hours. By the Act of 1905, the Corporation obtained powers to utilise the discharge of compensation water for the purpose of generating power to be used on the works, and this is accomplished by means of turbines placed on the pipes conveying the compensation water from the reservoir to the river. The compensation and power houses are situated immediately below the dam at Caban Coch. They are constructed on both sides of the river, the works on the two sides being duplicates of each other. The works on each side are sufficient for the normal discharge of 27 million gallons; but when the reserve water is discharged, the works on both sides are required simultaneously to their full capacity. The compensation water is drawn off at a level of 720 ft O.D., and the turbines are calculated to work at full duty under a head of 26 ft, leaving 76 ft depth of water to be drawn off before there is any curtailment of power.
 Each turbine house contains two installations:

(1) 75 hp utilised for generating electricity at 525 volts for power purposes on the filter beds
(2) 25 hp which serves –
    (*a*) to pump into the hydraulic accumulator providing a pressure of 700 lbs to the square inch, used for working valves in connection with the Caban Coch Dam and at the Foel Valve Tower (q.v.), and
    (*b*) to generate electricity at 220 volts utilised direct or through a system of storage batteries for lighting at the Caban Coch Dam, Foel Valve Tower, Filter Beds, and in the village.

Submerged Dam at Careg-Ddu (No. 2) (see diagram below)

The Caban Coch Reservoir, as has already been remarked, fulfils the double purpose of providing water for compensation and for supply. The compensation water is discharged at the Caban Dam at a level of 720 ft above O.D. The point of delivery at the Birmingham end of the aqueduct is 600 ft above O.D., and in order to ensure a proper fall on the aqueduct it was necessary that the water for supply should be drawn off at a consider-

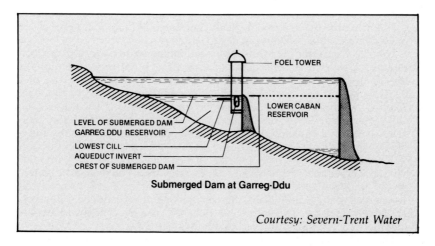

FOEL TOWER

LOWER CABAN RESERVOIR

LEVEL OF SUBMERGED DAM
GARREG DDU RESERVOIR

LOWEST CILL
AQUEDUCT INVERT
CREST OF SUBMERGED DAM

Submerged Dam at Garreg-Ddu

Courtesy: Severn-Trent Water

ably higher level than 720 ft O.D. The point fixed upon was Careg-ddu, where the aqueduct starts with an invert level of 770 ft O.D. at a point on the left bank of the reservoir, 1½ miles above the Caban Coch Dam. From the levels given above it is evident that, if the reservoir were continuous, the water level could never have been drawn below 780 ft O.D.; that is, the point of submergence of the entrance to the aqueduct, and, under these circumstances, the whole of the water stored below that level would be entirely useless. In view of this the device has been resorted to of constructing a subsidiary dam immediately down-stream of the head of the aqueduct, and having a weir level of 782 ft O.D. A viaduct is built by Parliamentary requirement over the submerged dam to carry a road giving access to the Claerwen Valley.

By means of the submerged dam, the Caban Coch Reservoir is divided into three portions:

(*a*) A stratum of 40 ft thick from 822 ft to 782 ft O.D., extending over the whole area of the reservoir, and containing 4,585 million gallons. This quantity is available both for compensation and supply.

(*b*) The portion of the reservoir below the weir level of the submerged dam (782 ft O.D.) and situate between that dam and the Caban Coch Dam. This second portion has a capacity of 2,565 million gallons, and is available for compensation only.

(c) The section of the reservoir up-stream, and below the weir level of the submerged dam. This section must always be kept full in order to charge the aqueduct, and when the Caban Coch Reservoir is drawn down to the 782 ft O.D. level, that level will be maintained in this third section by drawing from the Pen-y-gareg and Craig Goch Reservoirs on the River Elan, and also, by means of the Dol-y-mynach Tunnel (see below) from the Dol-y-mynach and other reservoirs on the River Claerwen.

Dol-y-Mynach Dam (No. 3)

Following the road across the viaduct of Careg-Ddu for a distance of 1½ miles, the incomplete Dol-y-mynach Dam is reached.

The site fixed upon for this dam is submerged when the Caban Coch reservoir is full. It was consequently necessary to put in the foundations of this dam during the construction of the works comprised in the first instalment, and this has been done, the dam being carried to the level 830 ft O.D. It will eventually be carried up to 900 ft O.D. At present the Dol-y-mynach reservoir has an area of 26 acres and contains 150 million gallons. When completed it will have a top water area of 148 acres and a capacity of 1,640 million gallons. A short distance up-stream from the Dol-y-mynach Dam a low tower marks the entrance to the Dol-y-mynach Tunnel. This tunnel is constructed for the purpose of conveying the waters of the Claerwen into the Caban Coch reservoir at a point above the submerged dam (Careg-ddu) thereby making the Claerwen reservoirs available for supply. This tunnel is 1 mile 437 yds long. The invert level at the inlet is 823 ft O.D., and at the outlet 802 ft O.D.

The following will be the particulars of the Dol-y-mynach Reservoir when completed:

    Height of dam, 101 ft.
    Length of dam, 938 ft.
    Top water level above O.D., 900 ft.
    Top water area, 148 acres.
    Capacity, 1,640,000,000 gallons.

Foel Valve Tower (No. 7)

The head of the aqueduct is marked by the Foel Valve Tower, situated immediately up-stream of the Careg-ddu Viaduct. The level of the summit of the dome is 877 ft O.D., that is, 55 ft above the top water level of the reservoir. The draw-off pipes in the base of the tower have an invert level of 770 ft O.D. The entire height of the tower above the draw-off is, therefore, 107 ft, of which 52 ft are submerged and 55 ft are above water. In the walls of the tower there is a series of orifices at different depths, providing free communication with the body of water in the reservoir. Within the tower is a dry well constructed of blue bricks and having an internal diameter of 12 ft. Between the outer wall of the tower and the dry well are three upstand pipes. Each of these is 5 ft 6 in. in diameter, and is composed of cylinders 6 ft in length, except the bottom section of each, which are respectively two, four, and six feet long with an adjusting length on the top section. Each column of cylinders is capable of being raised so as to form an opening between any two lengths. This device provides the means of drawing water from one or other of the three cylinders at steps of two feet throughout the whole depth of the reservoir down to 770 ft O.D. All of the pipes terminate in the inlet chamber of the aqueduct. They are controlled by valves, and each of them is capable of discharging the entire maximum supply of 75 million gallons per day under the minimum head provided at 782 ft O.D. The apparatus for lifting the cylinders and working the valves is operated by hydraulic power at a pressure of 700 lb. to the sq.in., accumulated in the turbine houses below the Caban Dam.

Above the entrance to the Tower a tablet in cast bronze is fixed, bearing the following inscription:

CITY OF BIRMINGHAM WATER DEPARTMENT, ELAN SUPPLY WORKS. June 27th, 1892. – The Act of Parliament authorizing the construction of the Works received the Royal Assent. Edward Lawley Parker, Mayor. Sir Thomas Martineau, Chairman of the Water Committee. Edward Orford Smith, Town Clerk. James Mansergh, Member Council Inst.C.E., Engineer and Originator of the Scheme.

July 21st, 1904 – His Majesty King Edward VII., accompanied by Her Majesty Queen Alexandra, visited and inspected the Elan Valley Works, when His Majesty opened the valves admitting the water to the Aqueduct through which it passes for a distance of 73 miles to the Service Reservoirs and Works at Frankley, near Birmingham. Sir Hallewell Rogers, Lord Mayor. Edward Lawley Parker, Chairman of the Water Committee. Edward Orford Smith, Town Clerk. Ebenezer Antony Lees, Secretary. James Mansergh, Past President Inst.C.E., F.R.S., Ernest Lawson Mansergh, M.Inst.C.E., Walter Leahy Mansergh, A.M.Inst.C.E., Engineers. George Nicholas Yourdi, M.Inst.C.E., Resident Engineer.

There is a rising main with a diameter of 18 in. from the Pumping Station to each of these reservoirs. In consequence of the rapid growth of the population in the high-level districts served from these reservoirs an additional engine has recently been put down to supplement the three originally provided. The water distributed by gravitation is taken into distribution by means of three 42 in. mains, one to the low level and two to the middle level. Each of these at the point of leaving the valve house is fitted with a Venturi meter with self-recording apparatus showing the quantity of water passing. The two rising mains from the pumping engines are also fitted with self-recording Venturi meters.

The whole of the houses and works are lighted by electricity generated in the engine house. The principal valves, penstocks, etc., are operated by hydraulic power distributed from the central station at a presure of 700 lb. to the square inch.

Cost of the Scheme

The Parliamentary estimate of the cost of the entire scheme was £5,851,000, and the estimate for the works originally included in the first instalment was £3,755,350. As the works progressed it became apparent that the cost would considerably exceed the estimate. It became, moreover, necessary to include certain additional works, such as the filter beds at the Foel, not originally provided for; also the foundations of the Dol-y-mynach Dam were undertaken, which had not been included in the estimate of the first instalment. Revised estimates were then prepared, and the Water Committee submitted to the City Council on March 4th, 1902, a report reviewing the circumstances and submitting an estimate of £5,884,918 as the estimate of the ultimate cost of the first instalment, being £2,129,568 in excess of the Parliamentary estimate. Of this excess £750,000 was stated by the Engineer to represent the cost of works not included in the original estimate for the first instalment. The works on the watershed account for £756,425 of the excess. This was explained by the Engineer on the following grounds:

(1) The necessity of making the foundations of all the dams deeper and longer than was anticipated.
(2) The failure to find suitable building stone in the neighbourhood of any of the dams except Caban Coch.
(3) The necessity of importing considerable quantities of stone, owing to restricted local facilities, in consequence of only the two quarries at Caban Coch being available.
(4) Considerable increase in wages and material over the rates prevailing when the original estimate was prepared.

The works carried out by contract on the aqueduct and at Frankley account for the remainder of the excess, which is attributable in part to obligations imposed by Parliament, general increase in cost of material and labour, and to various special local circumstances.

The expenditure on the scheme up to March 31st, 1908, was £5,762,853, as against the ultimate estimate of £5,884,918.

Two further dams were proposed on the Claerwen Valley (Cil-Oerwynt Dam and Nant-y-Beddau Dam) but were never constructed, being superseded by one large dam finished in 1952 and named the Claerwen Dam. This was the largest of all the dams holding over 48,302 megalitres of water (almost the combined capacity of the three Elan reservoirs). Its height is 56 metres from stream bed to crest (half as high again as the Elan dams) and 6 kilometres across the top face, a truly enormous constructional feat.

As important as the construction of the dams was the building of the aqueduct and pipeline to carry the water from Elan to Birmingham, and a section plan is enclosed of this 73 mile pipeline. One can see this pipeline running through the countryside today and the size of the two pipes can be ascertained in *Plate 99*. The water flows by gravitational means with a total fall of 170 ft meaning the average gradient is a mere 1 in 2300, one of the salient points (in economy terms) about the scheme when presented to the Water Committee in 1892. Inverted siphons carry the water across the larger valleys. At an

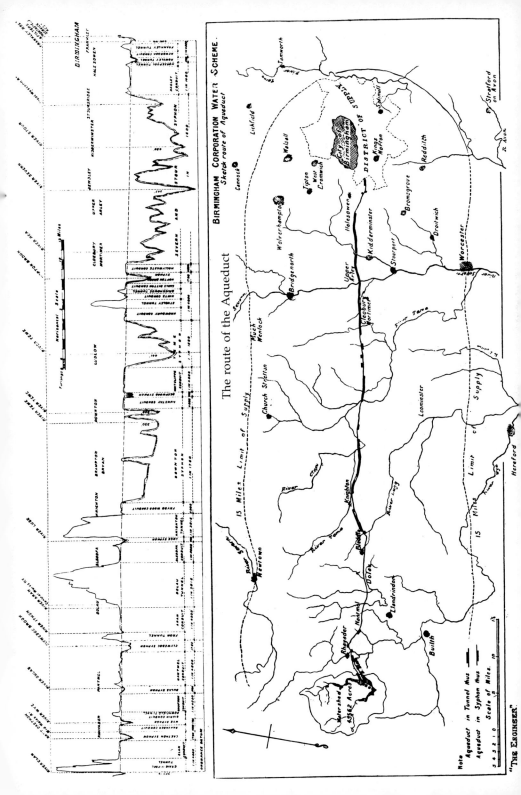

BIRMINGHAM CORPORATION WATER SCHEME.
Sketch route of Aqueduct

The route of the Aqueduct

"THE ENGINEER."

elevation of 600 ft Birmingham is amongst the highest urban areas in the country, so the beginning of the aqueduct had to be at a height of 770 ft. Since the bottom of Caban Coch Dam is only 700 ft high, a submerged dam was constructed in the reservoir to hold back the water at a height of 82 ft above the reservoir bed. The construction of the pipeline and its associated railway and villages would make a book on its own, perhaps!

Plate 99: Several unused sections of the main pipeline to Birmingham at the Elan Valley Visitors Centre site.   *Author's Collection*

Plate 100: A large postcard view of the Caban Coch Dam in full flood, photo-graphed from the Filter Bed site in 1908 when the main line was still in use but all sidings had disappeared. The single line on the valley floor was the end of Railway No. 1, and has two box vans and one BCWW brake van in view.   *Collection Mr C. Edwards, Rhayader*

Plate 101: This magnificent view of the Careg-Ddu Dam with the Foel Tower on the right, taken in the 1930s beautifully portrays the tranquility of the area.
Reproduced by permission of the Reference Library, Birmingham

Plate 102: A 1910's view showing the new road bridge and roads built during the dam's construction. Railway No. 4 is on the right hand side and can be seen climbing the gradient to "Devil's Gulch" (just to the right of the tower) on the headland promentary. The wooden shed beside the bridge is still in existence today inside the carpark. *Collection Mr C. Edwards, Rhayader*

Plate 103: Probably the most pleasing design of all the dams, and the only one with a truly curved construction, is the top dam of Craig-Goch. Railway No. 4 had a station/halt built at the roadway (bottom of photograph) at which the King alighted on his visit in July 1904.

Reproduced by permission of the Reference Library, Birmingham

Dol-y-Mynach Dam, Elan Valley.

Plate 104: The only view found of the small Dol-y-Mynach Dam built on the Claerwen river. This provides a head of water to feed the tunnel to Caban Coch Reservoir (*see map page 15*) and was never completed to its projected height. *Collection Mr. C. Edwards, Rhayader*

Plate 105: The enormous Claerwen Dam, completed in 1952 to increase the water capacity. This dam was built using road transport and no consideration was given to re-instating the railway as previously had been proposed. *Collection Mr C. Edwards, Rhayader*

Plate 102: The Cambrian engine used on the Royal Train of 21st July, 1904, a Sharps 4–4–0, No. 83.　　　　　　　*LGRP, Courtesy David & Charles*

Plate 103: The dignitaries loaded in their wagons proceeding up the Elan Valley for the Royal day. These ladies and gentlemen had just traversed in all their finery, the dank and dark Rhayader tunnel. Note the soldiers lining the route.　　　　　　　*LGRP, Courtesy David & Charles*

Chapter Nine

The Royal Visit – 21st July, 1904

Ho! citizens of Birmingham,
Ye loyal men and true,
Now hasten into Rhayader
Your waterworks to view.

An LNWR poem used on a publicity advert for the Royal Visit

The Birmingham Water supply scheme was certainly the most costly and probably the most ambitious of any of the great waterworks in the early 20th Century and it was appropriate and fitting that the opening of the water supply should be marked by a "memorable" ceremony. The Water Committee had asked that "all" the people of Birmingham should be able to take part, but as this proved impossible the Committee requested His Majesty King Edward VII and Queen Alexandra to perform the opening ceremony, which they duly accepted.

The build-up to this great event is recorded in the newspapers and periodicals of the day. The first extract sets the scene in the days leading up to the Royal Visit and although several other extracts cover the same scene, they allow the reader to savour the atmosphere of this colourful day that came just once to this small Welsh town.

> For days beforehand the passenger traffic had been exceptional – press men travelled over the line in a fine saloon lent by the Cambrian Railways, other less fortunate visitors contented themselves with goods wagons, across which boards had been nailed to form seats, and train-loads of officials, waiters and others were glad to avail themselves of any accommodation they could find, even the worst being preferable to the long and tiring walk from Rhayader. On the Wednesday evening a Great Western special train from Birmingham brought a large contingent of police; and we were much amused to notice the looks of amazement and the disparaging remarks which greeted the Corporation train as it backed down the platform; after the luxurious carriages in which the policemen had come from Birmingham, the dingy cushionless boxes were evidently not appreciated, though the matter was treated in a good humoured, bantering fashion by the men.

Another newspaper report recorded:

> The engines to be used on the Royal day are constructed on the side-tank principle, and are certainly not those powerful locomotives one would expect to see. It seems, however, that the smaller type of engine to be used on this Royal occasion are better adapted for curves and gradients of the Water Works Railway. The Directors' saloon is attached for the purpose of allowing the Directors and chief officials opportunity of seeing what the rolling stock can do, the working of the vacuum brakes, and so on.

On the trial trip, when the train arrived at Builth Road, the London and North Western engines were detached, and a Cambrian engine put on. From Builth Road the train was driven by Bob James* with E. Jones, fireman, both of Oswestry. The guards were Rees Lloyd (Oswestry) and Benjamin Newton, who acted as guard to the Royal train in 1896, when the King (then Prince of Wales) passed through Central Wales.

The Royal train remained at Rhayader station about an hour-and-a-half, while several of the railway officials proceeded by the Corporation train, up the Elan Valley.

Their Majesties are expected to arrive in Radnorshire from Swansea at noon, and, after a short wait here, the Royal train will be conveyed over the contractors' railway, as far as the Cabin Coch dam, where the water will be turned into the main pipe by the King.

Arrangements are being made for the school children to sing the National Anthem on the arrival of the Royal train at Rhayader. A deputation has approached Mr Denniss (*Manager, Cambrian Railways*), who has undertaken to do all in his power to have a platform erected for this purpose.

The *Western Mail* reported:

The visit to Rhayader

Rhayader station is in course of transformation. Painters have been set to work in all directions, signals, etc., have not been overlooked.

Alderman Lawley Parker, Chairman of the Birmingham Water Committee, and Mr E. Anthony Lees, Secretary, have been staying at the Elan Valley Hotel, arranging plans, and superintending preparations.

The erection of stands and platforms in the Valley has been let to a Birmingham contractor, who is also charged with the decorative work.

It is understood that on the conclusion of the inaugural ceremony the King and Queen will be taken to the extreme end of the valley to inspect the Craig-Goch dam. The luncheon will follow directly afterwards. It will be laid at a point near Elan Valley Hotel.

The Royal party will return to London via Welshpool, leaving Rhayader at 3.15.

Sleeping accommodation has been booked not only in Rhayader, but in the surrounding towns of Llanidloes, Llandrindod Wells, Builth Wells, Llanwrtyd Wells etc.

The Birmingham Corporation party will travel to the Valley in three special trains, preceding the Royal Train.

A platform is being laid half way across the top of the Cabin-Goch dam for the Royal party to walk over, and a large stand erected in front of the filter beds. It is understood that the women and children of the workers are to be admitted onto this stand by ticket.

---

* Robert James, Cambrian Railway Royal Driver born 14.3.1858, became Fireman on 23.5.1883 and Engineman 2.9.1891, and was based at Oswestry. He was paid a gratuity of 12s. by the Cambrian Railway Directors for his Royal duties.

View of West Street, showing decorations around Market Hall.

Besides the special trains which will be run on that date from different places to Rhayader, an excursion is to be run the following day from Birmingham.

Besides running excursion trains from Oswestry and Brecon, the Cambrian Railways Company will issue reduced fare tickets by the ordinary trains from the coast towns.

All the signals etc., on the Cambrian Railway from Builth Road over the length to be traversed by the royal party are being painted! A dozen hands have been employed on this work at the Rhayader station.

Mr W. Bowen Hamer, clerk to the Cwmdauddwr parish council, has now received a letter stating that their Majesties will be pleased to receive an address from his council, within whose jurisdiction the water-works are situated.

A body of picked men from the Montgomery Imperial Yeomanry will form an escort for the King and Queen at Rhayader and Elan Valley.

The Radnorshire County Council's address is to be presented in the vicinity of Rhayader railway station.

Birmingham Corporation contemplate despatching a troop of 400 police-constables for duty in the valley, and about 100 of them will be located at Rhayader.

A joint meeting of the justices for Radnorshire and the members of the County Council will be held at the Victoria Hall, Llandrindod Wells on Friday afternoon next, in connexion with the Royal visit.

The crowning day in the history of this short lived railway was without doubt Thursday 21st July, 1904, when the Royal visitors travelled to the site and over the private metals of the Corporation Railway. Seldom before or since had such types of engines, coaches or even track, the honour of transporting Royal visitors; but the little railway and its officials rose gallantly to the occasion and it was rewarded by the whole day passing off without any major hold-up or mishap.

The *Birmingham Mail* of 1904 gave an account of the scene in the morning at Rhayader:

The Morning Scene

Rhayader last night gave one the impression of tranquil hillside town which had just been transformed into a place of considerable importance by the invasion of a friendly military force with an external civilian following. The decorations in the quiet West Street suggested that a spirit of rejoicing was abroad, and the stir and bustle that prevailed on the evening had foreshadowed the great event of the morning. Officers in uniform lounged in the porticos of buildings and the crowds in the streets were freely dotted with men in khaki. The main street was in a state of congestion until long after the accustomed time of repose in Rhayader, and the inns and public houses, with which the town is well supplied, found its accommodation taxed to the utmost limit. The clatter of cavalry horses and the shouts of hostlers disturbed the peace of residents and visitors alike at an early hour this morning, but there was no disposition on the part of anyone to remain in bed with brilliant sunshine flooding the hills and with events of such magnitude near at hand. The streets began to fill up after seven, and the necessity for the notice so clearly displayed on lamp posts and venetian masts to "keep to the left" speedily became apparent. Belated shopkeepers hastened to put the finishing touches to their decorations, and military men were early astir completing the preparations for their share in the day's programme. The railway station, transfigured beyond recognition, was a centre of attraction long after the breakfast hour.

The *Railway Magazine* recorded the day's event with the following account:

Next morning all was bustle at Rhayader station; hosts of officials, under the personal supervision of Mr Gough (superintendent of the line) disposed as quickly as possible of the heavily-laden excursion trains – Cambrian, Midland, Great Western and North Western Railways – which continued to pour in from North and South. The Royal train, consisting of four-wheeled Cambrian stock, stood ready in a siding; and by the kindness of Mr Denniss we were permitted to photograph it for the *Railway Magazine*. First came a composite carriage, next the Royal saloon, followed by another saloon and a van, the whole newly painted in the Cambrian colours – white and green. Owing to the sharp curves and small allowance for clearance in places, it was not considered advisable to employ six to eight-wheeled stock on the Corporation line; hence the necessity for the Royal party changing at Rhayader, and for the employment of a somewhat antiquated type of carriage.

At length the trains from Birmingham, bringing the guests of the Corporation, commenced to arrive; these consisted of some of the finest dining saloons of the Great Western and London & North Western Railways between whom the traffic had been divided, and the platforms were soon crowded with Birmingham's most eminent citizens. As each special drew out of the station, there entered from the sidings such a train as few of those present had ever seen – a sturdy saddletank drawing a long string of goods wagons, each of which had boards nailed across it to serve as seats, reminding us very forcibly of the pictures we sometimes see depicting the trains of 70 or more years ago. Ladies and gentlemen were crowded into these primitive vehicles, ascending from the platform by small wooden ladders, and all was soon ready; a whistle dislodged tall hats and threw the passengers into each others' arms, as the couplings pulled tight and the train started for the valley. Just outside the station is a

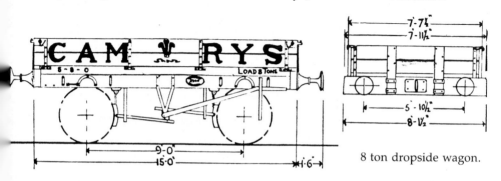

8 ton dropside wagon.

The style of wagon used for the conveyance of dignitaries to the Elan Valley site.

short tunnel, and it was easy to imagine that the elaborate summer attire of the ladies would not be improved by the time the open carriages emerged from it. But all were in high spirits and doubtless looked upon these small discomforts in the light of amusing novelties.

Nearer and nearer drew the time for the King's arrival and still the last train of guests had not arrived. At last it was seen approaching, and with all speed the passengers were transferred to the "open saloons" but, unfortunately for them, the Royal train was now due, and as it was feared that their passage along the line to the junction might delay His Majesty's arrival, they were ignominiously shunted into a siding, and kept there until the Royal special was well on its way to the Filter beds!

Travelling over the Central Wales line of the London & North Western Railway from Swansea, the King's train passed on to the Cambrian system at Builth Road, arriving at Rhayader at 12.25 pm. The engine was one of the standard four-coupled bogie express locomotives of the Cambrian Railways No. 83 (*plate 102*), and the train was that built for His Majesty's use by the London & North Western Railway in 1901*.

During the brief formalities at the station the little engine COEL was despatched "light-engine" along toward the Caban Coch site, to act as a pilot (*plate 104*) and ensure all was correct for the Royal Train. The locomotive CALETTWR with the Cambrian special saloons followed (*plate 105*) as the ROYAL TRAIN and there was no prouder man in all Wales than the man who drove the King. Harry Beckenham was his name. Burly of figure, beaming of face, he is one of the most popular men upon the Elan waterworks, where he has been employed for the last ten years, driving the locomotive CALETTWR, which is one of the eight Corporation locomotives.

Beckenham has spent his life in driving engines, so that the Corporation train was in the care of as experienced a hand as any driver of a Royal express. The only novelty was having Royal passengers behind him. Harry Beckenham was at one time employed in the locomotive department of the London and North-Western Railway, and for some time he ran an engine on the Holyhead section of the line. Then he went on to contractor's work, and was for some years under the Liverpool Corporation on the Vyrnwy lake construction.

All the locomotives taking part in this great event were tastefully decorated with bunting, smoke arresters and above all "spit and polish".

Along the whole of the route to the filter-beds the sides of the railway

---

* Apropos of the Royal visit, it is not generally known there was a slight hitch in connection with the Royal train. This had a decidedly humerous side to it, and was thus described by an eye-witness:

It is probable, he said, the Cambrian train bringing the Royal party to Rhayader would not have come into that place but for the assistance of a locomotive belonging to the Birmingham Corporation. There is a steep gradient coming into Rhayader, and it appears the Royal train, a heavy one, was pulled up this gradient.

Repeated attempts were made by the Cambrian engine to restart it, but without avail. It was then that a little locomotive belonging to the Corporation came to the rescue, and pluckily assisted in pulling the royal train up the gradient.

Plate 104: The diminutive locomotive COEL (with smoke arrester) with bunting strung twixt chimney and cab, a soldier standing on the side (with gun) and floral decorations on the smoke box, performing its duties on this most important day by the "pilot" engine proceeding the Royal Train, seen here near Noyadd Sidings.   *LGRP, Courtesy David & Charles*

Plate 105: The Royal Train of July 1904 seen here near Noyadd Sidings on the Elan Valley line with CALETTWR (with smoke arrester) at its head. The Shropshire Light Infantry can be seen lining the track side (supposedly every 15 ft) and "presenting arms" as the King passed.   *LGRP, Courtesy David & Charles*

were lined with police and soldiery; and as the train passed slowly along, an excellent view of the King and Queen was obtained by the thousands of excursionists who had taken up their position along those portions of the main road which run parallel with the line.

As the junction with the branch to the filter beds, where the ceremony of turning on the water took place (*plate 106*), faced descending trains, the Royal special was obliged to reverse at that point, being drawn along the branch by locomotive RHIWNANT.

By this time it was about two o'clock when their Majesties arrived at the field of Nant Madog (*plate 108*) and entered the sumptuously arranged luncheon tent to partake of refreshments in the presence of a small but distinguished company, who had received the honour of invitation to lunch in the Royal pavilion. The following menu was provided by the Lord Mayor for his illustrious guests:

Croutons of Caviare.
(Hot) Lamb Cutlets. Saute Potatoes.
Medaillons of Quails a la Royale.
Cold Lamb.
Roast Chicken. York Ham. Tongue.
Galantine of Chicken Truffled.
Pressed Beef.
Potatoes. Salads.
Strawberries and Cream. Helene Ices.
Dessert. Coffee.

During the repast both their Majesties chatted pleasantly with those around, thus putting everybody completely at their ease. The luncheon was, as a matter of fact, by no means a cold and formal function. It was pleasant, genial and agreeable. Ceremonial, of course, there was, but this was reduced to the briefest character. It fell upon the Bishop of St David's to say grace, and the only toast on the list was that of the health of their Majesties the King and Queen.

Their Majesties then re-entered the train and were taken up the valley to the terminus of the line at Craig-Goch (*plate 107*), where a platform had been erected for their accommodation. An inspection of the dam and the fine view obtained from it occupied only a few minutes, and at 3.30 Rhayader was reached again, the Royal party changing once more into the North Western train, which speedily whirled them away from the scene of the day's adventures.

Plate 106: A fine view of the Royal Party at the filter beds high above the Elan village. The effort of hauling the Royal Train up the gradients to this site must have been well worth watching!

Reproduced by permission of the Reference Library, Birmingham

Plate 107: The Royal party at the terminus of Railway No. 4 having just alighted onto the specially constructed platform, for a walk across the Craig Goch Dam. Note CALETTWR has the Royal Crest on the front and a polished plate reading "B.C.W.W." on the smokebox. The decorative smoke arrester is worthy of note. *Reproduced by permission of the Reference Library, Birmingham*

Plate 108: The temporary marquee site at Nant Madog where the Royal party enjoyed their luncheon. *Courtesy: Severn-Trent Water*

Plate 109: The Ceremonial wheel turned by the King to allow water to flow to Birmingham. The Inscription states: "Birmingham Corporation Waterworks; Elan Supply. Inaugurated by their most gracious Majesties King Edward VII and Queen Alexandra at the Elan Valley June 21st, 1904". The four spokes had the names of James Mansergh (Engineer), Edward Lawley Parker (Chairman), Edward Smith (Town Clerk) and Hallewell Rogers (Lord Mayor). *Courtesy: Severn-Trent Water*

The *Evening Despatch* recorded the whole day's events as follows:

RHAYADER'S GREAT DAY

Royal Visitors at Elan
KING'S WEATHER
His Majesty recognises a Great Work

(By our special representatives)

Rhayader, Thursday 9 am.

The Great day has come, and Rhayader is truly elated. The dull grey of the little village is hidden in a gorgeous effusion of many coloured bunting to which the finishing touches are now being put.

It is indeed King's weather. The mists are gone, and following a night lit by a crescent moon, a warm sun shines clearly while a gentle breeze comes over the hills to relieve the oppressive heat.

What yesterday was a scene of dreary dampness is now gay to a degree, the sun touches reds and yellows, blues and crimsons, glares on big banners fixed on central arches and great mottoes of welcome on house sides. It matters not to the men of Rhayader, apparently, that His Majesty will only catch a fleeting glance at the little town in the dip, and will not see one-eighth of the decorations. They are quite proud of the display, and intend to make the occasion one of general holiday-making and merriment.

Never has there been so great a throng within the village streets as there is this morning. Ladies in muslin, men in their regulation frock coats and silk hats sweltering in the sunshine, redcoats with plumes, motor men and cyclists, and by many a horse vehicle the natives of neighbourning parts make a brave, if strangely mixed, show. They walk about beneath the sun in the flickering shade of flag and banner, and talk of the day's doings.

POLICE AND MILITARY TRAINS.

Towards seven o'clock commenced the bustling activity which was to characterise Rhayader Station throughout the day. Earliest to arrive was the first of the Birmingham police trains, which brought just over 200 officers and men. They were drawn up on the platform, and veal, ham and egg pies were served out to them to be stowed away in haversacks for their lunch. Approximately 1,300 of these pies, weighing 2 lb. each, were secured for "rationing" the police and volunteers. Close on the heels of these came a second train, containing the remainder of the Birmingham force, which all told numbered 436 of all ranks, from the Chief Constable downwards. With them came 100 of the 1st Voluntary Brigade of the Warwickshire Artillery, with their officers, half of whom were to do duty from the filter beds to Caban Coch. In addition there were on board thirty-four ambulance men, with their equipment, under the command of Chief Superintendent Gilbert, who had as a very able lieutenant Superintendent Tozer (superintendent of stores). All the occupants of this train were also drawn up, served with rations, and then despatched up the valley in Corporation trains. Next in were the Birmingham Volunteers, of whom there were 350, some to form a guard of honour at the filter beds, and some to keep the luncheon field at Nant Madog and to assist The Shropshire Light Infantry already in place. After the volunteers had been sent on up the valley there came a considerable interval without anything connected officially with the day's proceedings, but meanwhile the bustle and excitement within the town itself were steadily increasing, cycles, carts and all kinds of conveyances began to pour onto the streets from the surrounding districts and all began to set out in the general direction of the Elan Valley. All the thoroughfares were well policed due to the narrowness of the streets where problems of serious obstruction could occur. A Birmingham policeman, PC Shipton (32E) was formed up with the mounted detachment outside the station, and had just mounted, when his horse reared. The animal and the man rolled over on the roadway. The constable was taken to the Elan Valley Corporation Hospital and had a serious fracture of the pelvis. It is doubtful whether he will see any more police duty.

Arrival of the Royal Train

There will be a great crowd up the valley today. Much attention has been paid to all the fences along the route which will keep the general public from mixing with the special parties, but though thousands come and swarm the roads they must sink into practical insignificance amid the mountains.

Other Arrivals

As the day advanced greater activity prevailed and trains brought in their loads of people hoping to catch a glimpse of His Majesty during his short visit at the station, and crowds thronged the banking to the station, while all who had taken precaution to obtain tickets were allowed on the platform. Enthusiasts who were honoured to own motor cars travelled from surrounding Cities and to add to the attractions of the day – The Band of the Montgomery Yeomans paraded through Rhayader prior to heading the procession to the station. Every train arriving at Rhayader, and there were many, was eagerly cheered by an expectant multitude. The first detachment of the Birmingham party was due at Rhayader at 9.50 and arrived a few minutes late while the second did not get in until 20 minutes past 11, an hour late, the third and last, not coming in until 5 minutes to 12 instead of 10.40. The result was that while the two first trains (the "Red" and "White" trains) went on to the filter beds the last train (named "the Blue train") was kept back, and, unfortunately for the passengers, shunted some distance down the line, so that the occupants did not get an opportunity of seeing their Majesties and the reception on the platform. The journey from Birmingham had been taken all to no purpose, and the chagrin of visitors can better be imagined than described. Prior to this the covered stand erected beside the platform was crowded, and large numbers congregated on the platform, but were speedily moved on.

Arrival of the Royal Train

Just before 12 o'clock the guard of honour, consisting of a company of the 1st Hereford Volunteers, was marched onto the platform of the Rhayader Railway Station and took its stand just below the spot where the King and Queen were to alight, the band playing martial airs. The public waited with expectancy for the coming of the Royal train. Seated on a raised platform were the children of the Rhayader and Cwmdauddwr Schools, and they whiled away the time by singing national airs. The train was later than anticipated, but half past twelve it was seen approaching, and as the engine steamed into the station the people rose *en masse* and gave vent to hearty cheers. His Majesty, attired in a grey morning suit, with grey tall hat, and looking in the best of health, alighted, and handed out Her Majesty, who was also evidently in good health, and looked as charming as ever. The Queen wore a dress of silver and black, brocaded silk and a bunch of carnations, a black and white stole, and a cream toque, trimmed with black.

Immediately on alighting His Majesty proceeded to walk briskly along the platform, and inspected the guard of honour, while the Queen chatted pleasantly meanwhile to the privileged few assembled under the awning. The school children struck up the National Anthem, and the sun bursting forth at the same moment from behind a bank of clouds, the scene was most picturesque and pleasing.

A Novel Journey

The departure of the Corporation trains for the scene of the ceremony was somewhat delayed in consequence of the late arrival of the "Red" excursion from New Street, but once the latter had steamed into Rhayader Station little time was lost in loading and getting it away to the filter bed. To the majority of the passengers, consisting as they did to a larger extent of specially invited guests, Yeomanry officers and Corporation officials, the trip from Rhayader to Foel was a decidedly novel experience. The train consisted of open trucks which had been specially fitted for the occasion with seats of rough boards of primitive kind of accommodation reminiscent of the early days of railway travelling, but in spite of the inconvenience some of the ladies experienced in climbing to their allotted seats, a task performed by the aid of short cord ladders, the majority of them seemed thoroughly to enjoy the novelty of the situation. With a sudden jerk, which resulted in the displacement of many silk hats, and provoked several slight screams from a few of the more timid of the ladies, the first train started on its journey to the filter beds at about 10.15, amid a hearty outburst of cheering from the group of prettily dressed school children, and a general waving of Union Jacks. Notwithstanding the character of the vehicles, the journey up the charming valley between lines of hills and verdant woodlands was by no means the least enjoyable incident of the day's proceedings, though after being rained upon with showers of ashes from the engine, the light summer costumes of the lady passengers and the silk hats, frock coats, and colourful waistcoats of the gentlemen looked somewhat less prim at the close of the journey than when the party started from Rhayader. The railway up to the scene of the ceremony was guarded by lines of police and members of the Shropshire and Warwickshire Volunteers, picketed at very short intervals, while the traffic on the roadway – by this time beginning to assume considerable proportions – was regulated by a detachment of mounted police. Though at least a couple of hours must elapse before the passage of the Royal train, spectators were already beginning to line the side of the road closest to the railway and a few energetic youths had even taken possession of the cross-trees of the telegraph poles.

At the Filter Beds

Immediately on the arrival of the trains at Foel the passengers were conducted to their respective seats on the gaily decorated stands erected on each side of the filter beds, and as the view of the valley was obstructed, and there was no music to relieve the monotony, the long period of waiting which followed became somewhat irksome. The fact that long after the time fixed for the arrival of the "White" and "Blue" trains nothing had been seen or heard of either, began to occasion some apprehension as to the possible cause of the delay, and a few of the occupants of the stands who had friends coming by the later trains betrayed a certain amount of anxiety. This was allayed, however, when about 12 o'clock, the reassuring message was sent round by the Chief Constable that the Royal train was on the way, and the other was following close behind. The complement of the "White" train consisted chiefly of members of the City Council and representatives of the leading Birmingham institutions. Among the first to alight were Sir Oliver Lodge and Alderman Lloyd. Alderman Lawley Parker, Sir James Smith and Alderman Beale had arrived earlier and were occupying positions on the Royal dais where a cinematograph apparatus had been erected to take animated pictures of the ceremony. The occupants of the "Blue" train were exceedingly unfortunate.

Their departure from Rhayader was delayed to such an extent as to make it impossible to get through without interfering with the progress of the Royal train. The only course open to the railway official was, therefore to shunt them on to a siding. A momentary view of the Royal party was vouchsafed to them as the Royal train passed, but they were obliged to forego entirely the privilege of witnessing the whole ceremony.

The great day over, the Elan Valley once more was given back to the solitude of the area; but a day to remember for all concerned.

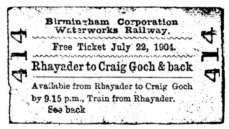

A free passenger ticket for the BCWR, issued in 1904 (a day after the Royal visit).

Appendix One
Walking the "Line" today

At the time of writing it is possible today to walk nearly the whole length of the track bed which used to be the "main line" of the Birmingham Waterworks Railway, and a start can be made from several points along its route.

By being driven to the Craig Goch Dam at map reference 894686*, you can start your walk (after crossing the dam wall) from the terminus of the old railway No. 4 (*plate 107*), continuing along and around the Pen-y-Garreg Reservoir, passing through the deep rock cutting of "Devil's Gulch" on the point of the "L" shaped reservoir (903675), on down the reservoir side to a fine brick railway bridge, spanning one of the feed rivers of Nant Hesgog (910676) before reaching the second dam of Pen-y-Garreg (912675). The gradient of this walk can be seen on page 107.

Walking past this dam you continue down the trackbed, either progressing on towards the Garreg-Ddu Reservoir (now appearing on your right), or by dropping down a steep path to your right through the trees to the road below (916674). Here you can rejoin your friends (if you wish) in the car, who will have travelled down the road towards Rhayader, near the Guest House, The Flickering Lamp, just over the road bridge (915671). There is a public telephone at this point.

If you choose to continue to walk the trackbed you will start to drop down through woodland and curving to the right. On down to the Junction of Railway No. 4 and Railway No. 3, which was situated on the road crossing (916666). Here there are picnic tables on the track-bed for a refreshing pause.

From here you again follow the water's edge of the Garreg-Ddu Reservoir right through to the Garreg-Ddu Dam (approx. 2½ miles) (911640).

On the way be careful of two original wooden bridges (described in Chapter Four, The Route Described), which are at present standing but in a dangerous condition, the one at map reference 914660 being the trickiest. Both can be by-passed by dropping down or climbing up and around them.

The road follows your course at a higher level through the trees and you can rejoin this road just before the "Foel Tower" at the Garreg-Ddu Dam by climbing up the bank and through the fence (911642). Again your friendly car driver will be able to pick you up from here, otherwise the remainder of the walk to the Visitors Centre is along the road.

---

* Ordnance Survey Map No. 147 (1 : 50,000) ELAN VALLEY and BUILTH WELLS (Landranger Series) to be used throughout.

NOTE: A small diversion across the Garreg-Ddu Dam top to the Baptist Church on the far bank will be well worth the time (909638).

The last section of the railway from the Garreg-Ddu dam to the top of the Caban Coch dam cannot be walked, but the Rangers from the Elan Valley Visitors Centre are hoping to rectify this during 1988. Do remember the railway line was intended to be just above the high water level and so please be extremely careful on these walks as the dams are *very* deep water and cold!

Finally, for those who would like to see the reservoirs and dams without leaving their car, one can see all these and railway trackbed on a circular car tour, starting out from Rhayader. From the centre crossroads of Rhayader (971680) the sign post indicates the ELAN VALLEY. Taking this road, one passes the Lion Royal Hotel on your right with the Police Station on the left, just beyond. Continue over the River Wye, with Station Road on your right. A brief excursion up this road is well worth it, to see the old Cambrian Station buildings of Rhayader Station, now a Council Office. Return to the main road and on round a right hand bend. Here can be seen the earthwork of the embankments of the old Cambrian main line where a bridge over the road once stood. The main road beyond here curves to the left with a junction on your right (965678). This is the point you will finally return to but I recommend you carry on the main road (to your left) towards the Elan Village and travel the route this way round.

The journey from here will *not* be described in detail as it will be breath-taking enough but the following points are worthy of mention. Note the railway trackbed on your left following the road up to Elan Valley Centre. Do call in at the Elan Valley Visitors Centre (928647) to see the Museum explaining the whole waterworks project and also to partake in their local walks (*see Appendix Two*). Now take. the road to the left at map reference 911640 over the top of the submerged Garreg-Ddu dam, on round to the newest and largest of the dams at Claerwen (871636), a drive through woods and open moorland, with waterfalls and streams abounding. Returning on the same road back to the Garreg-Ddu Dam and after re-passing over the top of the dam, turn left at the junction (911640) back on to the main route. Note the railway trackbed at this point with gates at each end (near the Foel Tower).

The road climbs up along the Garreg-Ddu reservoir and then drops down to the water's edge. You will note at reference 916666, the road crosses the old railway trackbed. This was the old No. 3 and No. 4 railway junction. Should you wish to, stop at the second dam of Pen-y-Garreg where a car park and telephone are situated, also several short walks are rewarded by spectacular views (915673). Continue up past the reservoir of Pen-y-Garreg negotiating several spectacular horse-shoe bends to the top dam of Craig Goch (894686). Park carefully on the roadside and after a short walk across the top of this magnificent curved dam you will be situated at the exact point where the King stood in 1904 (*see Plate 107*). Return to your car and drive up through the wild moorland to a road junction (at the top of a steep set of hairpin bends (905716). Turn right here to return to Rhayader and after a short climb to 488 metres you drop back down past magnificent waterfalls, giving beautiful views of the valley and lake below, on through woods to the junction (965678), where you rejoin the main road into Rhayader.

This is a drive of approximately 20 miles (plus 4½ miles extra to the Claerwen Dam) being one of the most spectacular and exciting anywhere in Wales. I hope you enjoy it as much as I have on my many visits to the area, whilst researching this book.

Buzzard

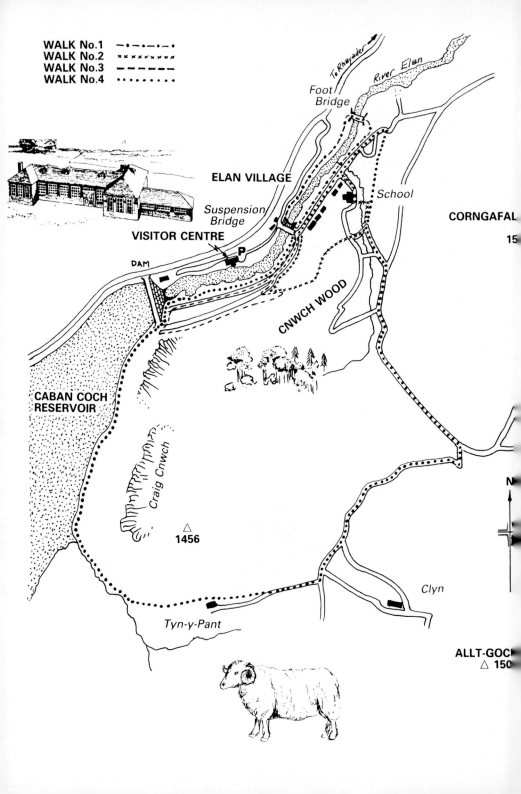

WALK No.1 ·—·—·—·
WALK No.2 xxxxxxx
WALK No.3 — — — —
WALK No.4 ·········

To Rhayader

River Elan

Foot Bridge

ELAN VILLAGE

Suspension Bridge

VISITOR CENTRE

School

CORNGAFAL

15

P

DAM

CNWCH WOOD

CABAN COCH RESERVOIR

Craig Cnwch

△ 1456

N

Clyn

Tyn-y-Pant

ALLT-GOC
△ 150

Appendix Two

Walks from the Elan Visitors' Centre

Nestling under the massive Caban Coch Dam lies the New Visitor Centre, Elan Valley, Rhayader, Powys (where all facilities are accessible for the disabled), tastefully converted from former BCWWR workshops (*see plate 13*). This centre publishes a series of brochures, one of which depicts four walks to and from the centre and is included in this book (*with permission*) so that the reader may enjoy the atmosphere of this unique part of Wales, and even be encouraged to visit the centre and participate in these walks.

I have included in Walks 1, 2, 3 and 4 extra detail where the walk is actually on the old track bed of several of the railways and have stated the map references using the Ordnance Survey map No. 147 (1 : 50,000) ELAN VALLEY and BUILTH WELLS (in the Landranger series of Great Britain). The Walks No. 1, 2, 3 and 4 are all suitable for the whole family but because of the nature of the ground, unfortunately unsuitable for wheelchairs and pushchairs.

The first three walks are reasonably short but Walk 4 is certainly strenuous and requires stout shoes (amply rewarded though with the magnificent views *en route*). At the time of writing (1987) all the walks are marked with yellow arrows and the appropriate walk number.

WALK 1 (approx. 1 mile, ½ hour)

From the visitor centre (928647) walk downstream along the river bank and cross the suspension bridge (930648). Turn left and follow along the road. This was the road of the Model Village described in Chapter Three.

At first sight the village houses all appear to be built to the same pattern, but a closer look reveals that no two are identical, with differences in the shape and position of windows, gables, and doorways. Notice also the typical Victorian attention to detail and decorations in the finely finished window surrounds, stonework, etc.

When you reach the cattle grid, TURN LEFT across the green towards a footbridge over the Elan river (934653) which you now cross. At the far side TURN SHARPLY LEFT and follow a rocky footpath along the bank, back to the suspension bridge, and regain the road by crossing the stile.

WALK 2 (approx. 1 mile, ½ hour)

From the visitor centre (928647) walk downstream and cross the suspension bridge (930648).

Pass through the large gate immediately in front of you (being sure to close it afterwards) and TURN RIGHT to follow a gently sloping track uphill. TURN SHARPLY LEFT (929646). At this point you are on one of the railway levels that brought the railway up from the dam bottom to the top of the dam (*see plate 37*).

Follow the path which soon becomes narrower and passes behind the village. Go through the small gate and cross the stream. Shortly, BEAR LEFT down to a footbridge, crossing two stiles and passing to the RIGHT of the old school (now an outdoor pursuits centre), and turn LEFT (933650) on the road back to the suspension bridge (930648).

WALK 3 *(approx 1 mile, 1 hour)*

From the visitor centre (928647) walk downstream and cross the suspension bridge (930648).

At the far side TURN RIGHT through the small white gate (please be sure to close it behind you) and follow the grassy track once the bed of a construction railway, through a wooded area of oaks and birches, which provides a rich habitat for many species of woodland birds. You will shortly arrive at the foot of 122 ft high Caban Coch Dam (925644). Water is released through the stone building on your right-hand side to maintain and regulate the flow in the Elan River. This is called compensation water (29 million gallons per day) and is also used to power turbines which provide electricity for the water treatment works and the village, with any surplus being fed into the National Grid. (Please keep to the marked path at this point and do not venture into the "No Public Access" areas.)

Walk up the short but steep path to your left and cross the stile at the top. From here you can look across the crest of the dam, and much of the 500 acre expanse of Caban Coch Reservoir. When full the top water level is 822 ft above sea level, and following periods of heavy rainfall the water flows over the top of the dam in a most spectacular fashion. The highest overflow rate so far recorded was in September 1946 when the depth of water on the crest of the dam reached 35.9 inches – a flow of 196 million gallons per hour! On each side of the dam you can see the quarries from which the stone was obtained for the construction.

To return to the visitor centre follow the wide track (which was the course of the top railway built for the transport of materials to the site) back down the valley, via a short zig-zag path to the suspension bridge, and thence to the centre.

WALK 4 *(approximately 4 miles, 2 hours)*

Strong shoes or boots are recommended for this one as previously pointed out.

Follow the directions for *WALK 3* to the top of Caban Coch Dam (925644) but keep going and continue along the shores of the reservoir. This is a rocky path and very uneven underfoot, and in parts is rather narrow, and once was the trackbed of the construction railway to the Dol-y-Mynach Dam site. Evidence of sleeper ruts can easily be seen on this section. Notice the outcrops of rock whose layers are standing upright, rather like a pack of playing cards on edge. These layers were originally horizontal, and were later forced up by the enormous forces at work within the earth during the period, many millions of years ago, when many of the world's mountains were formed.

The path bends around into a small inlet (922635) and then passes uphill and along the edge of a plantation of large trees. The concrete emplacement, and the remains of the small Nant-y-Gro Dam (923634) can be seen. (This dam was the first built to hold water for the Elan "Model" Village.)

At the top of this rather steep section the path broadens out and becomes rather less strenuous. This is the ideal spot to regain your breath and enjoy the sweeping views over Caban Coch Reservoir and the Garreg-ddu viaduct and reservoir. To the south-west the long ridge forms the boundary of the Elan Estate. In reasonably clear weather the high point of this ridge (some 6 miles distant as the crow flies) known as Drygan Fawr (862584) can be seen. At 641 m (2115 ft above sea level) this is the highest point on the estate.

Follow the grassy track until it joins a surfaced road at the mountain gate (929632) (make sure you close it behind you). In about 1 mile TURN LEFT at the T-junction (938638) and follow this road through an area of oak woodland, past the entrance to Cnwch Farm (934645).

Shortly after this take the grassy track marked, which bears left (934647) down through the woods to the village. Turn left along the green to the suspension bridge and then back to the Visitors' Centre.

Appendix Three
Richard Eustace Tickell

I, Eustace Tickell, count myself lucky to have been involved in the Elan Water Scheme since the early days. In 1891, I was employed by Mr Mansergh and his son Walter, carried out field surveys of the Elan and Claerwen watersheds and section of the Aqueduct route. Our work fixed the boundary of the land purchase by the Corporation. In early 1893, I was back employed by Mr Mansergh as a surveyor. In 1894 saw me supervising building the Nant-y-Gro Dam which provided water for the Navvies village. In 1895, I was on Mr Yourdi's staff where I managed the Cost Department. On the 1st May, 1896, I was placed in charge of the construction of the Pen-y-Gareg dam, which took five years to complete.

Throughout my life I enjoyed drawing and writing and I decided to celebrate the area in a book called "The Vale of Nant Gwilt – a submerged valley". I did the drawings from which the copper plate etchings have been made, with pen and ink in the field, and the book was published in 1894 (*plates 1, 3 and 4*).

Copy of a letter in the Elan Valley Visitor Centre

Plate 110: Richard Eustace Tickell: born 29th April, 1864, died 8th September, 1943, pictured here in 1900 alongside the dam for which he was Resident Engineer for the Pen-y-Gareg. The railway line in front of him was the mainline (Railway No. 4). *Courtesy: Severn-Trent Water*

Appendix Four

Alterations to the 1892 City of Birmingham Water Act

a) Birmingham Corporation Water Act 1896 for empowering the Corporation of Birmingham to make certain deviations of the Aqueducts to the Act of 1892 and to construct an additional short line railway and to acquire additional lands. Royal Assent 2nd July, 1896 (59 & 60 Vict.).

b) Birmingham Corporation Water Act 1902 authorised extension of time for construction of works, road diversions, a limited capitalization of interest and a postponement of the commencement of the sinking fund but without deferring the ultimate date of repayment.

c) Birmingham Corporation Water Act of 1905 (Part IV) authorised the utilisation of the compensation water for the purpose of generating power or light.

d) Birmingham Corporation Water Act 1907 which authorised a further postponement of the 1902 Act.

CITY OF BIRMINGHAM WATER DEPARTMENT.

ELAN SUPPLY.

We shall be obliged, if, in consigning this traffic, you should be able to select the route

via .... ,

as our arrangements with the Cambrian Railways will be facilitated thereby.

E. ANTONY LEES,

Secretary.

A wagon label used for consigning the cement traffic.

Appendix Five

Cambrian Traffic Statement (1893–1895)

Statement showing the number of wagons (goods & coal) received at Rhayader, and handed over to the Birmingham Corporation Water Works Railway, August 1893 to January 1895.

Months	No. of Goods Wagons	No. of Coal Wagons	Total
1893			
August	50	–	50
September	63	–	63
October	123	–	123
November	101	–	101
December	64	1	65
	401	1	402
1894			
January	86	1	87
February	78	2	80
March	192	6	198
April	418	3	421
May	250	3	253
June	141	8	149
July	123	5	128
August	187	19	206
September	233	22	255
October	321	26	347
November	176	20	196
December	245	24	269
	2,450	139	2,589
1895			
January	78	13	91
TOTAL	2,929	153	3,082

Appendix Six

The Cambrian Railways siding at Cerrig Gwynion

The Cambrian Railways installed a siding from the main Mid-Wales line at Cerrig Gwynion, mid-way between Elan Junction and Doldowlod station, to serve the large quarry that existed there. The siding was controlled by a 2 lever ground frame and tablet release. It was inspected and passed for use by Inspector Yorke on 4th January, 1897, with his recommendation that "staging should be put round the ground frame to protect it". This was done by 28th January, 1897 and the siding brought into use to supply stone to the dam construction sites. The only proviso for operation was that the locomotive carrying out the operation should shunt from the lower end (Doldowlod).

The plan shows the siding (protected by a catchpoint), a location plan and the loading stage to which the stone was brought down by road; see *plate 111* for view of the siding.

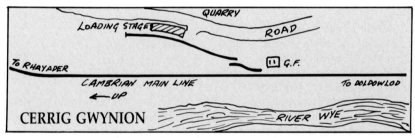

Source Reference: Public Record Office, Kew, RAIL MT6/2009/3 and RAIL MT6/770/3.

Plate 111: A postcard view showing the Cerrig Gwynion siding which was protected by a white gate (*middle*). *Courtesy M. Christiansen*

Acknowledgements

I am indebted to the following for their help in compiling this book:
Mike Christiansen
Mr & Mrs C. Edwards
G. Fox
Frank Jones
Roger Kidner
Ian Kennedy
The late Eric Mountford
C.R. Potts
K.P. Plant
Kevin Robertson
J.N. Slinn
Ken Smith
Lens of Sutton
T. Ingram
Real Photographs
The staff of the following Establishments are also thanked for their help:
Public Record Office, Kew
House of Lords Record Office
Walsall Public Libraries
Wolverhampton Public Libraries
British Library, Collindale
Elan Valley Visitors Centre and in particular Mrs Krysia Bass, Mike Couling and John Waddington without whose help this book would certainly not have been possible.
The Hunslet Company Ltd, Liverpool and in particular Mr G. Horsman.
The Birmingham Reference Library with special thanks to Maisie Tranter (*Deputy Librarian, Local Studies Department*).
The Severn–Trent Water Authority, with a special thank you to Miss Diane Williams for her research and help.
Special thanks to Sue Potts and Julie Lewis for deciphering the handwritten manuscript and typing the result.
Extracts from: *The Engineer*
The Railway Magazine
The Locomotive Magazine
Model Railway Constructor
GWR Magazine
S.L.S. Journal
Newspapers of the Period
Minutes of the Birmingham Corporation Water Committee
The Village under the Water by E. Tickell

Index

(heavy type denotes page for illustration)

Aberdovey 181
Abernant Turnout 94,
  97 (*pl.49*)
Accidents 54, 170
Aqueduct **19** (*pl.9*), 21,
  198
Ashbury Railway Carriage
  and Iron Co. 151,
  152, 154
Baptist Chapel
  Nant Gwilt **8** (*pl.5*), 10
  Llan Fadog **9** (*pl.6*), 10,
  17
Birmingham Corporation
  146
  Water Act 14, 227
  Mayor 30
Birmingham Water
  Committee 11, 13,
  26, 41, **42**, 53, 54,
  178, 193, 205
Board of Trade 41, 79
Brake Vans **175** (*pl.94 &*
  95), **201** (*pl.100*)
Brass Band 72
Bridge
  Aber Caethon **85** (*pl.32*),
  86 (*pl.33*), 167
  Nant Hesgog 101,
  106 (*pl.65*)
Bristol Wagon and Carriage
  Works
  Wagon Plate **153**
Builth Road 29, 30, 210
Caban Work site 24, 37,
  38 (*pl.12*), 47, 58, 87,
  88 (*pl.37*), 134, 165
Cambrian Railway 17, 22,
  29, 30, 36, 39, 41, 47,
  49, 53, 65, 79, 140,
  141, **151** (*pl.84*), 152,
  163, 165, 167, 174,
  228
Cambrian Rly. Timetable
  184
Canteen 72
Cardiff Corporation 136,
  154
Careg-Ddu Junction
  100 (*pl.54*)

Cement Traffic 181, 227
Ceremonial Wheel
  214 (*pl.109*)
Cerrig Gwynion siding
  229 (*pl.111*)
Chamberlain (Joseph) 14,
  47
Coal 142
Cranes 37, 160,
  162 (*pl.90*),
  163 (*pl.91 & 92*)
Cwm Elan House 5,
  6 (*pl.2*), 39,
  100 (*pl.55*)
Cwm Elan Mine 5, 111
Cwm Elan Turnout 94,
  100 (*pl.55*),
  170 (*pl.93*)
Dams
  Caban Coch 37, 51,
    93 (*pl.43*), 94,
    96 (*pl.47 & 48*),
    201 (*pl.100*), 220
  Careg Ddu 8, 94,
    98 (*pl.51*), **99** (*pl.52*),
    195, **201** (*pl.101*), 219
  Cil-Oerwynt 15, 198
  Claerwen 198,
    203 (*pl.105*), 221
  Craig Goch 49, 101,
    108 (*pl.68*),
    110 (*pl.70*), 136,
    159 (*pl.89*),
    202 (*pl.103*), 219
  Dol-y-Mynach 87, 90,
    92 (*pl.41*), 196,
    203 (*pl.104*)
  Nant-y-Beddau 15, 198
  Nant-y-Gro 58, 225
  Pen-y-Gareg **105** (*pl.63*),
    136, **202** (*pl.102*),
    226 (*pl.110*)
Dam Busters (R.A.F.) 58
Dean (William)G.W.R.
  145, 146
Devil's Gulch 48 (*pl.14 &*
  15), 49, 101,
  107 (*pl.66*),
  108 (*pl.67*), 219
Dol-Faenog Junction 101,
  136

Dol-Faenog Turnout 101
Dol-Falau **104** (*pl.60*), 111
Doss House
  Elan 59, **63** (*pl.19 & 20*),
    88 (*pl.36*)
  Standedge 62
Drawings
  Aqueduct **199**
  Locomotives
    Elan and Claerwen **118**
    Rhiwnant and Calettwr
    130
    Coel **138**
  Locomotive shed **135**
  Livery **134**
  Passenger Coach **148**
  Wagon **209**
Dutton Signal Co. 167,
  168

Earl of Dudley's Railway
  137
Ebbw Vale Steel Co. 35,
  36, 39, 40
Elan Valley Hotel 53, 65,
  77, **86** (*pl.34*)
Elan Valley Railway
  Junction 22, 30, 36,
  39, 79
  Signal Cabin **83** (*pl.30*),
  85 (*pl.31*), 165, 174
Elan Visitor Centre
  38 (*pl.13*), 220, 223
Excursions 190, 191
Filter Beds 90, 94,
  95 (*pl.46*), 212,
  213 (*pl.106*)
Fire Brigade 77
Foel (The) 90, 94
Foel Tower **99** (*pl.53*), 196,
  101, 219
Foxfield Light Railway
  133
Gigfran Quarry 39,
  88 (*pl.37*), 94, 136,
  150 (*pl.82*)
Great Western Railway
  33, 34, 41, 47, 145,
  146, 149, **151** (*pl.83*),
  152

Guard House 62 (*pl.18*)
Hospital 67, **69** (*pl.21*), 70,
 216
Hunslet Engine Co. Leeds
 113, 114, 119, 120,
 124, 126, 136, 140
Industries and Iron Journal
 29
Leeds Corporation Water
 Dept. 55
Lion Hotel 13, 54, 220
Liveries 120, 122, 134,
 152, 157
Lloyd (Lewis) 51, 59
Llyn Clap 101, **102** (*pl.57*),
 103 (*pl.58 & 59*)
Locomotives
 BIRMINGHAM
  CORPORATION
  RAILWAY 113, 144
  BANNER 115
  CALETTWR 130, 131,
   132 (*pl.78*), 173, 210,
   211 (*pl.105*),
   213 (*pl.107*)
  CARINGTON 115,
   116 (*pl.72*)
  CLAERWEN 115,
   117 (*pl.73*), 118, 119,
   120 (*pl.24*),
   156 (*pl.86*), 173
  COEL 136, **175** (*pl.94*),
   189 (*pl.97*), 210,
   211 (*pl.104*)
  ELAN 115, **116** (*pl.71*),
   118, 119, **170** (*pl.93*)
  LAUCHOPE 125
  MARCHNANT 134,
   137, 139, 144
  METHAN 122,
   124 (*pl.77*), 134
  NANT GWYLLT 120,
   121, 122, **123** (*pl.75 &*
   76), 134, **159** (*pl.89*),
   175 (*pl.95*)
  RHIWNANT 130, 131,
   132 (*pl.79*),
   133 (*pl.80*), 212
  VICTORY 115
  CAMBRIAN RAILWAY
   MAGLONA **85** (*pl.31*)
   No.22 **140** (*pl.81*), 141
   SEAHAM CLASS 176
   SHARPS No.83
   204 (*pl.102*), 210
  CONTRACTORS
   THE SCOTT 36
  Locomotive Shed 37,
   38 (*pl.12*), 134, 135
  London North Western
   Railway 65, 66, 67,
   154, 172, 173, 205,

Lovatt (Henry) Contractor
 32, 33, 34, 36, 39
Mail Train **151** (*pl.82*),
 181, 188, **189** (*pl.96*)
Manning Wardle & Co.
 Leeds 113, 117,
 125, 126, 130, 136
Mansergh (James) 12, 13,
 17, **18**, 27, 30
Mason's Yard **90** (*pl.38*),
 161
Mid-Wales Railway 13,
 16, 29, 160
Monorail Railway (Filter
 Beds) 90

Nant Gwillt
 Vale 5, 226
 House **6** (*pl.3*), 32, 39
 Capel **6** (*pl.4*), 10, 40
 Baptist Chapel **8** (*pl.5*),
  10, 25, **99** (*pl.52*)
 Village **9** (*pl.7*)
 School 10
 Site Offices **25** (*pl.10*)
Nant Hesgog **106** (*pl.65*)
Nant Madog 212,
 214 (*pl.108*), 216
Nant-y-Car Mine 5
Navvy Mission 54
Noyadd Sidings 79, **84**,
 141, 165, 167, 180
Passenger Coaches 145,
 148, 150, **151** (*pl.83 &*
 84), 152, **170** (*pl.93*),
 189 (*pl.97*),
 191 (*pl.98*)
Peckett and Sons Ltd.
 113, 114
Quarry Incline **91** (*pl.40*)
Railways
 Tenders 29, 30, 31, 33
 No. 1 16, 28, 34, 36, 40,
  49, **87** (*pl.35*),
  88 (*pl.36*)
 No. 2 35, 47, 49, 87,
  88 (*pl.36*), 94
 No. 3 49, 94, **100** (*pl.54*
  & 55), 101, 150
 No. 4 49, 101, **108** (*pl.61*
  & 62), 156, 213, 219
Recreation Hall **76** (*pl.24*)
Reservoirs
 Caban Coch **8** (*pl.5*), 16,
  193
 Cil-Oerwynt 16
 Craig-yr-Allt Goch 16,
  194
 Dol-y-Mynach 16
 Garreg-Ddu 219
 Nant-y-Gro 58
 Nant-y-Beddau 16

Pen-y-Gareg 16,
 108 (*pl.67*),
 109 (*pl.69*), 194, 219
Rhayader 5, 13, **18** (*pl.8*),
 19 (*pl.9*), 28, 41, 47,
 51, 53, 66, 79,
 82 (*pl.27 & 28*),
 83 (*pl.29*), 177, 205,
 207, 220
Rivers
 Claerwen 5, 14
 Elan 5, 14
 Wye 5
Royal Visit 151,
 204 (*pl.103*), 205
School 53, 70, 72,
 73 (*pl.22 & 23*)
Shelley 5
Sir Thomas Martineau 12,
 14
Sir Robert Rawlinson 12
Stables **87** (*pl.35*)
Stables Junction 87
Stockton and Middles-
 borough Waterboard
 26
Suspension Bridge 41, 59,
 60 (*pl.16 & 17*), 87
Tan-y-Foel Yard **97** (*pl.49*)
Three Cocks Station 29
Tickell (R.E.) 21, 226
 Etchings **6** (*pl.1*), **7** (*pl.3*
  & 4)
Ticket **218**
Topping Out Ceremony
 157 (*pl.87*),
 158 (*pl.88*)
Tunnel Junction 41,
 83 (*pl.30*)
Van Branch 140
Village 24, 51, 58, 66, 72,
 76 (*pl.25*), **77** (*pl.26*),
 223
Vyrnwy 22, 23, 210
Walking 219
Wagons 152, **155** (*pl.85*),
 157, 159
Walsall Corporation Gas
 Works 141
Water Wells Birmingham
 12
Weighbridge 41
Welshpool 29
Whistle Codes 172
Williams (Stephen) 24, 26,
 32
Working Timetables 171,
 172
Workman's Trains 182
Yourdi (G.N.) **25** (*pl.11*),
 26, 27, 32, 41, 173,
 175 (*pl.94*)